Teach Yourself VISUAL

WordPress®

3rd Edition

George Plumley

Visual
A Wiley Brand

Teach Yourself VISUALLY™ WordPress® 3rd Edition

Published by
John Wiley & Sons, Inc.
10475 Crosspoint Boulevard
Indianapolis, IN 46256

www.wiley.com

Published simultaneously in Canada

Wiley publishes in a variety of print and electronic formats and by print-on-demand. Some material included with standard print versions of this book may not be included in e-books or in print-on-demand. If this book refers to media such as a CD or DVD that is not included in the version you purchased, you may download this material at http://booksupport.wiley.com. For more information about Wiley products, visit www.wiley.com.

The Library of Congress Control Number is available from the publisher.

ISBN: 978-1-119-04775-9 (pbk); ISBN: 978-1-119-04765-0 (ebk); ISBN: 978-1-119-04784-1 (ebk)

Manufactured in the United States of America

10 9 8 7 6 5 4 3 2 1

Trademark Acknowledgments

Contact Us

For general information on our other products and services, please contact our Customer Care Department within the U.S. at 877-762-2974, outside the U.S. at 317-572-3993 or fax 317-572-4002.

For technical support please visit www.wiley.com/techsupport.

Sales | Contact Wiley at (877) 762-2974 or fax (317) 572-4002.

Credits

Acquisitions Editor
Aaron Black

Project Editor
Sarah Hellert

Technical Editor
Donna L. Baker

Copy Editor
Scott Tullis

Project Coordinator
Suresh Srinivasan

Manager, Content Development & Assembly
Mary Beth Wakefield

Vice President, Professional Technology Strategy
Barry Pruett

About the Author

George Plumley has been building websites for over 20 years, working exclusively with WordPress since 2007. He is the author of several books and video courses on WordPress, as well as running the help site SeeHowSupport.com where he does site makeovers and group coaching for clients. When he isn't in front of a screen, he enjoys hiking Canada's west coast.

Author's Acknowledgments

I want to thank my wife, Kim, and daughters Grace and Ella, for being patient, once more, with a somewhat absentee and absent-minded husband and father; my sister Patricia, and my in-laws, Gord and Carole, for their unwavering support; at Wiley, acquisitions editor Aaron Black, project editor Sarah Hellert, copy editor Scott Tullis, and technical editor Donna Baker were so helpful bringing me up to speed and then so patient when schedules were bent; my agent, Carole Jelen, who finds me wonderful projects like this; my clients and students over the years, who have helped me hone explanations and discover new ones; and finally, to the tens of thousands of active WordPress users who share their knowledge, produce amazing software, and have a lot of fun doing it.

How to Use This Book

Who This Book Is For

This book is for the reader who has never used this particular technology or software application. It is also for readers who want to expand their knowledge.

The Conventions in This Book

① Steps

This book uses a step-by-step format to guide you easily through each task. Numbered steps are actions you must do; bulleted steps clarify a point, step, or optional feature; and indented steps give you the result.

② Notes

Notes give additional information — special conditions that may occur during an operation, a situation that you want to avoid, or a cross reference to a related area of the book.

③ Icons and Buttons

Icons and buttons show you exactly what you need to click to perform a step.

④ Tips

Tips offer additional information, including warnings and shortcuts.

⑤ Bold

Bold type shows command names, options, and text or numbers you must type.

⑥ Italics

Italic type introduces and defines a new term.

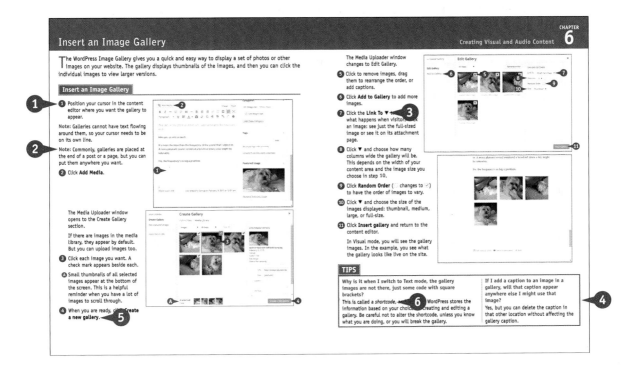

Table of Contents

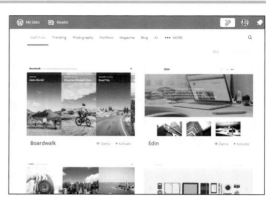

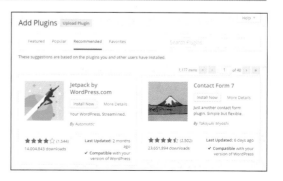

Chapter 4 Knowing Your Administration Tools

Chapter 5 Creating Written Content

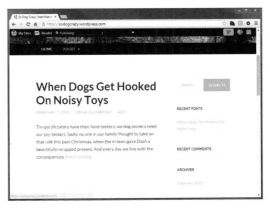

Table of Contents

Chapter 6   Creating Visual and Audio Content

Chapter 7   Organizing and Managing Your Site Content

Table of Contents

Chapter 10   Adding Functionality with Plugins

Chapter 11   Making Your Site Social

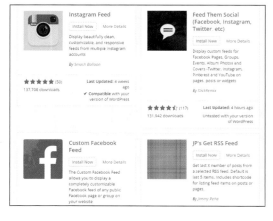

CHAPTER 1

Introducing WordPress

WordPress is the world's most popular content management system for websites. Not only is it easy to set up and use, but its flexibility and expandability make it a powerful tool for virtually any small business or personal website.

Choose a Version of WordPress

WordPress comes in two versions: a fully managed and hosted version at WordPress.com, and a self-hosted, self-managed version you can download at WordPress.org. Which version is best for you depends on your current and future needs, so it is important to understand the goals and requirements of your website.

It is possible to move your content from one version to the other, so you can change your mind later. But as you will see, it would mean giving up different kinds of functionality.

About WordPress

WordPress is *open-source* software, meaning anyone can download it, use it, and change it, generally for free and with few restrictions. It has been around since 2003 as a program for self-hosted sites, and this book uses version 4.1. The organization that developed around the software, WordPress.org, later started WordPress.com for people who did not want to host their own sites.

Our Bill of Rights

WordPress is licensed under the General Public License (GPLv2 or four core freedoms, consider this as the WordPress "bill of rights":

- The freedom to run the program, for any purpose.
- The freedom to study how the program works, and change it to m wish.
- The freedom to redistribute.
- The freedom to distribute copies of your modified versions to othe

Why WordPress?

What separates WordPress from other free blogging or content management tools is the size of the community. Yes, it is easy to use, but more importantly, so many people use WordPress that the number of resources available far outstrips any other platform. Whether it is troubleshooting an installation, helping with your design, or needing added functionality, it is easy to find a free or paid solution.

WordPress Platform Powers 23 Percent Of Websites In The World, Statistics Say

WordPress.com — Managed Hosting

WordPress.com provides hosting for your site and takes care of all updates. It offers a good selection of designs and a useful set of functions, such as forms, social sharing, polls, and more. WordPress.com is constantly adding to its list of designs and functions, but you cannot add your own.

WordPress.org — Self-Hosted

WordPress.org provides you with software that you then need to host, set up, and maintain. None of these tasks is difficult, but they do require time and/or money. The tradeoff for doing everything yourself is that you can customize WordPress in virtually limitless ways: Make it look exactly the way you want, using free, paid, or custom *themes*, or add as many functions as you want using free, paid, or custom *plugins*, which are small programs you literally plug in to the core software.

Key Differences: Design

WordPress.com offers a good selection of free or paid themes to make your site look good. There is even a paid option that allows you to tweak your theme to get exact colors and so on. Wordpress.org, on the other hand, allows you to put in any theme you want, and thousands of free and paid themes are available. You can even create your own theme from scratch, or modify an existing theme as much as you want.

Key Differences: Functionality

WordPress.com has good basic functionality built in, such as the ability to create a contact form, share your site on social media, and more. But your site is limited to whatever is currently offered. WordPress.org allows you to add as much functionality as you want using plugins. You can choose from more than 50,000 free and paid plugins, or you can create your own.

Key Differences: Ads

WordPress.com allows affiliate text links and sponsored posts, but no image ads or ad networks (unless you join its in-house ad network). Also, unless you pay to have them removed, WordPress.com may place its own ads on your site. With a WordPress.org site, you have complete control over the type and amount of advertising you place on your site.

Key Differences: Cost

WordPress itself is free, whether you download it to self-host or sign up for a WordPress.com account. The difference in cost is that WordPress.com offers a small number of paid features, such as using your own domain name, customizing the look of your theme, or enabling e-commerce. For WordPress.org sites, you need to pay for a hosting account, but beyond that, any costs would involve paid themes or plugins or hiring someone to do custom work.

Key Differences: Support

Both WordPress.org and WordPress.com offer free support in documentation and in forums. WordPress.com offers its own paid support service; Wordpress.org users can get additional support through paid themes or plugins or third-party support services.

Choose a Site Topic

Being clear in your mind about your site's purpose and audience means you are more likely to communicate that information both to visitors and to search engines. Clarity about your site means you also understand what theme and what plugins you will need for WordPress. Following are some example types of sites to help you focus what your site is about and what it is intended to accomplish.

Personal Sites

Whether you want to focus on a hobby or a broad range of personal interests, a blog can be a great way to share your thoughts as well as your images and videos.

Organization Sites

A website is the perfect way for any organization, large or small, to get the word out to the public and help members stay in touch.

Business Sites — Information

Websites that explain what a company does and invite visitors to make contact in various ways are the most common type of business site. Using WordPress posts, you can keep visitors up to date on company and industry news.

Business Sites — E-Commerce

Whether you offer a couple of services or a large catalog of items, selling directly from a website is a powerful tool for many businesses. There are many ways to make your WordPress site an e-commerce site, including a paid package on WordPress.com.

Dineamic Online Store Gift Voucher

Author and Artist Sites

A website is the perfect way for authors and artists to showcase their work (and even sell them directly). In the case of authors, you may want to have a separate website for individual books or series, and for artists you could even have a separate site for a particular exhibit.

Directory Sites

Helping people find things on the Internet or in the real world is a valuable service. Creating a directory site is a great way to organize and present information.

Instructional Sites

Websites that focus on providing courses or other types of instruction have become increasingly popular. They may be free or paid or a combination of the two. Payment is usually taken in the form of a membership for a period of time.

Entertainment Sites

Creating a website that entertains is a great way to draw a lot of visitors and either sell something related to the entertainment, or sell advertising if you have very high numbers for a particular audience. For example, you might produce an online graphic novel series that appeals to young adults, or develop a set of animated games that help kids learn as they play.

Understand WordPress and Website Terms

Learning a few WordPress and website terms before you dive in makes the process easier to follow.

Posts versus Pages

WordPress has two main types of content: posts and pages. *Posts* are pieces of content which get grouped together into *categories*, such as press releases. New posts are constantly being added. WordPress *pages* typically are used for singular content which changes very little, such as the history of a company or the description of a service. Do not confuse a WordPress page with a website page. Individual WordPress posts, for example, are displayed as web pages.

Plugins

A *plugin* is a piece of software that you literally plug in to WordPress to add new functionality. A form plugin, for example, would allow you to add a contact form to your site. At WordPress.com, a very limited, but useful set of plugins is built in to the system, whereas with WordPress.org you can choose from tens of thousands of possible plugins.

Themes

A *theme* is a piece of software that determines not only the look of your WordPress site, but to some extent the functionality. A theme controls the layout, colors, typography, and graphics for the design, but it could also add, say, the ability to put testimonials on your site or display a portfolio of your work.

Widgets

A *widget* is content or functionality you can add to your site, usually somewhere outside the main content area, such as in a sidebar or the footer. For example, widgets can display your most recent posts or connect to your social media accounts and display your latest activity there.

Dashboard

The *dashboard* is the home page of the WordPress administration area. It offers an overview of your site content, and provides notifications of pending comments, draft content, and news from the WordPress community.

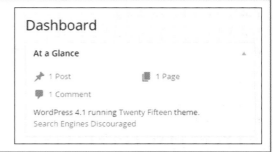

Media Library

Every media file you upload to WordPress (images, documents, video, and so on) is listed in the *media library*. From there you can edit, delete, select, and insert media files.

CSS

This stands for *cascading stylesheet,* which is the primary way of controlling the look of a website. Stylesheet rules can govern the elements of HTML as well as specially named classes and IDs.

```
blockquote {
        border-left: 4px solid #707070;
        border-left: 4px solid rgba(51, 51, 51, 0.7);
        color: #707070;
        color: rgba(51, 51, 51, 0.7);
        font-size: 18px;
        font-size: 1.8rem;
        font-style: italic;
        line-height: 1.6667;
        margin-bottom: 1.6667em;
        padding-left: 0.7778em;
}
```

SEO

This stands for *search engine optimization.* Anything that helps search engines find, index, and rank web pages can be called an SEO technique — for example, making sure your page title and content use the same keywords.

More news for seo

Search engine optimization - Wikipedia,
en.wikipedia.org/wiki/Search_engine_optimization
Search engine optimization (SEO) is the process of aff
or a web page in a search engine's "natural" or un-paid
Backlink - Google Webmaster Tools - Seo - Vertical se

Plan Your Site's Content

Planning your site's content consists of two stages: the initial site launch and the ongoing addition of material. Some of these suggestions apply to both.

Focus

Every web page needs to have a clear focus. A contact page should not go into your company history, for example. If you offer three distinct services, then have at least one page for each. Several posts may belong to the same category, but they should each have a clear focus distinct from the others.

Benefits of a Raw Food Diet for Dogs

Putting your dog on a raw food diet has many benefits. but you need to make sure it's the proper mix of foods:

- Increased Stimulation
- Improved Skin and Coat
- Stronger Immune System
- Leaner Body Mass

Make It Easy to Find

Part of content planning is mapping out how visitors will find the content. A clear navigation structure is crucial. If you have more than a few web pages, you need to organize the menu so that it shows an overview of your site, with submenu items that lead to more details within each area. Linking to your own material is also very helpful to visitors. If you write about prepping your garden for winter, include a link to a post you wrote the year before about how to protect plants from frost.

Consider Post Length

Posts should be only as long as they need to be. In other words, you need to be succinct whether writing 3 paragraphs or 30. Assuming you have a focused topic, say what you have to say as quickly as possible, while still being clear and accurate. If you have anything more than 7 or 8 paragraphs, be sure to ask yourself whether the post is truly focused and whether it could be broken into 2 or more parts.

p
Word count: 648

Be Visual

Images and video are powerful ways of engaging your visitors. In fact, the content on every web page should contain at least one image. Be on the lookout for photo opportunities, even if you are not sure how you would later use the image. Similarly, you should be thinking of videos, no matter how short, that you could record now and use later for content. Consider subscribing to a stock photography site, such as dollarphotoclub.com, if you plan on doing a lot of posting.

Benefits of a Raw Food Diet for Dogs

Consider Post Frequency

Visitors and search engines want to know that you are still active, so spread out your posts whenever possible. If you have a lot of ideas when you first start your site, do not post them all at once. A good rule of thumb is to post something new at least once every couple of weeks. WordPress has a scheduling feature, so you could write a lot of material at one sitting, but have it publish over a number of weeks.

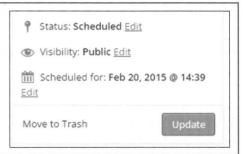

Create an Editorial Calendar

To help ease the burden of coming up with new content, as well as to target your audience at appropriate times, develop an editorial calendar. Map out important dates and events, both generally (Christmas, summer vacation, and so on) and within your field (trade shows, seasonal issues, and so on).

Link to Other Sites

Always be on the lookout for valuable content you can link to. The web is a vast store of information, and helping your visitors find useful or entertaining material is a great way of supplementing your own thoughts. In fact, you can create entire posts out of pointing visitors to a valuable site. But do not just link; summarize or give a quote of what you think is of value and even add your own comments.

Listen and Keep Notes

What questions are your customers asking? What topics are your friends discussing on social media? What are your competitors writing about, and how can you offer a new perspective? If you listen to those around you, you will never be short on content, and what you write about will be relevant to your audience. Even if you do not have something to say on the topic right now, make a note of what you heard and save it for those days when you need inspiration.

Research Site Titles

Naming your site well is vital, whether to maintain an existing brand or to create a new one. If you have a product, company, or organization, you already have a focus for your site title. You have more options if the site has no existing ties, but there are still some rules to keep in mind.

Site Title versus Domain

Your *site title* appears in the header of your web pages. A *domain name* is the part of a web address that includes *.com, .net, .info,* or one of the other domain name extensions. You can read about buying a domain name in the next section, "Buy a Domain Name."

Corresponding Names

It is important for your site title and domain name to match, or at least to correspond closely, so that people can find you more easily. From hearing the name of your company, organization, or personal blog, people should be able to easily look you up on the web.

Spelling Counts

A domain name that exactly matches your company name is one way to make it easy for people to remember, but what if the name is hard

oceansideaccommodation.com

oceansideaccomodation.com

to spell? You can buy a second domain with the incorrect spelling and point it to your site as well. Or avoid the spelling issue by going with a name that focuses on your product or service instead. Shorter is easier, unless you have a memorable, easy to spell, exact match, such as thegreatlittlebreadcompany.com.

Brainstorm Names

If you have an existing company, product, or
organization name, stick as closely to that as
you can. Consistency is more important than
being clever. If this is a new venture or a personal website, then brainstorming is crucial. Focus on what
you do or what you are going to write about. If your subject is dogs, start by narrowing the focus: training
dogs versus dog breeds versus my dog's adventures. Start brainstorming from there.

> **dogcrazy   crazyaboutdogs   crazyfordogs**
> **sodoggonecrazy   sodogcrazy**

Try for a Unique Name

Increase your odds of having a unique
site title by typing your proposed
title into a search engine, and look
for sites that use your title in full or
in part. If you are signing up at
WordPress.com, it automatically
checks if your site title is taken
within its system (it also lets you
know if the domain of that same name is available).

> Is Your Dog Crazy? 15 Nutty Behaviors Explained - CBS News
> www.cbsnews.com/.../is-your-**dog-crazy**-15-nutty-behaviors-explained/ ▾
> Is your **dog** idiosyncratic? Ridiculous? Eccentric? A lot of odd **dog** behavior can be
> traced to fears that took root in the early months of a puppy's life, says ...
>
> Occupational Dog Bite Prevention | How to Train a Puppy ...
> www.**dog**gone**crazy**.ca/ ▾
> Contact Doggone **Crazy** of Campbellville ON for How to Train a Puppy, **Dog** Bite
> Prevention, **Dog** Behavior Problems, How to Stop a **Dog** From Biting, Clicker ...

All the Good Names Are Taken!

With so many domain names already registered,
it can take a lot of creativity these days to find a
good one that is available. If your company or
product name is fairly unique, you stand a better
chance. With more generic names, try adding a
location (franksplumbingportland.com) or
additional relevant words (franksplumbingservice.
com) or get clever (callfrankforplumbing.com).
You can get help at sites such as panabee.com, bustaname.com, or dotomator.com, which also tell you when
related domain names are taken or available.

> dogcrazy.COM
>
> ⓘ Sorry, **dogcrazy.com** is not available.
>
> Here is a list of domains recommended for you:
>
> **Filter By**   1 - **10 of 92 results**   Show All

Avoid Duplication

Aside from possible legal issues, using the same site title as someone
else or registering a domain with the same name but different extension
just does not make any sense. Why run the risk of visitors confusing your
site with someone else's?

> dogcrazy.**website**
>
> dogcrazy.**link**
>
> dogcrazy.**click**
>
> dogcrazy.**bio**

Buy a Domain Name

If you are self-hosting your site, you need a domain name. WordPress.com has a paid option for using your own domain instead of yoursitename.wordpress.com.

Domain names can be registered for one or more years through what are called *registrars*. Although most hosting companies are also registrars, the functions are entirely separate. In other words, you do not have to register your domain through your hosting company.

Buy a Domain Name

1 Go to www.name.com in your web browser.

Note: This site is one of many where you can search for and buy domains. Your web host may give you a discounted price.

2 Type the name of your proposed domain in the field.

3 Click **Search** or press Enter.

A Domains with the name you searched appear in a scrollable strip near the bottom of the screen. Those already registered are marked *Taken*. Domains registered to someone else who is selling them at premium prices are labeled *Premium*.

Choosing *Backorder* means the registrar will try to snag the domain for you when its registration expires.

Suggested alternative domain names appear farther down on the page.

If none of the available or suggested domain names satisfies you, repeat steps **2** and **3** until you find one you want.

4 When you find a domain you want, click **Add** to add it to the cart.

B The cart displays the domain you chose, and any additional domains if you chose multiple names.

C Most registrars also offer additional features, such as privacy, email, and even hosting. None of these are required for registering a domain.

5 After you have added or removed items from your cart, click **Next Step**.

A new web page opens.

6 If you are an existing customer, you can log in here, or if this is your first purchase, create an account.

7 Proceed through the remaining screens until your registration and purchase are complete.

Note: If you register more than one domain over time, be sure to use the same registrar each time; it will save you a lot of potential headaches.

Do I have to buy a domain name?
No. But without a domain name, the URL of your site will include your web host's domain. If you ever switch hosts (which often happens) the URL of your site changes, breaking all existing links and losing all your search engine ranking. A domain name gives you continuity as well as identity.

Is the process the same for a WordPress.com site?
It can be, or you can buy your domain name through WordPress.com. Doing so eliminates a few steps in setup.

CHAPTER 2

Setting Up Your WordPress.com Site

In this chapter, you sign up with WordPress.com, get familiar with its workings, choose among settings, and select a theme for your new blog's appearance.

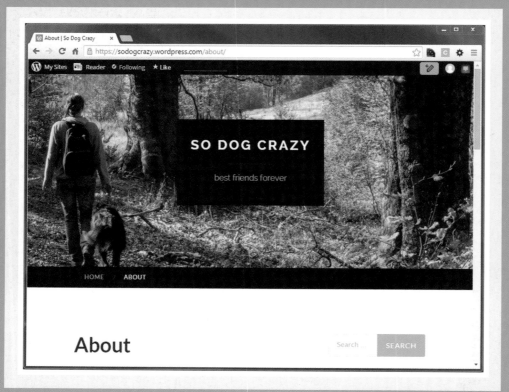

Sign Up with WordPress.com

With just a few simple steps, you can sign up with WordPress.com. A few steps more and you can have a website up and running at no cost.

Sign Up with WordPress.com

① Navigate to https://wordpress.com in your web browser.

② Click **Create Website**.

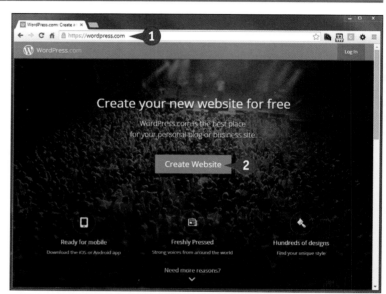

③ Type an email address where you can receive the activation link.

Note: A green check mark appears at each stage if your entry is accepted.

④ Type a username of lowercase letters and numbers.

⑤ Type a strong password.

⑥ Type the name you want as the address of your site.

Ⓐ A check mark appears if the name is available.

Ⓑ A dropdown offers to sell you available, similar domains as an option.

⑦ Click **No thanks, I'll use the free address**. (*yourname*.wordpress.com) and continue scrolling down.

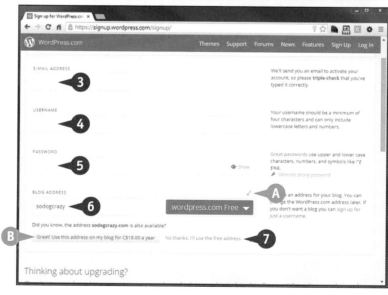

18

C A table shows you what features are available for free and for paid upgrades.

8 Click **Create Blog** to use the free website option.

The next screen begins the process of setting up your site, which is covered in the next section, "Set Up Your New Site."

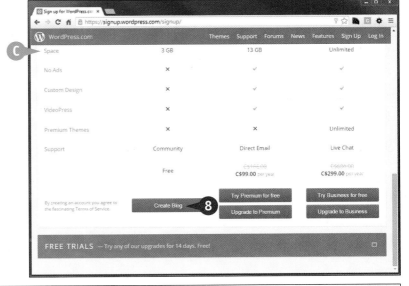

9 Click the link in the email you receive to confirm your account.

If the email is opened on a different device than you are signing up with, you are asked to log in to WordPress.com.

Note: WordPress sends you a second email informing you that the account is set up and offering a link to its tutorials.

Howdy georgetyv

Thank you for signing up with WordPress.com. Click the button below to confirm your email address and start publishing posts.

Confirm Email Address **9**

You can also confirm your email address by copying and pasting this address into your address bar: https://signup.wordpress.com/activate/630bb124b96def94

Please save this email. If you get locked out of your account in the future, this email will help us restore access to your account.

TIPS

Can I just sign up without starting a blog?

Yes. You can add your own blog or site later. To sign up without starting a blog, click **Sign up for just a username** under the Username box, and follow the sign-up instructions.

Now that I am a member, how do I sign in?

You can go to the home page at WordPress.com and sign in at the top of the page; you can type your blog's address plus **/wp-admin**, such as **example.wordpress.com/wp-admin**; or, if you have a Meta section on your blog, you can go to your blog's home page and click the **Log in** link.

Set Up Your New Site

Even while WordPress.com is sending out your confirmation email, you can start setting up your site.

Set Up Your New Site

1 Type a blog title.

The blog title appears in the header of all pages.

2 Type an optional tagline.

The tagline is a few words that further describe your site. The tagline appears below your title.

3 Click the **Language** ▼ and choose a language for your site. The default is English.

4 Click **Next Step**.

You can scroll through several hundred possible themes.

5 When you find a theme you like, click it to highlight it.

Ⓐ Some themes require payment, but most are free.

6 Click **Next Step**.

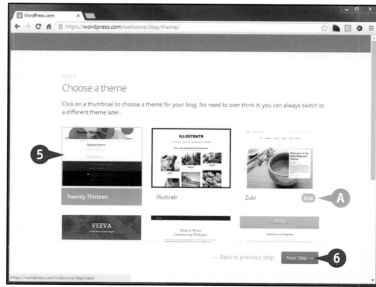

B You see a sample of the theme with a description and its features.

7 Click **Customize It**.

C If you choose not to customize at this time, you can click **Next Step**.

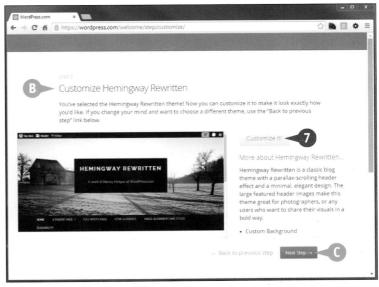

A new screen with customization options appears.

D You see your site as it will look with the chosen theme.

E A menu appears on the right with possible customization options for your theme.

F When you choose an option — in this case, Header — a new section of screen slides out. Here, you are given instructions for changing the header image.

8 Click **Add new image** and another window appears for uploading your header image. When you click **Select and Crop**, the window closes.

9 After you finish making all your theme customizations, click **Save**.

10 On the Customize screen, click **Next Step**.

G You can click one of these buttons to open a dialog box for entering your account information for other social media sites.

11 Click **Next Step** to begin entering content for your site.

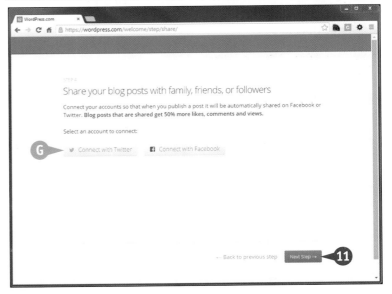

View Your New Site

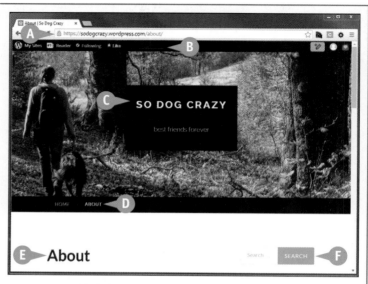

Ⓐ Address

View your site by entering the site name you signed up with, followed by ".wordpress.com."

Ⓑ Toolbar

You can quickly access your WordPress.com site's administrative screens from this toolbar.

Ⓒ Header

In addition to your site title and tagline, this area may contain a background image or your logo, depending on your theme.

Ⓓ Menu

All themes include a navigation menu of your site's pages.

Ⓔ Page or Post Title

The title of the current content, whether it is a page or a post.

Ⓕ Sidebar

The sidebar is comprised of widgets, which perform various functions, like this search function.

Ⓐ Page or Post Content

This is the actual content of the page or post. It can consist of text, images, video, documents, or any combination of those.

Ⓑ Sidebar Widgets

Widgets provide a wide variety of functions, such as displaying your latest posts or social media feeds.

Ⓒ Sharing Buttons

Your visitors can share your content with various social media.

Ⓓ Edit

This link — visible only when you are signed in — takes you to the administrative area for the current web page. Visitors cannot see this.

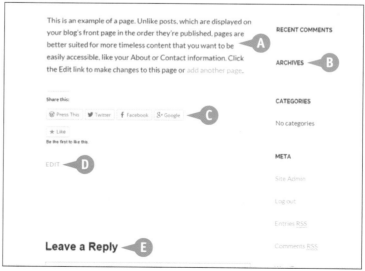

Ⓔ Comments Area

This title marks the start of the comments area, where visitors can leave a comment about this page or post.

Ⓐ Comments Box

The box where visitors enter their comments. Comments which you approve will appear below this box.

Ⓑ Footer

Every theme has a footer area at the bottom of the screen. Usually it contains widgets.

Ⓒ Footer Widget

Widgets are not just for sidebars.

Ⓐ Widget

Another example of a widget that automatically shows content when some is available. No categories have been created yet, so nothing appears. You can remove widgets that currently have no content and then put them back when there is.

Ⓑ Logout/Login

The Meta widget contains a link for logging in to your site, so you do not need to go to the WordPress.com home page to do that. When you are logged in, the link changes to enable you to log out.

Ⓒ Footer Credits

In the free version of WordPress.com, there is a link here encouraging visitors to get their own website.

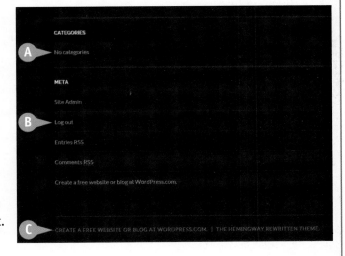

My Site Looks Nothing Like This

WordPress themes vary a great deal, so do not worry if your site looks quite different from the screenshots on these two pages. What you will have is the same basic structure: header, content, sidebar, footer, and the toolbar at the top, so become familiar with those.

Where Is the Blog?

WordPress.com used to create a sample post as well as a sample page, but that is no longer the case. Because no posts have been entered on the So Dog Crazy site, no blog area is showing at this point. That is why the sample page is being shown here.

Get to Know Your Site's Dashboard

The Dashboard can be thought of as the home page for the administrative area of your site. It has a number of helpful sections, like statistics, which show you the current state of your site.

When you first sign up for WordPress.com, the Dashboard displays a comprehensive Help menu to get you started, and which you can turn off when not needed.

Access Your Site's Dashboard

Ⓐ In your browser's address bar, you can add **/wp-admin** to your WordPress domain name, and if you are logged in, you are taken to the Dashboard. If you are not logged in, you see the login screen. In this example, you would type **http://sodogcrazy. wordpress.com/wp-admin**.

Ⓑ From your website, you can click **Site Admin** if you are already logged in.

Ⓒ This Log Out link would show as Log In if you were not signed in to WordPress.com. Note: The widget that displays the login/logout links — displays the login/logout links — called the Meta widget — may not be visible on your site, but you can add it to any widget area.

Ⓐ When you click the **My Sites** link — visible all the time in the toolbar — you get a screen that looks like this.

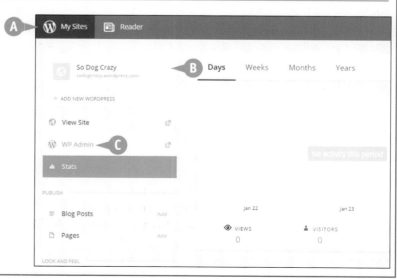

Ⓑ The WordPress.com site you are currently working on appears in this box. If you have more than one site, you can choose which one to administer. You can also add a new site from this box.

Ⓒ Click **WP Admin** to be taken to the Dashboard of your site.

Tour the Dashboard

Ⓐ Left Admin Menu

Every admin screen is accessible from this menu, located on the left side of the screen. When you mouse over a menu item, submenu items appear, and when you are in a menu section, the submenu items are visible. Note: You can collapse the menu to a set of icons by clicking the **Collapse Menu** link at the very bottom.

Ⓑ At a Glance

In this box, you find a summary of how many pages, posts, drafts, and comments you have. In addition, it tells you what theme you are using and how much space your media files (images, documents, and so on) are taking up.

Ⓒ Activity

Shows your latest posts and visitor comments on the WordPress.com website for this Dashboard.

Ⓓ Your Stuff

Shows your recent activity on any WordPress.com website, whether you are commenting on someone else's site or publishing a post to one of your other sites. Note: Just below Your Stuff, and not visible on this screenshot, is another box, What's Hot, that displays news from the WordPress.com team, as well

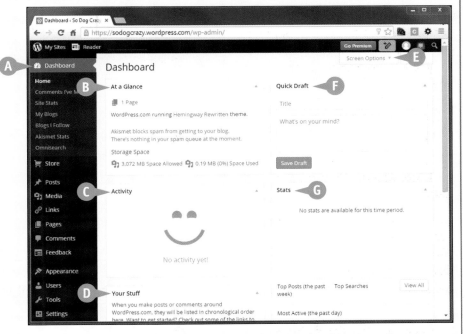

as recent posts and comments from top sites on WordPress.com.

Ⓔ Screen Options

Hide any of the boxes on the Dashboard and then restore them in the future.

Ⓕ Quick Draft

Had a sudden idea for a post? Enter some notes here and get a draft started right away.

Ⓖ Stats

WordPress.com provides statistics for your website, so you know how many visitors you are getting, what posts they are reading the most, and much more.

Understand the WordPress.com Toolbar

When you are logged in at WordPress.com, the toolbar at the top of all screens provides a wealth of options. With just a click, you can start a new blog post, visit other blogs, and do a whole lot more. Some toolbar offerings vary depending on where you are on your own site or other WordPress.com sites.

Ⓐ My Sites

Mouse over this menu item to view a comprehensive set of administrative links, covered in detail below.

Ⓑ Reader

The WordPress.com Reader is your guide to all the other sites on the platform. Mouse over this menu item to view links to various functions of the Reader, covered in detail below.

Ⓒ Statistics Graph

Known as the *Sparkline*, this graph represents the last 48 hours of visitors viewing pages on your site.

Darker lines represent nighttime page views, and if you mouse over the graph, the number you see is the highest amount of views per hour.

Ⓓ Go Premium

Click this link to see your options for upgrading to a different WordPress.com plan.

Ⓔ Add New Post

Click this icon to go to the Add New Post screen.

Ⓕ My Account

Mouse over this menu icon to view links relating to your account, covered in detail below.

Ⓖ Notifications

Click to view a list of notifications about your activity on WordPress.com.

Ⓗ Search

Click to reveal a search box.

My Sites Submenu

Ⓐ Current Site

Shows the site you are administering and a Switch Site menu if you have others on WordPress.com.

Ⓑ View Site

Click to view the front end of your site, as the public sees it.

Ⓒ WP Admin

Click to go to the Dashboard of the current site.

Ⓓ Stats

Click to view your detailed WordPress.com site statistics.

Ⓔ Comments

Click to go to your comments management screen.

Ⓕ Content Links

You can view a list of your Blog Posts, Pages, or Media files. From those lists you can manage individual content items.

Ⓖ Look and Feel Links

You can view available Themes, Customize your current theme, or manage your Menus.

Ⓗ Configuration Links

You can manage your Sharing settings, your Users, the site's Settings, or your Upgrades.

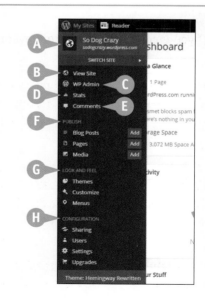

Reader Submenu

Ⓐ Blogs I Follow

Check what is new on sites you have chosen to follow, and not just from WordPress.com.

Ⓑ Freshly Pressed

See what posts the staff have picked as noteworthy from the hundreds of thousands of sites on WordPress.com.

Ⓒ Recommended Blogs

Browse a list of staff-recommended WordPress.com sites by topic.

Ⓓ Find Friends

See which of your social media friends are on WordPress.com.

Ⓔ My Comments

See your most recent comments on WordPress.com sites.

Ⓕ My Likes

Access any posts you have liked on WordPress.com.

My Account Submenu

Ⓐ Your Gravatar Image

If you uploaded an image to Gravatar.com, it appears here.

Ⓑ Sign Out

Log out of your site and WordPress.com. There is also a link to your Gravatar.com account (which was automatically created when you signed up with WordPress.com).

Ⓒ Profile Links

Click **Account Settings** to access your WordPress.com account information, such as Profile, password, security settings, and more. Click **Trophy Case** to view your achievements on WordPress.com (writing your first post earns you your first trophy). Click **Billing** to see a complete history of any billing transactions.

Ⓓ Extras Links

Click **Help** to access the extensive support system for WordPress.com. Click **Find Friends** to see which of your social media friends is on WordPress.com.

Select Your General Settings

The General Settings screen enables you to control basic elements of your site identity and operation. And if you do not like your choices, you can always change them later.

Select Your General Settings

1 On the left admin menu under Settings, click **General**.

2 Change the title of your site, which you entered during setup, from here.

3 Change the tagline of your site, also entered during setup, from here. You can leave the tagline blank if you want.

A You can have an image or an icon associated with your site across WordPress.com.

4 Click **Choose File** to select an image from your device.

5 Click **Upload Image**.

B The image you uploaded appears with a white crop box on a new screen.

6 Resize the box by using the drag handles around the edges.

7 When you have selected the area of the image you want to use, click **Crop Image**.

Note: A confirmation screen opens to show your cropped image. Click **Back to Blog Options** to return to General Settings.

⊙ The cropped image now appears at the top right of General Settings.

⊙ You can choose and upload a new image any time, or you can simply remove the current image.

8 Click the **Timezone ▼** and select a city in your time zone from the dropdown or your time relative to UTC (*coordinated universal time*).

Note: Scroll up in the pop-up list to find cities. If you choose a UTC setting, you must manually reset the zone for daylight savings time.

9 Click a date format (○ changes to ◉).

10 Click a time format (○ changes to ◉).

11 Click the **Week Starts On ▼** and change the day that WordPress uses as the start of a new week.

12 If you plan to write in a language other than English, click the **Language ▼** and choose it.

13 Click **Save Changes** when you finish.

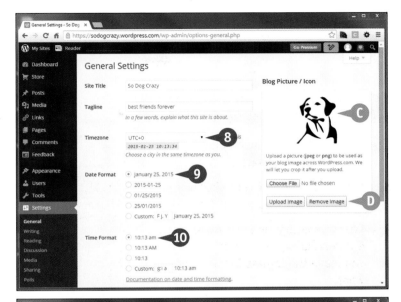

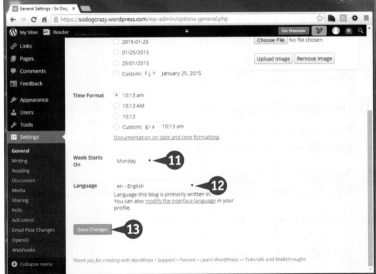

TIP

What is the difference between the Gravatar on the My Public Profile page and the Blog Picture/Icon on the General Settings page?

Gravatar stands for *globally recognized avatar*, and is associated with a particular email address. Any service in the world that uses Gravatar.com now displays that image whenever you use the email address. The Blog Picture/Icon on this page — known as *blavatar* to indicate a *blog* avatar — is an icon for your website. It appears as the favicon in visitors' browsers, as well as in the WordPress.com toolbar. You can have the same image for both, but you would still need to upload the file separately.

Choose Your Personal Settings

The Personal Settings screen enables you to personalize elements of the administration area.

Choose Your Personal Settings

1 On the left admin menu under Users, click **Personal Settings**.

2 If you were looking for My Public Profile, click here.

3 Click here to get an Akismet key.

4 Click a color scheme for your administration area (○ changes to ⊙).

5 Click **Keyboard Shortcuts** (☐ changes to ☑) to enable keyboard shortcuts for comment moderation.

6 Use this section to post your Twitter updates directly to your site.

7 To use a secure browser connection (HTTPS) when working in the administration area, click this option (☐ changes to ☑).

8 Click the **Interface Language** ▼ and choose which language to use for the administrative area.

9 If you have more than one WordPress.com site, click ▼ and select which is primary (which appears by default under My Sites).

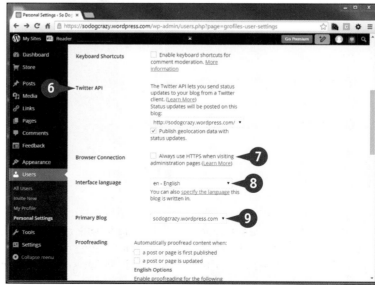

10 Click these options to have WordPress.com automatically proofread your content when you publish or update (☐ changes to ☑).

11 Click proofreading options for English, such as checking for Clichés or Jargon (☐ changes to ☑).

12 If you will be writing in different languages, click this option to have WordPress.com automatically detect the language (☐ changes to ☑).

13 Click here to change your WordPress.com username. It is possible to change this, but you are warned of the consequences.

14 Update your administrative email here.

15 Update the website to which your comments are linked here.

16 Update your password here.

17 Click this button to automatically generate a strong password.

Ⓐ This is an example of a generated password.

18 Click **Save Changes** when you are done.

TIPS

How does my Profile differ from Personal Settings?
Personal Settings are for your administrative area, whereas your Profile controls what the public sees about you on WordPress.com.

What is the two-factor authentication that WordPress.com sometimes mentions in tips?
Having a bank card and a PIN is a type of two-factor authentication: You need both to access your account. WordPress.com offers a version of this which works through an app on your smartphone. It generates a special code that is valid for only 60 seconds, which you use in addition to your username and password.

Create Your Public Profile

Your WordPress.com public profile allows you to tell the world who you are through words, pictures, and links. This information is shown to visitors and displayed at Gravatar.com, so do not include any information you want to keep private.

Create Your Public Profile

1 On the left admin menu under Users, click **My Profile**.

A This area explains that the information entered here is public and where it will appear.

2 If you were looking for Personal Settings rather than My Public Profile, click here.

3 Type your first name.

4 Type your last name.

5 Type your full name.

6 Choose which version of your name you want displayed publicly.

7 Click **Change your Gravatar**.

A new tab opens in your browser, displaying your account at Gravatar.com. The account was automatically created when you signed up with WordPress.com.

B You have a number of options for uploading your image, including linking to an existing image online or using your webcam.

You can crop the image you choose and then approve the final result. When you are done, close the tab.

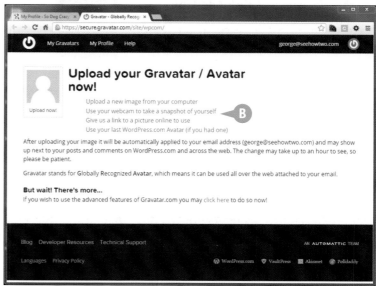

c You should see your new Gravatar in the toolbar as well as at the top of the My Public Profile screen.

8 Enter as much location information as you want the public to see.

9 Enter a bit about yourself (the bit you want to be public).

10 Under Contacts, you can enter as many or as few methods for the public to get in touch: email, social media, and phone numbers.

11 Click **Update Profile** when you are done.

D You can add more than one profile image at Gravatar.com. Those additional images appear here, and you can delete any of them from here as well.

E You can have additional links appear on your public profile. Enter a title and the URL here and click **Add Link**.

F You can verify your accounts at various other services, such as Twitter, Vimeo, Goodreads, and others. This helps confirm you are who you say you are. Choose a service and click **Verify Through** Gravatar.com.

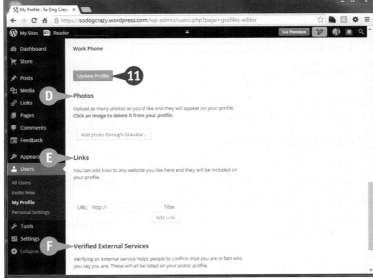

TIPS

Where does my profile appear?
Any website or application that uses the services of Gravatar.com, such as Hootsuite or Disqus. And of course your Gravatar and pop-up profile, or *hovercard*, appears with comments you make on WordPress.com blogs and on posts where you click **Like**. It is associated with your email address.

I do not want my picture and information all over the place. Can I opt out?
Not exactly, because you automatically have a Gravatar account when you sign up with WordPress. However, you can leave your profile information blank, and only a symbol and your username appear when you comment or like a post.

Consider Premium Features

Whereas a basic site at WordPress.com is free, there are a number of paid features available, either individually or bundled with several plans. These features allow you to do more with your site, such as use your own domain name, customize your theme, and even sell products or services.

You can view or order paid features using the **Store** link on the left admin menu or by entering https://store.wordpress.com in your browser's address bar. Paid plans bundle a number of paid features into a single, yearly fee. Most business websites are likely going to need one or the other paid plans. You can upgrade from one plan to another at any time, and WordPress.com offers a free trial of any upgrade. Note: Prices are shown based on the country you are in.

You can also upgrade your account anytime with individual features, which are bought for a 1-year term. But if you are considering even a couple of features, it is probably worth looking at one of the bundled plans.

WordPress.com Plans

Ⓐ Basic

This is the plan which all people get when they sign up for WordPress.com. It is free for life.

Ⓑ Premium

The key features in addition to the Basic plan are:

- You get your own domain name.
- You can customize fonts, colors, and even your CSS.
- You get 10GB of additional storage, including access to VideoPress, which enables you to store video files.
- Your site will never have WordPress.com ads on it.
- You get email support from WordPress.com, not just access to the support forums.

Ⓒ Business

The key features in addition to the Premium plan are:

- You get unlimited storage, including unlimited video file space.
- You can sell products on your site.
- You have access to all Premium themes (50+).
- You get live chat support.

Individual Features

Custom Design

In addition to triggering user-friendly interfaces for changing fonts and colors, purchasing this feature enables you or your designer to change the stylesheet for your theme.

No Ads

On free websites, WordPress.com may occasionally show advertisements. Purchasing this feature ensures that your site will be ad-free.

Unlimited Themes

Whereas anyone can purchase a paid theme, this feature allows you to use any paid theme and switch them as often as you want.

VideoPress

This service enables you to play your videos without any ads or popovers, and to let others share and embed them anywhere on the web (based on your privacy settings). You upload videos up to 1GB in size, and you get unlimited bandwidth.

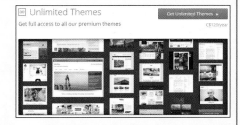

Custom Domain

Instead of a URL ending in wordpress.com, your site can have its own unique domain.

CHAPTER 3

Setting Up Your WordPress.org Site

Your self-hosted WordPress site requires a little more effort, but the payoff is in total control of the look and function of your site.

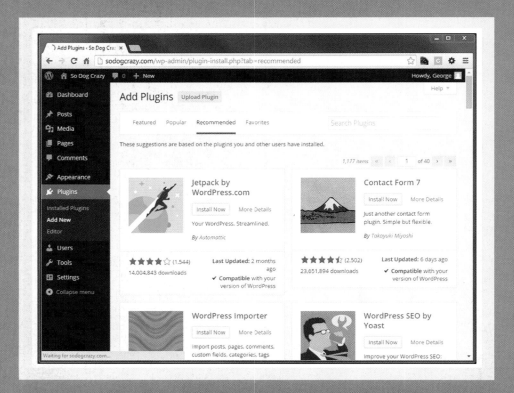

Choose a Host for Your Site

A self-hosted WordPress site requires two things: a domain name, which was covered in Chapter 1, and a web hosting account. Choosing a good web host is important to ensure that your site is always available.

What Web Hosts Do

A web host provides a server (a computer with specialized software) that stores your site's files and databases, and makes them available over the Internet. They also provide control panels which make it easy for you to manage a wide range of functions, such as managing site files or setting up email accounts.

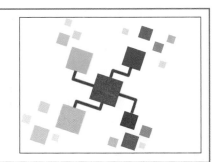

WordPress Requirements

Running WordPress 4.1 requires that your web host provide two basic software packages: PHP version 5.2.4 or greater, and MySQL version 5.0 or greater. PHP is a scripting language, and MySQL is database software. Virtually any server today will meet these requirements, but it is always good to check. WordPress also recommends, but does not require, Apache or Nginx as the server software.

To run WordPress your host just needs :

- PHP version 5.2.4 or greater
- MySQL version 5.0 or greater

That's really it. We recommend Apache or Ngin> for running WordPress, but any server that supp

can't test every possible environment and each

Your Requirements

Choosing a web host also depends on your requirements. Try to anticipate your future needs as much as possible. Will you be needing e-commerce? How many visitors are you trying to attract? Will you need to store a lot of large documents over time? Will you have the skills and time to manage your account and WordPress installation?

Happy Ninja
★★★★★
£18.00

Add to cart

Types of Servers

There are three basic types of servers that web hosts offer: *shared*, *VPS* (virtual private server), and *dedicated*. On a shared server your site will be one of hundreds. On a dedicated server yours is the only site. VPS falls between the two: You share the server with a few other sites, but you are each separated in a way that is close to having a dedicated server. A good shared account is fine for most personal or small business sites.

Ignore Bright Shiny Hosting Objects

Do not pay attention to ads touting unlimited storage or bandwidth, and in particular, ignore ads with "super low" prices. Any good shared hosting account will allow you to store a lot of files and have a lot of visitors, but it is always limited. If you have an extremely large number of visitors, for example, you are asked to move up to a VPS or dedicated server. As for price, if you cannot afford $7 or more per month to promote your business, you need a new business plan. If that is too much for a personal site, consider using WordPress.com instead.

- Unlimited **Web space**
- Unlimited **Traffic**
- Unlimited **Email Accounts**
- Unlimited **SQL Databases**
- Unlimited **Websites**

Managed WordPress Hosting

Many web hosts now offer a special type of shared hosting account aimed at WordPress users. Typically they provide automatic updating of WordPress, automatic backups, tools to ensure your site loads quickly for visitors, and specialized support for WordPress itself. These packages cost more — typically two to three times more than a regular shared hosting account — but they can save you a lot of time and potential headaches.

You create your own WordPress site. We do the work with fully-managed hosting, setup and security.

99.9% uptime guarantee*

Checking Them Out

WordPress.org has a list of recommended hosts, which makes a good starting point. You should also search for online reviews and be sure to include "WordPress" in your search terms. Do not use hosting review sites, because many of them are just advertising; look for independent reviewers who go into the pros and cons. Then go to the support forum of a host you are interested in, and see what problems people are having and whether the problems are being resolved quickly.

WORDPRESS.ORG

Showcase   Themes   Plugins   Mobile   Support

WordPress Web Hosting

There are hundreds of thousands of web hosts out minimum requirements, and choosing one from th

What If It All Goes Wrong?

Computers break down, people make mistakes; the best web hosts sometimes have problems and maybe your website will be affected. Not to worry. If things go wrong, you simply move to a new host and point your domain name there. In fact, your new host will usually move your account for free.

ERROR 404 - PAGE NOT FOUND

Why am I seeing this page?

How to find the correct spelling and folder

Install WordPress via Your Host's Auto-Installer

Virtually all web hosts today offer one-click installation of WordPress, so do not make this the reason for choosing a host.

In this example, the host offers an installer called Softaculous, but there are other installers, such as Simple Scripts or Fantastico.

Install WordPress via Your Host's Auto-Installer

① After you log on to your hosting account and go to its control panel, look for a section called Software or something similar.

② Look for and click a link to an installer; in this case, **Softaculous Apps Installer**. Check the help function if you are not sure.

Note: Some hosts have a specific link for installing WordPress.

The script installer window opens.

Ⓐ In this example, WordPress is already on the Softaculous short list.

③ If WordPress is not visible, look under a CMS or Blog category, depending on the installer.

④ If all else fails, try searching for WordPress.

⑤ After you have located WordPress, click **Install**.

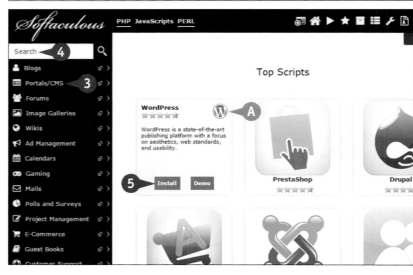

6 If you have more than one domain on this hosting account, make sure you are on the correct one.

7 Softaculous automatically inserts a directory name of "wp," but in most cases you do not want WordPress in a special directory, so delete this.

8 Type the name of the database to be created.

9 The default prefix added to database tables is wp_. You can change this for a bit of extra security.

10 Type the name of the site.

11 Type the site description or tagline.

Ⓑ If multisite is offered, leave it unchecked.

12 Type your administrative username for logging into WordPress.

Note: Do not use "admin."

13 Type your administrative password, making sure it triggers the Strong indicator.

14 Type the administrative email.

15 Click ▼ and choose the language for the administrative area.

16 Click **Install**.

The success screen has links to your new site and to the WordPress admin login.

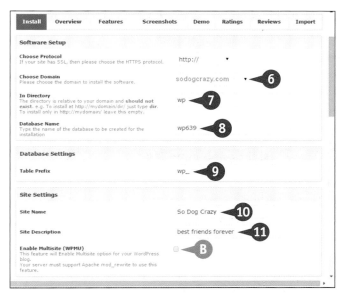

Do I need to choose plugins, themes, or other advanced options at this point?

Leave all of these until after WordPress is installed. You will have a greater choice of plugins, and choosing themes is much easier from the administration screens. Any advanced options will be available on your settings screens.

I forgot to write down my password during installation — how do I get into WordPress?

As long as you have access to the administrative email you entered, you can use the WordPress password recovery function when you try to log in.

Get an FTP Application for Manual Installation

An *FTP program*, or file transfer protocol program, lets you easily move files from your computer to your web host. You need it to do a manual WordPress installation. Your host may provide an FTP utility through its control panel, but using an FTP program on your computer is usually faster.

FileZilla Client is a free, open-source FTP program that works with Windows, Macintosh, and Linux computers.

Get an FTP Application for Manual Installation

1 After starting your web browser, go to http://filezilla-project.org.

2 Click **Download FileZilla Client**. Do not click on FileZilla Server.

The FileZilla Client Download window opens.

3 Review the download options to find the version for your computer's operating system.

4 Click the link to the version you need.

A download window opens. Follow the usual steps for installing a program to your computer.

Note: You will use your FTP client to upload files to your web host by way of your FTP address. Your FTP address is probably ftp://*yourdomain*.com as opposed to http://*yourdomain*.com, which is used to view your website. Check with your web host if you are not sure.

Download WordPress Software

Before you can upload WordPress to your web host for a manual installation, you first must download the software from WordPress.org. After this simple process, you are ready to complete your manual WordPress installation.

Download WordPress Software

1 In your browser, go to https:// wordpress.org/download.

You can also click the **Download WordPress** button at the top right of every page at WordPress.org.

2 Click **Download WordPress 4.1**. The button displays the most current stable version number.

A download window, which varies with your computer's operating system, opens.

Note: Be sure to save the file to a logical location on your computer, and make a note of that location. You will need it later during the uploading process.

A The file you download is a Zip file, so you will need to extract or unarchive the files, depending on your operating system.

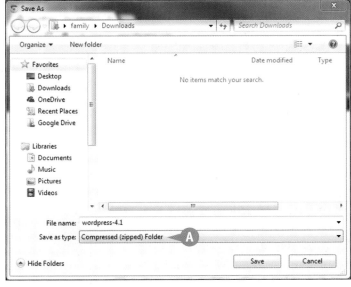

Set Up the MySQL Database

You need a MySQL database to run WordPress. No database, no site, so you need to set up the database before running a manual installation.

Go to your web host and log on to its control panel to get started. This example shows the widely used cPanel control panel, but every web host has an equivalent. Check with technical support at your host if you cannot find the appropriate link.

Set Up the MySQL Database

1 Click the MySQL set-up link for your hosting control panel. For cPanel, you would click **MySQL Database Wizard**.

2 Begin by typing a name for your database.

Ⓐ Most shared servers have a beginning portion of the database name which you do not control. Typically, this is your hosting account's username.

Note: You need the full name (both parts) for your WordPress install.

3 Click **Next Step**.

4 Type a username.

Ⓑ As with the database name in the section "Install WordPress via Your Host's Auto-Installer" (see step **9**), the first portion of the username is determined by the server.

5 Type a password, making sure it shows Strong or Very Strong in the strength indicator.

6 Retype the password.

Note: Save looking them up later by recording the full username and password.

7 Click **Create User**.

ⓒ The next window confirms the creation of the user.

ⓓ At various points in the process, you may see the full database and usernames. If you have not yet recorded these, now is your chance.

⑧ To give the user you created — that is you, the administrator — all the privileges you require to set up and operate the database, click **All Privileges** (☐ changes to ☑).

⑨ Click **Next Step** at the bottom of the screen (not shown).

A new screen confirms the user was added to the database.

⑩ Click **Return Home**.

You are back at the cPanel home.

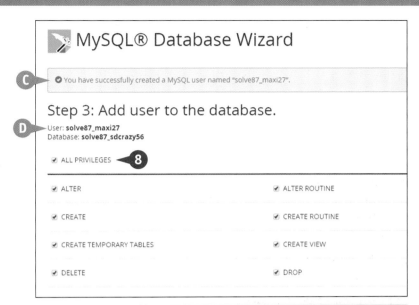

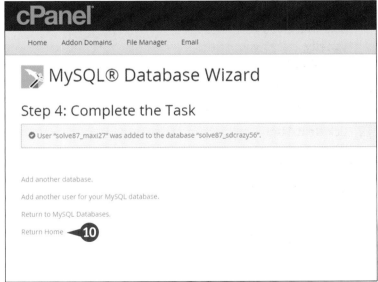

What should I name my database?
Give it a name that you readily associate with your site so that you will recognize it in the future. This is particularly important if you have more than one site on your hosting account, with multiple databases.

Can I use the same username and password that I used for WordPress?
It is better to use different ones for greater security.

Upload the WordPress Files

Time now to upload the files that you downloaded and unzipped from WordPress.org. Only after uploading these files to your server can the installation process begin.

Upload the WordPress Files

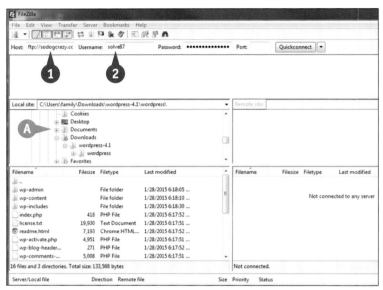

(A) When you open your FTP client, FileZilla in this example, the files on your local computer appear in the lower left panel.

1 Type your host name into the Host field.

Note: The host is just your domain name. If that does not work, check with your host.

2 Type your username in the Username field.

Normally this is the username for your hosting account.

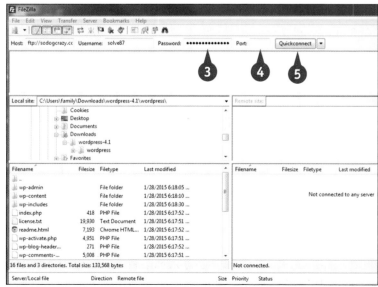

3 Type your password in the Password field.

Normally this is the password for your hosting account.

4 The Port field can be left empty unless you want to use secure file transfer (SFTP). Check with your host for that port number.

5 Click **Quickconnect**.

46

B FileZilla shows the progress of the connection.

C When connected, your web host directory appears in the right panel.

6 Navigate in the left panel until you find the folder containing the WordPress files you downloaded and extracted, and open that folder by double-clicking it.

7 In the right panel, open the public_html folder. It will most likely be empty, except for a folder called cgi-bin.

Note: public_html is the most common name, but another is httpdocs.

8 In the left panel, select all the WordPress folders and files.

9 Drag the highlighted items to the right panel.

D The upload process takes several minutes, and you can watch the progress in the bottom pane of the FileZilla window.

E When uploading is complete, you see all the WordPress files in the right panel.

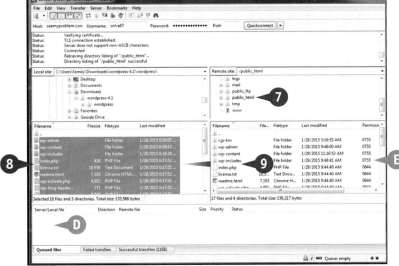

TIPS

I do not feel comfortable working with FTP. Is there another way to upload these files?

Most hosting control panels have a File Manager. These work in much the same way as an FTP program does, but they usually do not show your computer files in the handy split panel, and they are sometimes slower than an FTP program.

How do I know what my site's root directory is?

If you have only one domain name on your hosting account, the root directory will be the public_html folder or httpdocs. If you have more than one domain name, it will be the folder with that domain name. If in doubt, ask your host.

Complete the Configuration and Installation

So far you have been getting ready to install WordPress. Now it is time to actually do the installation.

Complete the Configuration and Installation

1 Type your domain name in your browser and press **Enter**.

2 Choose a language for your WordPress site by scrolling and clicking on it to highlight it.

3 Click **Continue**.

A window opens and reminds you of the information WordPress needs to create your configuration file.

4 Review the list of needed information — which you created when you set up your MySQL database — and make sure you have it all available.

Ⓐ The table prefix is an optional item if you want a bit of extra security instead of using the default wp_ prefix.

5 Click **Let's go**.

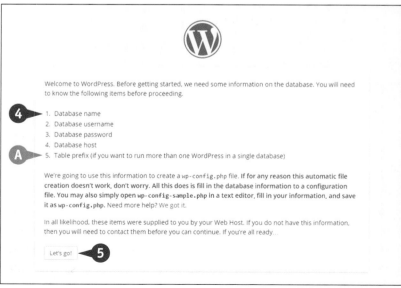

The connection details window opens.

6 Type your MySQL database name.

7 Type your database username.

8 Type your database user password.

B The default localhost is fine for most servers. Check with your host if you are not sure.

9 Click **Submit**.

10 If all went well, a confirmation appears. Click **Run the install**.

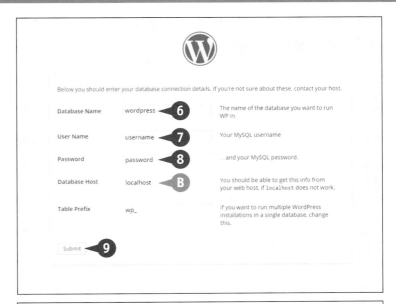

The Information Needed window opens.

11 Type your site title.

12 Type a username. Do not use "admin."

13 Type a password, making sure it is strong.

14 Type your email.

15 If you do not want search engines to index your site, click this option (☑ changes to ☐).

16 Click **Install WordPress**.

17 The Success window opens and shows your WordPress username. Click **Log In** if you are ready.

Note: WordPress emails your username to the email address you provided.

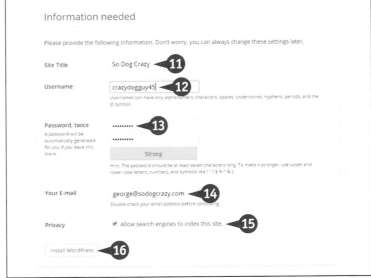

TIPS

Should I change the Table Prefix?
WordPress adds a prefix to all its database tables; default is wp_. Some people say you have a bit more security by using a unique prefix, such as yT5r_. There is no clear consensus about how effective this is for security.

What if my installation did not work?
Although even the manual installation is fairly simple, occasionally things can go wrong. The error message or messages you see will guide you. See the next section of this chapter, "Troubleshoot Installation Errors," for more information.

Troubleshoot Installation Errors

Things do not always go as planned, of course. When this happens with a manual WordPress installation, a bit of troubleshooting is usually all it takes to get back on track.

Trouble Uploading Files

Although the set of WordPress files is not very large (around 17MB), you might have a slow or interrupted connection. Most FTP programs are good at picking up where they left off, but if you are not sure it finished properly, just upload again, overwriting any existing files. Make sure you have entered your hosting account login for your FTP credentials (or whatever the hosting company gave you for FTP purposes). Do not create a new FTP account for this process, or you may run into file ownership issues.

Cannot See the First WordPress Install Screen

If you navigate to your site's URL, and instead of the first WordPress installation screen you get a message saying the site cannot be found or is under construction, you may have uploaded the WordPress *folder* you got from WordPress.org rather than its *contents*. If so, just move the files out of the folder using FileZilla or your host's file management utility.

This webpage is not available

Details

Cannot Select Database

During the installation process, WordPress may let you know that it cannot connect to the database using the credentials you entered. Make sure you are correctly typing the password in particular, and that you have the correct database host name. Check with your host, or consult a list of some popular hosts' hostnames at http://codex. wordpress.org/Editing_wp-config.php. If you think you may have copied the password incorrectly, go back to your hosting panel and re-enter the database user password.

Can't select database

We were able to connect to the database server (which able to select the mutt26_wp79 database.

- Are you sure it exists?
- Does the user mutt26_chris40 have permission
- On some systems the name of your database is username_mutt26_wp79. Could that be the proble

Other Error Messages

If you complete the installation but the first time you log in to WordPress you get error messages, you are possibly missing a file or a file got corrupted on upload. Using your FTP program, upload all the WordPress files again, telling the program to overwrite the existing files. Make sure the Transfer Type is set to Auto (the default) and not to Binary or ASCii.

Fatal error: Call to undefined function icl_register_string() in /data03/
/woocommerce_wpml.class.php on line 527

Never Change Permissions to 777

Sometimes you will read advice on the Internet to change the permissions on a file or folder to 777 in order to troubleshoot a problem. A numeric value of 777 for permissions means anyone can read, execute, or write, that is, change, a file. WordPress automatically sets all permissions during installation. Using your FTP program, it is possible to change permissions, but you should not need to and certainly never to 777.

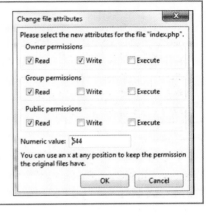

Go Automatic

Web hosts began offering auto-installers precisely because things do occasionally go wrong for manual installations. It may be time to switch to this method of installing WordPress if you are still having issues. If your host does not offer this service, consider switching hosts.

You Can Always Start Again

If all else fails, and you still want to do a manual installation, you can delete everything, including the database, using your hosting control panel and start again. Before doing so, double-check that your host meets the WordPress requirements. If you are still having trouble and your hosting company is not providing sufficient help, you can really start again by getting a new host, pointing your domain there, and trying the install with it.

FREE Website Transfer

We'll transfer your website for you, free of charge.

One of the biggest challenges for a web hosting customer is transferring their hosting provider. It's one of the most daunting tasks that a website owner can GreenGeeks offers a FREE Website Transfer service for all customers who have with another hosting provider and want to switch to us.

Log In to Your Site's Administrative Area

To manage your self-hosted WordPress site, you need to log in to the administration area. This section outlines the two main ways of doing this.

Do not go to WordPress.com and try to log in. Your site is self-hosted and has nothing to do with WordPress.com.

Log In to Your Site's Administrative Area

Log In from a URL

1 In your browser, type your domain name followed by **/wp-admin** and press `Enter`.

The browser takes you to your WordPress Log In page.

2 Type your WordPress username in the Username field.

3 Type your WordPress password in the Password field.

A If you want WordPress to remember your computer for 14 days rather than 2 days, click **Remember Me** (☐ changes to ☑).

Note: Do not use this if others can access your computer.

B You can click the **Lost your password** link if you have forgotten your password.

4 Click **Log In**.

The Dashboard opens.

C The lost password screen explains the process. After completing this screen, you receive an email with a link allowing you to change your password.

5 Type your username or administrative email.

6 Click **Get New Password**.

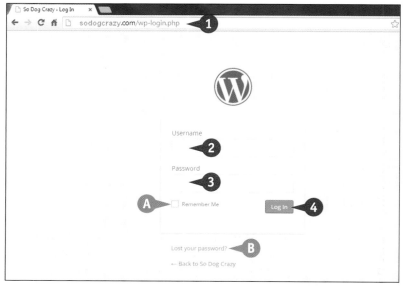

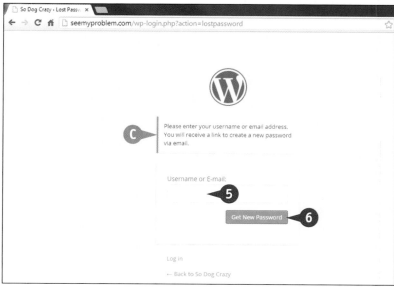

Log In from Your Site

1 Many WordPress themes have a default widget or a footer area that displays a Log In link. Click that link to get to the Login screen.

Note: If you want a Log In link on your site and it does not appear by default, you can add it using the Meta widget that comes with WordPress.

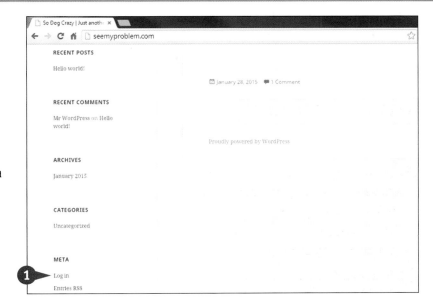

TIPS

I thought I typed my password right, but I am still having trouble logging in.

Your password is *case sensitive*, so be sure that you are typing capital or lowercase letters the same when you are logging in as you did when you created the password.

What do I do if the email I used during installation no longer works and I am the only administrator?

It is possible to go into the WordPress database and manually change the password of any user. However, you need to know what you are doing. You could hire a WordPress expert to do this for you or talk to your host.

View Your New Site

The moment you completed the installation of WordPress there is a website set up. It does not contain much at this point, but all the basics are there and it is important to become familiar with them.

Note: Not shown in this screenshot is a footer area that appears on all pages.

A The header area of the site contains items such as your site title, tagline, and possibly a header image or logo. Learn about controlling this area in Chapter 9.

B These are individual widgets grouped in a widget area. Learn about widgets and widget areas in Chapter 8.

C Whereas the default Twenty Fifteen theme does not show a menu by default, most themes do, and it usually appears somewhere in the header area. Learn about menus in Chapter 8.

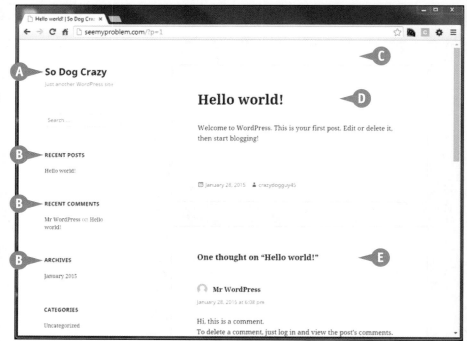

D This is a post, which is one type of content, the other being WordPress pages. Learn about creating written content in Chapter 5.

E The comments area for this post. Learn about managing comments in Chapter 11.

Know the Administrative Screen

The power of WordPress is to enable easy management of your site content, design, and functions. This is done through a series of administrative screens, also known as admin screens, all of which share some common elements.

Ⓐ The left admin menu runs the height of the left side of all screens. From here you control your content, settings, theme, plugins, widgets, comments, and more.

Ⓑ The toolbar is the black strip across the top of all admin screens and can also appear on the front end of the site while you are logged in.

Ⓒ A Screen Options link appears on most screens, allowing you to control the display of meta boxes and other elements.

Ⓓ Most admin screens have a Help link which displays information about that particular screen.

Ⓔ The large gray area is where you will find the administrative tools for any particular screen. Here you see a list of all posts.

Get to Know the Dashboard

The Dashboard is the administrative home page for your self-hosted, WordPress.org installation. From the Dashboard, you can get a snapshot of the state of your site as well as the WordPress community.

When starting out with WordPress, the Dashboard is an important part of getting to know the administrative area.

Ⓐ The Welcome to WordPress box has a series of links to key functions like adding posts or pages, or managing widgets or menus. You can dismiss this box when you are comfortable finding your way around.

Ⓑ At a Glance gives you overall totals for various types of content, as well as listing the version of WordPress you are running and what theme is active.

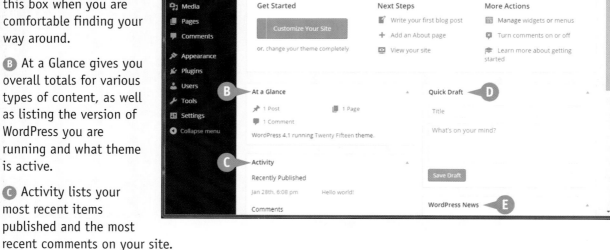

Ⓒ Activity lists your most recent items published and the most recent comments on your site.

Ⓓ Quick Draft allows you to make a quick draft post you can return to later and finish.

Ⓔ WordPress News keeps you up to date with what is happening in the WordPress community.

Get to Know the Toolbar

The toolbar for self-hosted sites, visible at the top of both the back end and front end of your site when you are logged in, gives you quick access to the administrative functions you most need. You can remove the toolbar from the front end of your site, as explained in the section "Select Your Profile Settings."

Ⓐ Drop-down menu links to information about WordPress.org and to support.

Ⓑ When on the front end of the site, this drop-down menu links to frequently used administrative modules. When on the back end of the site, clicking the site name takes you to the home page of the front end of the site.

Ⓒ Shows number of comments awaiting approval, if any, and goes directly to the Comments panel to moderate them.

Ⓓ The New drop-down menu on the toolbar makes it easy to add new posts, media file(s), pages, and users.

Ⓔ The Profile menu on the toolbar shows your username, along with your Gravatar image (or a generic icon, as in this case). From the dropdown you can also edit your profile or log out of WordPress.

Ⓕ Clicking the magnifying glass slides out a search box.

Check Your General Settings

Whereas some of your site's general settings were entered during the installation process, there are a few more you need to check before getting started on your site.

Check Your General Settings

1 On the left admin menu under Settings, click **General**.

2 The site title you entered during installation can be changed from here.

3 If you did an auto-install (see the section, "Install WordPress via Your Host's Auto-Installer"), the tagline should already be changed. On a manual installation, it show the default "Just another WordPress site," which you can change from here.

4 Do not change the WordPress address or site address unless you know what you are doing. It could break your site.

5 The administrative email address entered during installation can be changed here.

6 Leave the Membership option unchecked.

7 Leave the New User Default Role option at Subscriber.

8 Choose a city in your time zone from the drop-down menu.

9 Pick a date format (○ changes to ●).

10 Pick a time format (○ changes to ●).

11 Click ▼ and choose the day the week starts on.

12 The site language you chose during installation.

13 Click **Save Changes**.

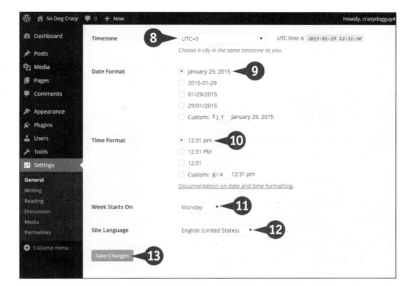

I do not see the tagline on my site. Do I need to change it?

Not all themes use the tagline, but it is used for creating the title tag that appears in browser tabs and which is used by search engines, so it is very important to change it from the default. At the very least leave it blank so you are not one of the tens of thousands of sites that show up in search engines under "Just another WordPress site."

Select Your Profile Settings

Your profile contains settings that control how you view the admin screens and the way you are identified to visitors to your site.

Select Your Profile Settings

1 Click **Your Profile** under Users.

Note: You can also access Your Profile from the top right of the toolbar.

2 Click this option to disable Visual mode of the content editor during writing (☐ changes to ☑).

Ⓐ Several color schemes are available for admin screens. See them in real time by clicking one (○ changes to ◉).

3 Click this option if you want keyboard shortcuts enabled when moderating comments (☐ changes to ☑). Unless you get a lot of comments, leave this unchecked.

4 Click this option to hide the toolbar while viewing your site (☑ changes to ☐).

Ⓑ Your username cannot be changed.

5 Type your first name.

6 Type your last name.

7 Type a nickname.

Note: The nickname defaults to your username; for security you should change it.

Ⓒ The Display Name Publicly As dropdown defaults to the username.

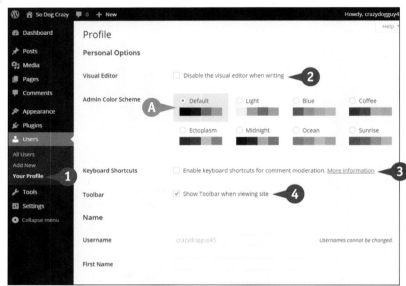

8 Once you have entered some names, the dropdown shows your choices. Click ▼ and choose the public identity you prefer.

9 Creating a user requires a username and an email address. You can update the email from here.

10 The website address entered here may be used by a theme when displaying site authors.

11 The short biography entered here is sometimes used by themes when listing authors on a site.

12 You can change your password here.

13 Re-enter your new password.

D The indicator shows how strong your password is based on the instructions.

E If you have logged in to WordPress on multiple devices, this button becomes active and logs you out of all other instances of WordPress.

14 Click **Update Profile**.

Your profile is saved and a confirmation message appears.

If you changed your public identity, the new name appears at the top right of the toolbar.

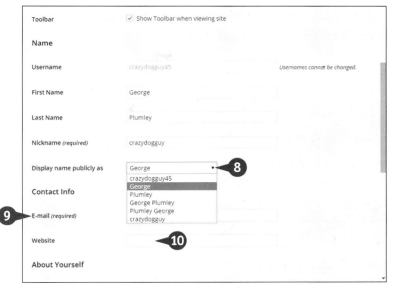

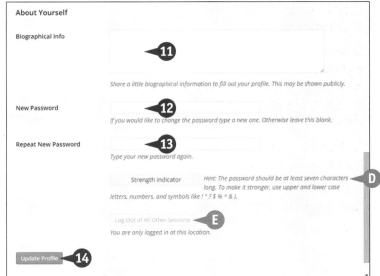

TIPS

What if I want to change my username?

You would need to create a new user. But keep in mind that user emails must be unique, so you would need a different email address for the new user. Once your new account is created, log in as that user and you can delete the old user.

Do I have to include contact information?

Only email is required — which is not public and is only for receiving email notices, such as when comments appear on your blog or when you forgot your password. You can add other contact or biographical information, but understand that it may become public, depending on your theme.

Choose a Theme

Self-hosted WordPress blogs have nearly limitless options when it comes to *themes* — the set of files that control the look and layout of your site. Finding a great-looking theme is easy these days, but you need to look beyond the bright shiny front ends. In this section, you find some key questions to be asked before you try or buy.

There are a couple of default themes that come with your WordPress installation. It is important to keep these in your theme library even if you are not using them. They can be important for backup or testing purposes in case of issues down the road.

Theme Types

Many themes are built to display content in specific ways or offer features that appeal to a particular kind of site owner. Consider the purpose and content of your site. If you are a photographer or ad agency, you might search for *portfolio* themes. If you are selling products, look for *catalog/e-commerce* themes. There are themes aimed at all kinds of businesses, from real estate to restaurants to bands.

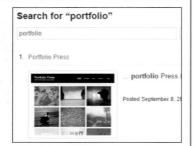

Ease of Use

Themes can take very different approaches to the way they are administered. You may find one approach easier than another. Therefore, it is important to try out the administrative side of a theme, not just view a demo of the front end. Fortunately, WordPress makes it easy to install, activate, and delete themes, so test-drive as many as you need.

It Is Not Just about Appearance

Although a theme controls the look of your site, it does much more. For example, WordPress has a menu system, but one theme may offer only a single menu location, whereas another offers three. Note: If the theme does not use the WordPress menu system, find another theme. Others do more than they should, such as search engine optimization (SEO), which is best handled by a *plugin*. Ask yourself if you would want the function even if you got rid of the theme; then it belongs in a plugin.

Theme Frameworks

One type of WordPress theme is called a *framework*. The idea is that there is a parent theme common to all kinds of child themes. The parent does most of the work, and the child themes give the site its appearance. The advantage here is that you do not have to lose functionality or learn new ways of doing things when you switch the look of your site. Those are common problems today because themes vary so greatly between different makers. A framework is a way of future-proofing your WordPress site, saving you time and money.

Responsive or Not?

A *responsive* theme means that it adapts to the type of device the visitor is using: desktop, tablet, smartphone, and so on. Most themes created since 2013 are responsive, but you always need to check. If you find a theme you like which is not responsive, WordPress can install a plugin fairly easily that will display your theme to mobile users using a special mobile theme.

Free Themes

There are only two places from which you should get a free theme: the Themes Directory at http://wordpress.org/extend/themes or a reputable commercial theme maker offering a free sample. Anywhere else and you risk getting not only a poor quality theme, but one with malware. You can search the Directory right from your WordPress installation by clicking **Appearance** in the left admin menu and then the **Install Themes** button to search.

Commercial Themes

Commercial or *premium* themes refer to themes you pay for. In addition to high quality features and coding, you should expect to get fast support, but none of this is guaranteed, so you still need to do your homework. These themes do not appear on your site's Appearance/Install Themes search. You can find links to commercial theme makers at http://wordpress.org/themes/commercial.

Commercially Supported GPL Themes

While our directory is full of fantastic themes, sometimes people want to use don't mind paying for that. Contrary to popular belief, GPL doesn't say that e the software or theme that it not restrict your freedoms in how you use it.

With that in mind, here are a collection of folks who provide GPL themes wit them you may pay for access, some of them are membership sites, some n support. What they all have in common is people behind them who support c

Custom Themes

You can get a custom theme in two ways: Take an existing theme and change its coding, or have a theme built from scratch. Customizing an existing theme is the less expensive and more common route to take, because typically you only need to change some aspects of design or add an additional function or two. Building a theme from scratch may be necessary, though, if you need a lot of very specific functionality.

```
<article id="post-<?php the_ID(); ?>" <?php post_class(); ?>>
        <?php twentyfifteen_post_thumbnail(); ?>

        <header class="entry-header">
                <?php the_title( sprintf( '<h2 class="entry-ti
href="%s" rel="bookmark">', esc_url( get_permalink() ) ), '</a
        </header><!-- .entry-header -->

        <div class="entry-summary">
                <?php the_excerpt(); ?>
        </div><!-- .entry-summary -->
```

In either case, you need to hire a designer and/or developer who is experienced with WordPress.

Install Your New Theme

You can install and activate free themes from the WordPress directory more easily than you can change your clothes. Installing commercial themes is only slightly more involved.

This section assumes you already chose a theme by following the guidance in the previous section, "Choose a Theme."

Install Your New Theme

Themes Selected through Install Themes on Your Site

1. Click **Appearance** on the left admin menu.

A. The Themes panel opens and displays all themes in your theme library. Which default WordPress themes are installed depends on the current version of WordPress.

2. Click **Add New**.

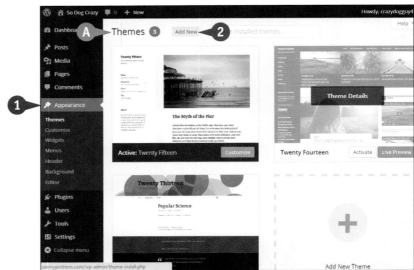

The Add Themes screen opens. You are now viewing the WordPress themes directory from within your administration area.

B. You can search through the directory using a number of filters.

Note: You see large thumbnails of each theme as you browse. Mouse over a theme and you see an Install and a Preview button. Clicking Preview shows you a demo of the theme.

3. Type the name of your chosen theme in the search box. When you finish typing, WordPress automatically searches.

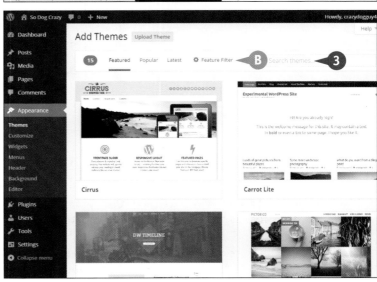

This example searches for the Carrot Lite theme.

You should see a large thumbnail of your theme. Mouse over to see the Install button.

4 Click **Install**.

C WordPress displays the completed steps as it installs the theme. This should take only a few seconds.

5 Click **Activate** to make the theme active.

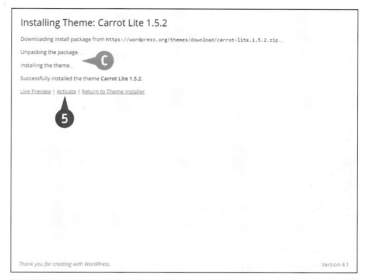

WordPress activates the theme and returns you to the Themes screen.

D A success message confirms that you have activated a new theme. Always watch for success messages when taking an action in WordPress.

E Your newly active theme appears at the top left of the list of installed themes.

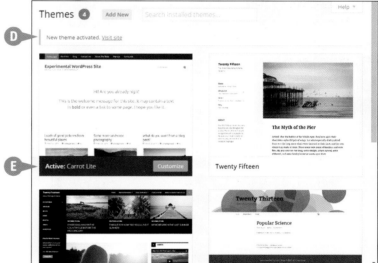

TIPS

Why did WordPress ask for FTP credentials when I tried to install my theme?
This means WordPress does not have correct ownership of its folders and files. If you don't want to enter FTP information every time, contact your host to correct the situation.

My theme does not look the way I expected. Why is that?
Themes are always promoted using home pages filled with content — in particular, great looking images. With no content or home page settings, your new site will rarely look much like the promotional shots or demos. Well-built themes provide you with instructions or documentation right in WordPress, often with support at the theme maker's website.

continued ▶

When you buy a theme or get a free theme from a commercial theme maker, you need to download the theme files and do a manual installation. Fortunately, WordPress makes the process very simple.

Install Your New Theme (continued)

Themes Installed Manually

1 Download the theme from the seller's site, or if you have been searching at WordPress.org, you can download a theme there. Themes should be in a zipped file.

2 Save the file to your computer.

Note: Do not extract it; leave it as a Zip file.

3 In the left admin menu, click **Appearance**.

4 Click **Themes**.

5 Click **Add New** at the top of the Themes screen.

The Add Themes screen opens.

6 Click **Upload Theme**.

The Add Themes screen changes to allow you to choose a file for upload.

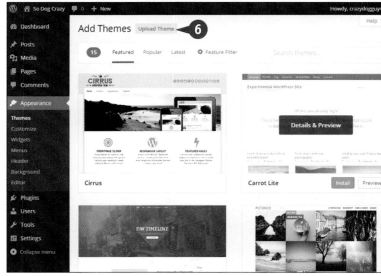

7 Click **Choose File** and browse your computer to find your theme's Zip file.

A When you have selected it, the file name appears beside the Choose File button.

8 Click **Install Now**.

WordPress lists the progress of your installation.

9 When the theme is successfully installed, click **Activate**.

The Themes screen opens with the new theme activated at the top left of all the installed themes.

When WordPress Says It Cannot Install the Theme

B Sometimes the Zip file you download from a commercial theme maker contains additional files, such as Photoshop files.

C Inside that downloaded Zip file is another Zip file, which is the actual theme, and the file that you need to upload to WordPress.

Note: Check inside the extracted theme folder for a ReadMe.txt file, which may have additional installation instructions.

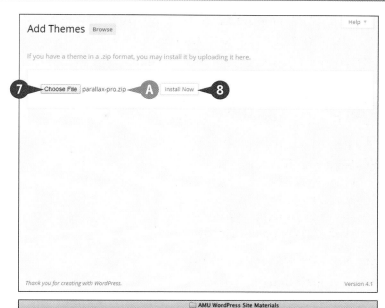

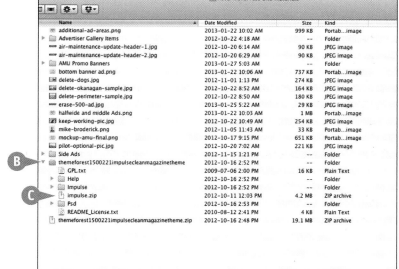

I got a bunch of gibberish on my screen when I clicked Activate. What happened?
There is a good chance the theme was activated anyway. Click **Themes** in the left menu bar, and see if your theme appears as the current theme. If not, try clicking **Preview** under the theme image, and then **Activate** in the preview window.

How can I tell if my cost-free theme is also problem-free?
Alas, virtually no theme, including paid ones, guarantees flawless performance. The ratings and comments on the WordPress.org theme pages and forums can help identify potential problem themes. For other themes, review the theme's home page to see whether it provides significant support.

CHAPTER 4

Knowing Your Administration Tools

The WordPress admin screens provide the tools and information you need to manage your website.

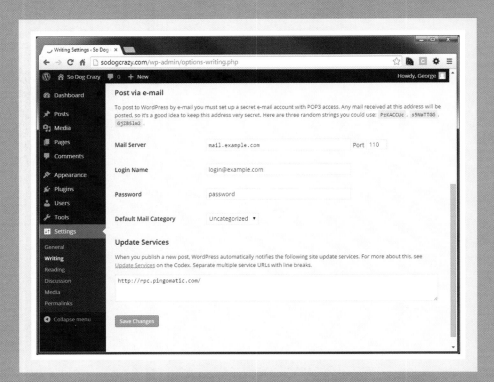

Customize Admin Screens

Wordpress makes it easy for you to customize the layout and organization of many admin screens so you can work more efficiently.

The boxed areas which appear on many admin screens are referred to as meta boxes.

Customize Admin Screens

Collapse Meta Boxes

1 Position your mouse pointer anywhere in the header area of a meta box — in this case, Activity.

A The arrow (▲) at the right is pointing up, indicating the meta box is open.

2 Click anywhere in the header to make the box collapse.

B The meta box collapses and only the heading appears. This meta box, At a Glance, is collapsed.

C In the exploded view, the indicator arrow at the right is now pointing downward (▼).

3 Click anywhere in the header to expand the meta box again.

Collapse the Left Admin Menu

1 Click **Collapse menu** at the bottom of the left admin menu to toggle between full mode and icon-only mode.

D In icon-only mode, the submenus still fly out with full text.

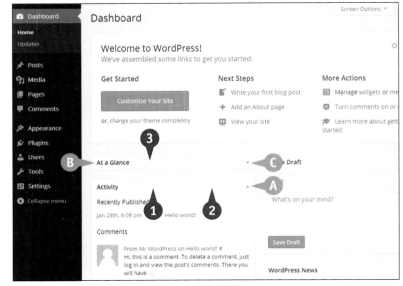

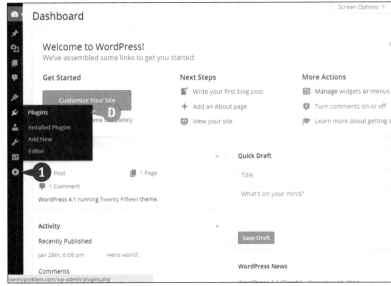

Rearrange Meta Boxes

1 Click and drag in the header area of a meta box.

E As you drag, you see a dashed outline of the box's original position.

F The box itself becomes transparent as you drag, so you can see what is below it on the screen.

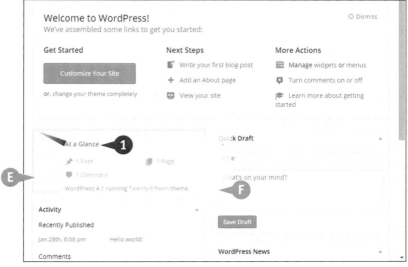

G As you drag the box around the screen, other boxes move out of the way.

H A potential new location for the box appears as a dashed outline. If that is where you want the box, let go of your mouse and the box falls into position.

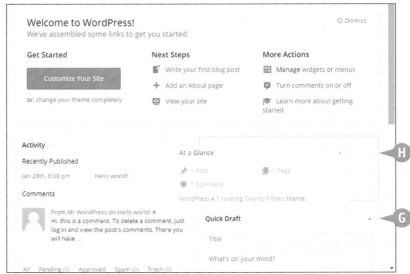

TIPS

Do I have to collapse or move boxes every time I am on a screen?
No. WordPress remembers any changes you have made and uses them on all screens of that type until you make a new change.

Why would I want to move a meta box?
If you always forget to select a featured image for your posts, for example, you could move the featured image box near the publish box. That way, whenever you go to publish a post, it will be obvious whether you remembered to select a featured image.

continued ▶

ere are more ways you can customize your admin screens so they match your work habits.

Customize Admin Screens (continued)

Change the Number of Columns

Note: Many admin screens — in this case, the Add New Post screen — have two columns of meta boxes. To reduce clutter, you can change that to one.

1 Click **Screen Options** at the top right.

A A drop-down area appears with ways to modify the screen.

Note: What you can do in Screen Options varies with different admin screens, and not all screens have a Screen Options section.

2 Under Screen Layout, look for Number of Columns and click **1** (○ changes to ◉).

3 Click **Screen Options** to close the dropdown.

B The screen now shows only one column of meta boxes.

C Meta boxes like Publish or Categories are not gone; they are lined up below the Content Editor.

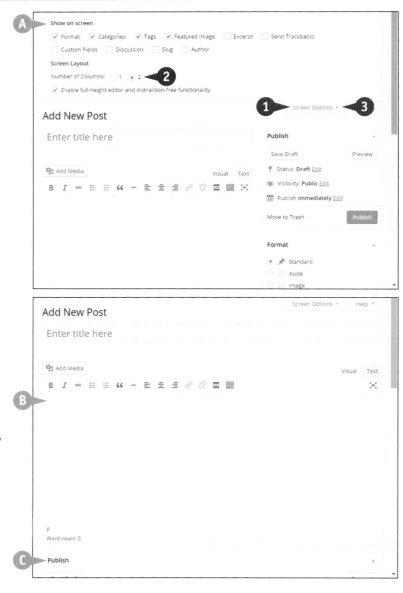

Hide Meta Boxes

Note: Sometimes you simply want to get rid of a meta box, not just collapse or move it.

1 Click **Screen Options** at the top right of the screen.

D If you see the meta box listed, that means you can hide or show it. This example hides the Welcome meta box.

2 Click **Welcome** (☑ changes to ☐).

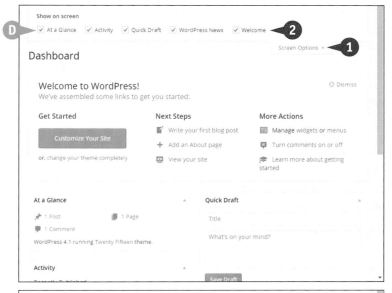

The Welcome box is no longer visible.

3 Click **Screen Options** to close the dropdown.

Note: WordPress by default hides boxes on certain admin screens to help reduce the initial clutter. Or, adding a plugin may create certain meta boxes which WordPress also hides by default. You can always see what is available by clicking **Screen Options**.

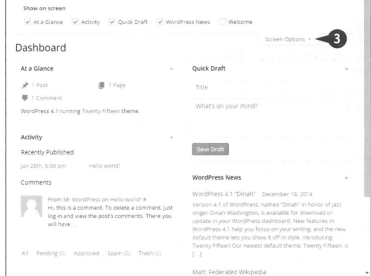

TIPS

Do I need to change the number of columns when I am on my mobile device?
No. WordPress automatically chooses the single column view if the width of the device's browser is less than on a desktop.

Could I just move meta boxes until they all line up in a single column?
Yes, but it is a lot of work. It is much simpler to use the columns function in Screen Options, particularly if you want to easily switch back to two columns again.

Review the Writing Settings

The writing settings you choose affect the mechanics of how you write your blog posts, whether you write directly into your WordPress interface or post by email or other means. Your writing settings also set your default blog post category. You can find Writing Settings by clicking the **Writing** link under Settings on the left admin menu.

On WordPress.com and WordPress.org

Ⓐ Formatting

Lets you select whether WordPress automatically inserts graphic emoticons as you type, such as replacing :-) with 😊. Also lets you decide if you want WordPress to correct bad markup, such as missing closing tags.

Ⓑ Default Post Category

If you do not choose at least one category for a post, WordPress defaults to this.

Ⓒ Default Post Format

Lets you choose the default format for posts. The choices vary by theme.

Ⓓ Press This

Lets you instantly start a new post while viewing any web page. The title of the post will be the title of that web page and a link, along with any text or image you have highlighted, will appear in the post.

Ⓔ Post via Email

Sets you up to post to your site from email.

On WordPress.com Only

Ⓐ Default Link Category

If you forget to categorize a link, WordPress defaults to this.

Ⓑ Markdown

Lets you choose whether to use this alternative to HTML tags as a way of marking up your content (bold, lists, and so on).

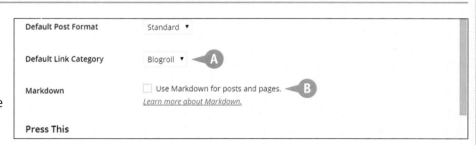

Set Up to Post by Email

Creating and publishing posts by email can be handy, particularly for smartphone users. It works by setting up a hard-to-guess email address. WordPress.com does this for you, although on self-hosted WordPress, you need to create the address through your hosting control panel.

You can find the Post by Email option by clicking the **Writing** link under Settings on the left admin menu.

Set Up to Post by Email

On a Self-Hosted Site

1 After you set up a special email account — instructions are given on screen — type the mail server information for that account in the Mail Server field.

Note: You can get server information from the provider of your special email address.

2 Type your special email address in the Login Name box.

3 Type the email account's password in the Password box.

4 Click ▼ and select the default category for your emailed posts.

5 Click **Save Changes**.

When you post by email, the subject line is used as the post's title.

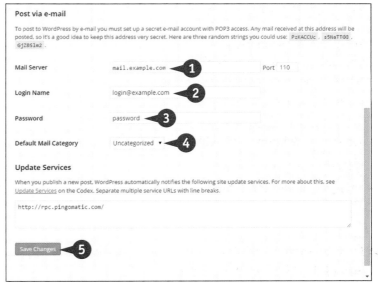

On WordPress.com

1 After clicking **My Blogs** on the Writing Settings page or Dashboard menu, click **Enable** under Post by Email.

An email address replaces the Enable button. Use that address to post via email.

A WordPress.com also offers Post by Voice.

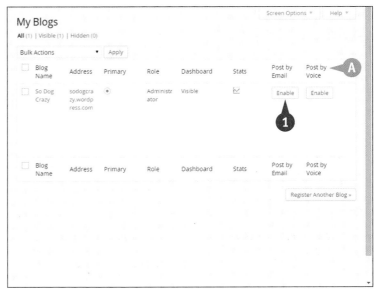

Choose the Discussion Settings

An important part of websites is interaction with visitors, and WordPress has a powerful built-in system for visitor comments. The Discussion Settings let you decide how that interaction works. Approving, or *moderating*, comments lets you avoid comment spam and block inflammatory comments.

You can find Discussion Settings by clicking the **Discussion** link under Settings on the left admin menu.

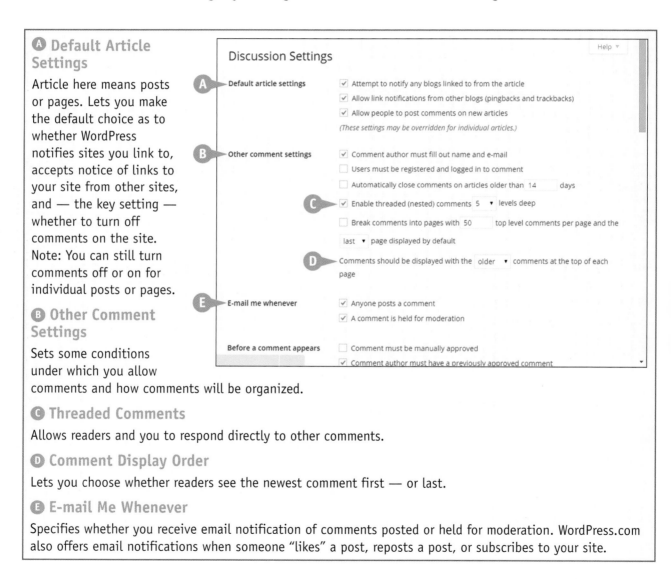

Ⓐ Default Article Settings

Article here means posts or pages. Lets you make the default choice as to whether WordPress notifies sites you link to, accepts notice of links to your site from other sites, and — the key setting — whether to turn off comments on the site. Note: You can still turn comments off or on for individual posts or pages.

Ⓑ Other Comment Settings

Sets some conditions under which you allow comments and how comments will be organized.

Ⓒ Threaded Comments

Allows readers and you to respond directly to other comments.

Ⓓ Comment Display Order

Lets you choose whether readers see the newest comment first — or last.

Ⓔ E-mail Me Whenever

Specifies whether you receive email notification of comments posted or held for moderation. WordPress.com also offers email notifications when someone "likes" a post, reposts a post, or subscribes to your site.

Ⓐ Before a Comment Appears

Lets you review all comments or automatically accept ones from a previously approved commenter.

Ⓑ Comment Moderation

Options include specifying the minimum number of links that trigger moderation and a box to list terms that may be signs of spam.

Ⓒ Comment Blacklist

Lets you list terms that automatically identify comments as spam. WordPress. com also lets you choose to respond to comments via email and to allow visitors to *subscribe to comments*, which notifies them of new comments to a post.

Ⓐ Before a comment appears	☐ Comment must be manually approved
	☑ Comment author must have a previously approved comment
Ⓑ Comment Moderation	Hold a comment in the queue if it contains 2 or more links. (A common characteristic of comment spam is a large number of hyperlinks.)
	When a comment contains any of these words in its content, name, URL, e-mail, or IP, it will be held in the moderation queue. One word or IP per line. It will match inside words, so "press" will match "WordPress".
Ⓒ Comment Blacklist	When a comment contains any of these words in its content, name, URL, e-mail, or IP, it will be marked as spam. One word or IP per line. It will match inside words, so "press" will match "WordPress".

Ⓐ Avatar Display

Indicates whether to show *avatars*, which are like personal logos associated with comment writers. Note: WordPress. com sites have a setting to allow hovercards to pop up when you mouse over a Gravatar.

Ⓑ Maximum Rating

Lets you choose the allowed level of rating, based on the user's setting at Gravatar.com.

Ⓒ Default Avatar

Allows you to pick a default image when no avatar exists. The *generated* image changes slightly for each commenter.

Avatars

An avatar is an image that follows you from weblog to weblog appearing beside your name when you comment on avatar enabled sites. Here you can enable the display of avatars for people who comment on your site.

Ⓐ Avatar Display	☑ Show Avatars
Ⓑ Maximum Rating	◉ G — Suitable for all audiences
	◯ PG — Possibly offensive, usually for audiences 13 and above
	◯ R — Intended for adult audiences above 17
	◯ X — Even more mature than above
Ⓒ Default Avatar	For users without a custom avatar of their own, you can either display a generic logo or a generated one based on their e-mail address.
	◉ Mystery Person
	◯ Blank
	◯ Gravatar Logo
	◯ Identicon (Generated)
	◯ Wavatar (Generated)
	◯ MonsterID (Generated)

Learn about Site Visibility Settings

By default, your WordPress site is visible to the public and can be indexed by search engines. There are settings that control these two types of visibility, depending on which version of WordPress you are using.

Self-Hosted Site Visibility

On self-hosted WordPress sites, the only site visibility setting deals with indexing by search engines. Even if you choose to discourage search engines, there is no guarantee your site will not be indexed. Using plugins, it is possible to make your entire self-hosted WordPress site visible only to people who are logged in.

> **5 things you're doing that drive your dog crazy | Cesar Millan**
> www.cesarsway.com/**dog**-behavior/basics/5-things-that-drive-us-**crazy** ▾
> Jan 15, 2015 - You might be surprised to learn that what you're doing to your **dog** is confusing him—maybe even driving him **crazy**. Here are five bad habits ...
>
> **30 Reasons That Dog People Are Completely Crazy**
> news.distractify.com/.../30-reasons-that-**dog**-people-are-completely-**craz**... ▾
> When you have a **dog** (or three), your life tends to revolve around them. And before you know it, you've started to display some bizarre behavior.

WordPress.com Site Visibility

WordPress.com offers the same site visibility as self-hosted blogs as well as a third option: letting you hide your site from the general public. By making your site private, only users registered at WordPress.com, and whom you have invited, will be able to see your site. The number of invites is limited, but you can add more users for a fee.

> https://sodogcrazy.wordpress.com/ is marked private by its owner. If you were invited to view this site, please **log in** below. Read more about privacy settings.

Visibility for Individual Posts or Pages

In addition to site-wide visibility settings, you can control the visibility of individual posts or pages. You could set a password just for that post or page, or you could hide it from visitors who are not logged in to WordPress. The details of those settings are covered in the section "Write and Publish Your First Post" in Chapter 5.

> 👁 Visibility: **Public**
> ◉ Public
>   ☐ Stick this post to the front page
> ○ Password protected
> ○ Private
>
> OK   Cancel

Select Your Site Visibility Settings

Search engines are constantly following links between web pages and websites, and indexing what they find. WordPress offers a setting which discourages them from doing this on your site. It may be that you do not want your site to be easily found, but more commonly this setting is used temporarily before the launch of a site.

You can find visibility settings through the Reading link under Settings on the left admin menu.

Select Your Site Visibility Settings

At WordPress.org

1 Click **Reading** under the Settings menu in the left admin menu.

2 Choose to ask search engines to index your site, or to ask them not to index your site (☐ changes to ☑).

3 Click **Save Changes**.

Note: If you intend to block search engines only temporarily, remember to change the setting back.

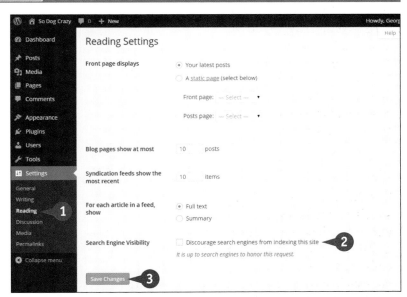

At WordPress.com

1 Click **Reading** under the Settings menu in the left admin menu.

2 Choose to ask search engines to index your site, or ask search engines not to index your site, or make your site private (○ changes to ◉).

A If you made your site private, a new section of the screen appears.

3 Click **Invite viewers to your blog**.

The Invite New Users to Your Private Blog screen opens, where you can invite only people who are registered with WordPress.com.

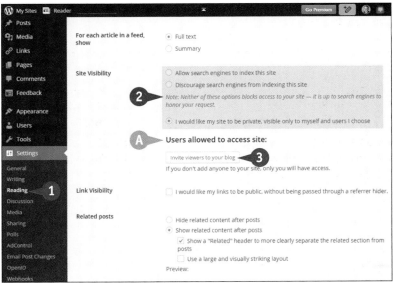

Set the Permalinks Structure

A *permalink* is short for permanent link, which means if someone links to a web page, the link always works. Every web page on a self-hosted WordPress site has a default permalink that looks something like this: http://sodogcrazy.com/?p=123.

The problem is, that URL is not very user-friendly, so self-hosted versions of WordPress enable you to choose what are referred to as *Pretty Permalinks*, resulting in links that look like this: http://sodogcrazy.com/about-me.

Set the Permalinks Structure

At WordPress.org

1 Expand the Settings menu, and click **Permalinks**.

2 Click your preferred permalink structure (○ changes to ◉).

Note: For most types of websites, the best permalink setting is Post Name.

Ⓐ The code for your selection appears in the Custom Structure code box at the bottom of the list.

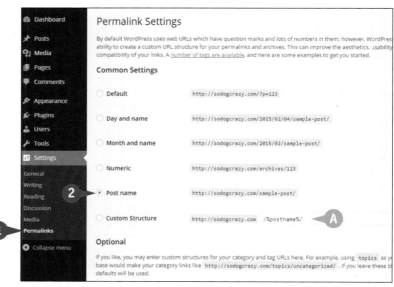

Ⓑ You can also create a custom base structure for category and tag URLs, but for most websites, just leave these blank.

3 Click **Save Changes**.

Note: Do not change your permalink setting after your site is launched, because that breaks any links people have made to your site.

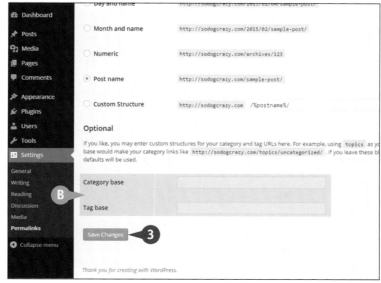

Consider Other Settings

The default settings in WordPress are fine for most sites, and you have seen some key ones that can be changed if needed. Throughout this book some additional settings will be discussed when required, but it is important to have an overview of the Settings menu for both WordPress.org and WordPress.com.

WordPress.org

The settings portion of the left admin menu varies greatly between self-hosted WordPress sites because as you add plugins, many of them add their own settings screens, either under Settings or elsewhere on the menu. Most but not all plugins also have a link to their settings screen in their listing under Plugins. Because the number and type of plugins you can add are virtually limitless, your Settings menu could be quite large!

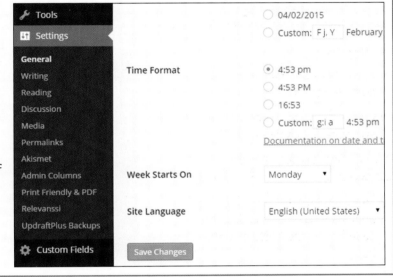

WordPress.com

Because you cannot add plugins to a WordPress.com site, the Settings menu is fixed, although new functions are added from time to time. Settings which appear here but not on default self-hosted sites are: Sharing, Polls, AdControl, Email Post Changes, Open ID, and Webhooks. See Chapter 11 for more about letting visitors share your content; for the rest, refer to the help screens at WordPress.com.

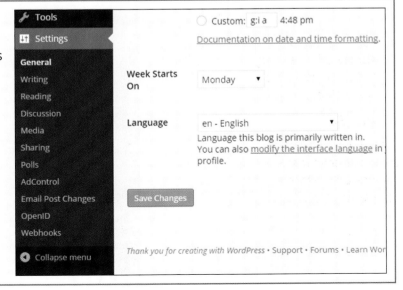

CHAPTER 5

Creating Written Content

With your site set up, you can begin the truly important part of running a website: creating content. The WordPress interface is very user-friendly and makes adding to or editing your content a breeze.

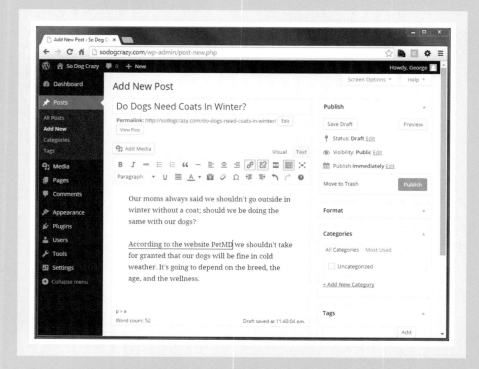

Get to Know the Add New Post Screen

The Add New Post screen is the primary location for creating new posts. After you save or publish a post, the title of the screen changes to Edit Post.

Find the Add New Post screen by clicking **Add New** under Posts in the left admin menu. You can also use the New menu on the toolbar and select **Post**.

ⓐ Title Box

Where you type your post's title.

ⓑ Add Media Button

Clicking this button opens the Media Uploader window where you can add images, documents, video, and audio, or select from previously uploaded content, all of which is covered in Chapter 6. WordPress.com has three more buttons here: Add Poll, Add Contact Form, and Add Location.

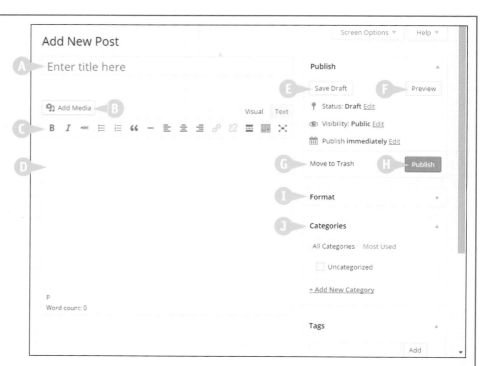

ⓒ Button Bar

Provides tools for styling and formatting text, adding links, and more. In Visual mode, the bar is a set of icons; in Text mode, the bar is a set of text buttons.

ⓓ Content Editor

Where you type and work with your content. The default display is like a word processor — what you see is what you get (WYSIWYG) — but you can also view content in pure HTML, the language of the Internet.

ⓔ Save Draft Button

Saves your content without publishing it to your site. Note: Each time you save a draft, WordPress keeps a copy of that revision.

ⓕ Preview Button

Displays how your draft post would look if published.

ⓖ Move to Trash Link

Puts an unwanted post into the Trash, but you can recover it within 30 days.

ⓗ Publish Button

Publishes the post to your site for visitors to read.

ⓘ Format Box

If your theme supports multiple formats for posts, you can select one here.

ⓙ Categories Box

Every post must be in at least one category, and here you find all available categories. You can also add new categories from here.

Ⓐ Writing Helper

WordPress.com offers these two writing tools: Copy a Post and Request Feedback, which solicits comments from other users.

Ⓑ Likes and Shares

WordPress.com has a built-in tool for choosing whether to display how many Likes your post has and buttons that make sharing your post easy. WordPress.org users can add these functions using plugins.

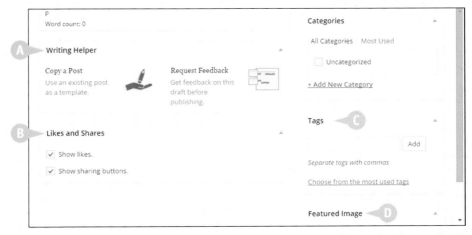

Ⓒ Tags Box

Lets you assign tags, which are more specific than categories, to your posts.

Ⓓ Featured Image

Lets you assign an image to be the thumbnail used in lists of posts and so on. How that thumbnail is used varies by theme.

Ⓐ Screen Options

Toggles the Screen Options panel open and closed. Not all meta boxes are shown by default on a Post screen. Screen Options allows you to choose which ones appear.

Ⓑ Custom Fields

WordPress.org has an area where users can edit additional fields used by plugins or themes. You can also add your own fields, but unless they are coded into theme files, nothing will happen.

Ⓒ Discussion

Lets you choose whether to allow comments on an individual post.

Overrides default selection under Discussion Settings.

Ⓓ Slug

Another way of editing the post's permalink.

Ⓔ Author

Presents a drop-down list of authors, which is helpful for multiauthor sites.

Ⓕ Excerpt

Provides a text area to write a summary or teaser for your post. It may be used in some themes or in RSS feeds.

Ⓖ Send Trackbacks

Lets you notify non-WordPress blogs when your post has linked to them.

Introducing the Visual Mode Button Bar

With the WordPress content editor, you can view your content two different ways. The default is called Visual mode and it looks like a word processor — *what you see is what you get* — or WYSIWYG. The button bar contains the functions for the content editor and varies depending on which mode you are in.

Mousing over any button shows the name of its function. Most buttons work like a toggle switch, turning the effect off or on.

A Visual Mode Tab

Is bright when active, which means you are using the WYSIWYG editor to write or edit your post. The other tab is Text mode and is described in the next section.

B Text Styling

These three buttons make text bold, italic, or strikethrough, respectively.

C Text Formatting

These three buttons format text in the following ways: bulleted list, numbered list, and *block quote*, used primarily when quoting others.

D Horizontal Line

Inserts a horizontal line.

E Text Alignment

Three buttons that align text to the left, center, or right.

F Links

Two buttons that allow you to insert or remove links.

G Read More

Inserts a *More* tag to tell WordPress where to stop displaying text and create a Read More link to the remainder of the post.

H More Buttons

Shows or hides an additional row of buttons. WordPress.com also has a spell-check button.

I Distraction-Free Writing

Removes all screen boxes except the content editor.

A Headings

Drop-down menu primarily used for the headings of sections of text.

B More Styles and Formats

Three buttons for underlined text, justified alignment, and coloring text.

Add New Post

Enter title here

Permalink: http://sodogcrazy.com/?p=5 | Change Permalinks | View Post

Add Media   Visual | Text

B *I* ABE ☰ ☷ 66 — ☰ ✎ ☰ ⊘ ⊘ ⊞ ▦ ✕

Paragraph ▾ U ☰ A ▾ 📷 ⊘ Ω ⊰ ⊱ ↶ ↷ ?

Lorem ipsum **or sit** et, ec adipiscing elit. Pellentesque dictum arcu diam, et tincidunt quam luctus non.

Suspendisse orci purus, vulputate sit amet

Screen Options ▾   Help ▾

Publish ▴

Save Draft | Preview

📌 Status: **Draft** Edit

👁 Visibility: **Public** Edit

📅 Publish immediately Edit

Move to Trash   **Publish**

Format ▾

Categories ▴

C Pasting Tool

Lets you paste text from browsers or other applications without formatting errors.

D Format Eraser

Removes formatting from selected text.

E Special Characters

Opens a pop-up window in which you can choose special characters such as mathematical operators, bullets, letters with accents — or *diacritics* — and dashes.

F More Indentions

Changes the indention on paragraphs you select but does not add bullets or block quote formats.

G Undo and Redo

Undoes actions in order since the last save/update, or redoes what was undone.

H Help

Provides added information about the visual editor, including keyboard shortcuts.

Introducing the Text Mode Button Bar

The WordPress content editor displays a WYSIWYG view of your content by default. If you want to work with the HTML underlying what appears in Visual mode, you can switch to Text mode.

You can find Text mode by clicking the **Text** tab at the top right of the content editor.

A Text Mode Tab

The lighter color tells you Text mode is active.

B Quicktag Buttons

Only a few of the buttons from Visual mode are available here. If you select text and then click a button, opening and closing HTML tags are inserted around the text. Simply clicking a button inserts an opening tag; when you are finished typing, click again to insert the closing tag. Note: You are not limited to the HTML tags created by these buttons.

C Distraction-Free Writing

Removes all screen boxes except the content editor.

D Content Editor

You see the post's content with only its HTML tags instead of how it would appear in a web browser. There is no syntax highlighting, but WordPress.org users can add a plugin to provide that.

As of early 2015, WordPress.com is making available an alternative version of the post admin screen. Some form of this will likely be the new default screen in the future.

A On WordPress.com, at the top of post screens, you see this message, inviting you to try a new version of the post admin screen. Click the link to be taken to the alternative post screen.

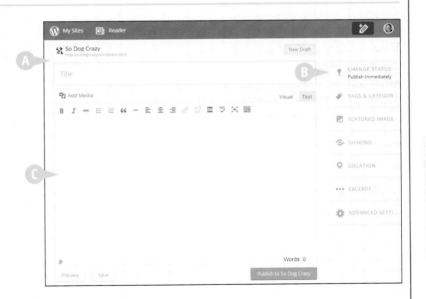

A No Left Admin Menu

There is no admin menu running down the left side of the screen. As of this writing, you must click **My Sites** and then click the **WP Admin** link to access other admin screens.

B Drop-Down Functions

Meta boxes have been replaced with a series of dropdowns which reveal the various functions for controlling the post you are working on, such as Publish, Categories, or Featured Image. Click a heading to reveal the functions. Click again to close.

C Content Editor

This functions the same way as the old design: Visual and Text modes, each with its respective button bar.

Write and Publish Your First Post

There may be many options in WordPress for writing and publishing a post, but there are only four steps you must take to make a post live on the web.

Write and Publish Your First Post

Write and Publish a Post

1 Click in the title box and start typing.

A If you have a permalinks structure other than the default one, your title will appear in the permalink area with dashes between each word. It is possible to edit that portion of the permalink before publishing.

2 Click in the text area of the content editor and type your post's content.

B If you want to see what your post will look like when published, click **Preview**.

3 You must choose at least one category for your post.

4 When you are finished, click **Publish** and watch for the success message. You can now see your post on your site.

C If the post is successfully published, you see this success message.

D The title of the screen changes to Edit Post.

E The main button in the Publish box changes to Update.

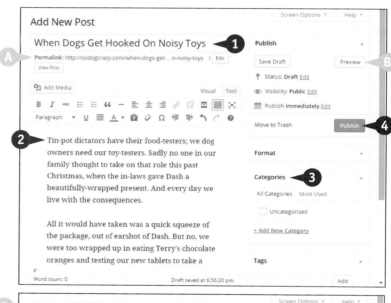

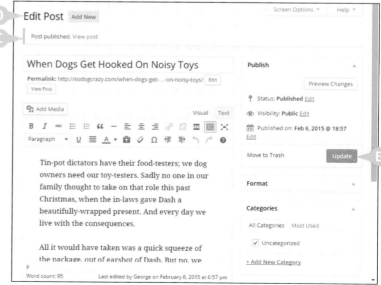

Publish Later

Ⓕ When adding a new post, a line appears in the Publish meta box that says Publish Immediately. A date selector drops down.

① Change the date and time.

② Click **OK**.

③ WordPress displays the scheduled time. The Publish button changes to read **Schedule**, which you click.

Change Visibility

Ⓖ WordPress defaults to making new posts publicly visible.

Ⓗ If you do not want your post to be moved off the home page by newer posts, click **Stick this post to the front page** (☐ changes to ☑).

Ⓘ Clicking **Password protected** (○ changes to ◉) limits viewing to visitors who have the unique password you enter here.

Ⓙ If you want only visitors logged in to WordPress to see the post, click **Private** (○ changes to ◉).

① Click **OK**.

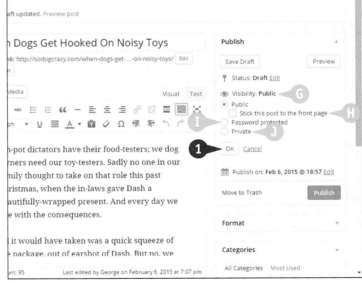

Can I use the keyboard shortcuts I use in all my other programs, such as copy and paste?
Yes. The content editor allows all the usual shortcuts and more. Click the Help button for a list.

Add Styling and Formatting to Your Text

Styling and formatting your text is partly about making it look good, but it is also about making it easy for visitors to read and understand.

Styling involves qualities like bold and italic, whereas formatting refers to the layout of the text, such as when creating lists.

Add Styling and Formatting to Your Text

Change Text Styling

1 Select the text you want to style.

2 Click the appropriate button on the button bar.

In this example, the Bold button is being clicked, but the process is the same for italic, strikethrough, and underline.

WordPress applies the styling to the selected text.

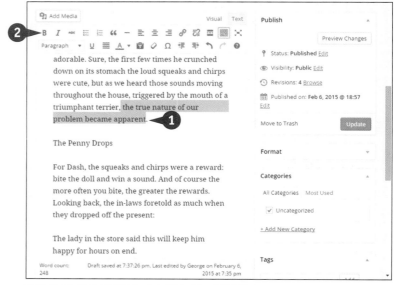

Change Text Formatting

1 Text formatting applies to paragraphs of text. You can select the whole paragraph, or position your mouse pointer anywhere inside the paragraph.

2 Click the appropriate button, or use the drop-down menu on the second row of the button bar.

In this example, the Block Quote button is being clicked.

WordPress formats the paragraph.

Create Subheadings

Note: It is important to create subheadings in your text when the post is long or has clearly separate ideas within it.

1 Make sure your heading text is on its own line.

2 Click ▼ on the second row of the button bar in Visual mode.

3 Choose from one of the heading levels other than Heading 1, which is generally reserved for your post title.

WordPress changes the paragraph format as you specified — in this example, as Heading 2.

4 Click **Preview Changes** to see how your changes will look.

5 Click **Update** to save changes.

View Your Changes

A An example of boldface.

B An example of a Heading 2.

C An example of a block quote.

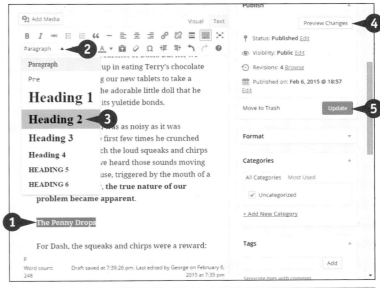

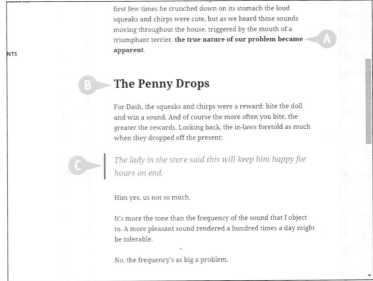

Should I use the Text Color button?

Only rarely and very carefully. First, use a color that complements your site's theme. Second, use the button very little, if ever. It creates HTML that overrides your theme. Even if the new text color looks good now, when you change themes, you need to remember all the places you used this button, and then go in and change them.

Add Text Hyperlinks to Your Content

A hyperlink allows visitors to jump to another location on the web — including elsewhere on your site. This allows visitors to verify a quote, read a recommended article, use an online tool that was reviewed, or take any number of valuable actions.

WordPress makes it easy for you to include links within your posts or pages.

Add Text Hyperlinks to Your Content

Link to Other Sites

1 Select the URL on the page you want to link to and copy it.

Note: With most browsers, you can copy the URL by pressing `Ctrl` + `C` (`⌘` + `C` on a Mac). Or, you can select **Copy** from the Edit menu.

2 Highlight the text that you want to make into a hyperlink.

3 Click the link icon (🔗) on the button bar. The Insert/Edit Link window appears over the top of your post.

4 In the Insert/Edit Link window, paste the URL in the URL field.

Note: Make sure you overwrite the default http:// in the field or you end up with two and break the link. The default is there just to remind you that a full URL is required.

5 Type a descriptive title for the page to which you are linking.

Note: Although the Title text is optional, readers see it when they mouse over the link, and search engines use it in assessing your content.

6 Click **Add Link**.

The Insert/Edit Link window closes.

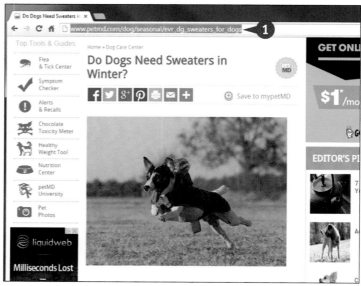

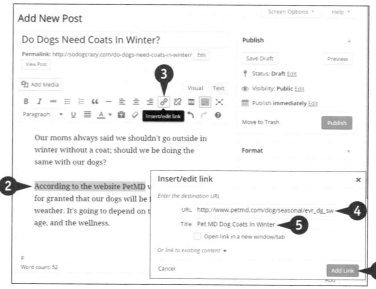

(A) The text you highlighted is now linked to the website you referred to in your post.

Link to Your Own Site

Note: The process of linking to your own site is no different, except WordPress provides an even handier tool.

1 In the Insert/Edit Link window, click the **Or link to existing content** link near the bottom.

(B) A search function and a scrollable list of all content drop down.

2 Click the item when it appears on the list.

(C) WordPress automatically fills in the URL and the content title for you.

3 Click **Add Link** to create the link on whatever text you highlighted in your content.

TIPS

What exactly should I put in the Title field?

The key is to describe in a few words what the visitor can expect to find by clicking the link. Just putting in the title of the site is not very useful, and sometimes even the title of the web page may not tell the story well. Imagine you are the visitor clicking the link: Do you get the content the link says you will get?

Can the link open in a new window or tab instead of taking me away from my site?

Yes. Simply click **Open link in a new window** (☐ changes to ☑). If not specified, WordPress sends readers to the linked page in the same window or tab where they were reading your site.

Use Distraction-Free Writing Mode

If you find the Add New Post screen a bit distracting for writing — crowded as it is with menus and meta boxes — then you will appreciate distraction-free writing mode.

Use Distraction-Free Writing Mode

1 With a post open, click the **Distraction-Free Writing** button (⟩⟨).

Note: The same button is on the button bars of Visual and Text modes. It toggles Distraction-Free Writing mode off and on.

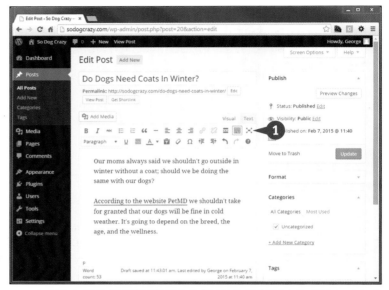

Clicking the Distraction-Free Writing button (⟩⟨) moves everything off-screen except for the title box and the content editor.

The screen remains minimized until you move your mouse outside the content editor.

Even though all elements are back on screen, they disappear again if you move the mouse back over the content editor.

However, if you click one of the elements while it is momentarily displayed, then the screen returns to normal.

The elements stay visible until you begin making additions or changes in the content area. Then they disappear again.

2 These actions continue until you click the **Distraction-Free Writing** button again (⟩⟨).

Publish from Your Mobile Device

With more and more people using smartphones and tablets, often as their primary device, being able to manage their website from these devices is crucial, and WordPress is mobile-friendly in a couple of ways.

Responsive Admin Screens for Smartphones

When your device has a very narrow screen, WordPress collapses the admin screens so that the menu drops down from the top. Although all functions can be run from a smartphone, some are complicated by the narrowness of the screen, such as trying to edit images.

Responsive Admin Screens for Tablets

Although tablets can vary greatly in screen width, a typical size produces a collapsed version of the left admin menu and a single column in the main content area. This is plenty of room to manage all WordPress functions.

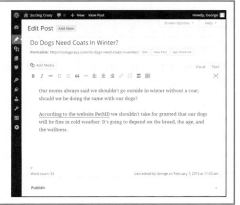

Apps for Administering WordPress

The ability of WordPress admin screens to conform to mobile devices means having to open a browser and log in, in addition to other functions that are awkward to perform on very small screens. That is why some people prefer using an app focused on key tasks like adding new posts, and WordPress has one each for iOS and Android.

Create Post Teasers

When WordPress lists posts, say, on the home page, most themes display the entire post. Instead of forcing visitors to scroll through the full content of each, it is better to use the Read More tag and give them a taste of each post.

Create Post Teasers

1 Position your cursor at the point in the text where you want to insert the Read More tag.

The content before your cursor will be visible to the public, and what comes after will be hidden until they click the resulting link to the full post.

2 Click the **Insert Read More tag** button (▦).

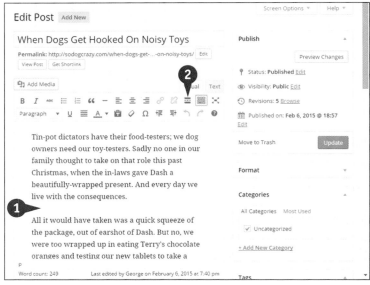

A A Read More tag appears at the point in the text that you chose.

3 Click **Update**.

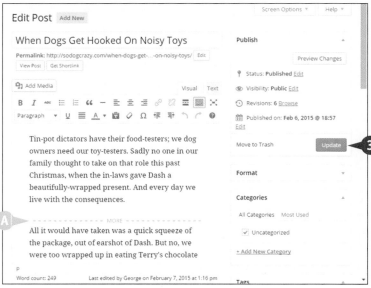

B On your site, the post now appears in listing pages with just the opening paragraph and a Continue Reading link to the full contents.

The wording of the Continue Reading link can vary by theme, and some themes allow you to change the wording yourself. On WordPress.org sites, there are also plugins that provide that function.

WordPress.com enables you to very easily change the wording of the Read More link.

In Text mode, you are able to modify the Read More tag. By default, it looks like this:

```
<!--more-->
```

C But by adding your own text, you can change the wording of the link:

```
<!--more Keep reading. . .-->
```

Note: Be careful not to change the opening and closing tags or you will break the function.

D The Read More link now uses the wording you specified.

How is the excerpt box related to the Read More tag?
It all depends on your theme. Most do not use the WordPress excerpt function, so the excerpt box has no effect; and the only way to show visitors a teaser is to use the Read More tag. If the theme does use the excerpt function, WordPress first looks for something in the excerpt meta box, and then looks for a Read More tag. If neither is present, it automatically uses the first 55 words of your post. If your posts have teasers without you having to do anything, you know your theme uses the excerpt function.

Write and Publish a Page

With the exception of personal blogging sites, WordPress *pages* play just as important a role — if not more so — as posts do. Although most of what you have learned about posts applies to the creation and editing of WordPress pages, there are some differences.

Find the Add New Page screen by clicking **Add New** under Pages in the left admin menu. You can also click the **New** menu on the toolbar and select **Page**.

Write and Publish a Page

1 Under Pages in the left admin menu, click **Add New**.

The Add New Page screen opens.

2 Type a title in the title field.

Note: Make your title descriptive of the page content. Do not worry if it does not fit on the navigation menu because WordPress lets you customize the navigation label.

3 Type your text in the content editor.

4 Click **Save Draft**.

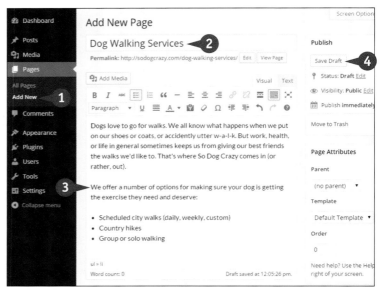

Ⓐ Watch for the success message to indicate that your page was saved.

Ⓑ The screen title changes to Edit Page.

Ⓒ If pretty permalinks are turned on, as shown in the section "Set the Permalinks Structure" in Chapter 4, and you need to edit this page's link, do it before publishing.

Note: If you have a good descriptive title, the permalink should need no editing.

5 Click the **Parent ▼**.

The default setting is (no parent).

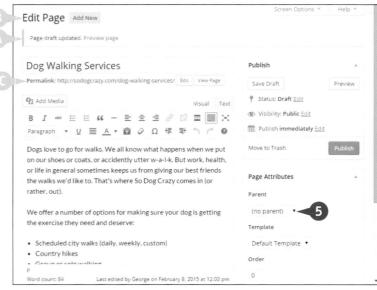

6 Click ▼ and click a page from the dropdown to make that page the parent of the new page you just created. If you prefer to keep your page as a main page rather than a subpage, simply collapse the menu and proceed.

D Pages usually appear in alphabetical order in default WordPress page listings, but you can assign each page a number to specify the order.

E If your theme offers more than one page layout, called *templates*, then a drop-down menu appears here. The number of templates varies widely. Simply choose the template you want for this page.

7 When you are ready to publish your page to your website, click **Publish**.

Note: The Publish box works the same for pages as it does for posts. See the section "Write and Publish Your First Post" for more.

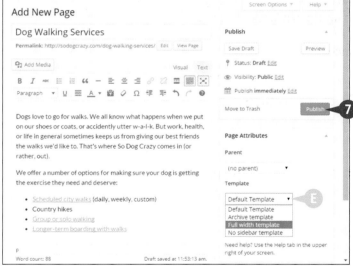

I still do not understand the difference between posts and pages.
One way to think of it is in terms of time. Posts are intended for groups of content in which the latest content is the most important; press releases are a good example. Pages, on the other hand, are for content that is not time-dependent, such as a company profile or a description of a particular service.

What exactly happens if I make one page the child of another?
If you let WordPress generate your site's navigation automatically, parent pages appear on the menu, whereas child pages appear as drop-down submenu items, but creating menus manually lets you choose.

Restore an Earlier Version of Posts or Pages

The WordPress content editor has an undo function, but once you have saved a draft or published, the ability to go back with undo is lost. However, WordPress also keeps copies of saved revisions so you can go back and retrieve what you had written earlier.

WordPress.com saves the last 25 revisions of a post or page. On WordPress.org sites, the number of revisions is unlimited, but there are plugins to set a limit.

Restore an Earlier Version of Posts or Pages

Note: You can access the revisions screen in two ways, if any revisions exist. In the Publish box, you see the number of revisions available.

1 Click **Browse** to get to the revisions screen.

A Alternatively, you can click **Screen Options** and then click **Revisions** (☐ changes to ✔).

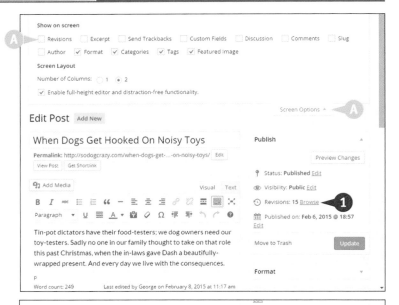

2 Scroll to the bottom of your Edit Post screen.

B A list of post revisions appears.

3 Click the version that you think you would like to restore.

WordPress opens the revision screen with that version selected.

C WordPress displays two consecutive versions side by side and highlights places in which the two versions are different. The older version is on the left, the newer on the right.

D A timeline of all revisions appears. Mouse over it to see the date and time of each revision.

E Moving the indicator along the timeline changes the revisions that appear.

F If you want to compare two nonconsecutive revisions, click this option (☐ changes to ☑) and two indicators appear on the timeline.

4 When you have identified the desired previous version and it appears on the right-hand side, click **Restore This Revision**.

G WordPress restores the desired version and returns you to the Edit Post page. Check the success message for the correct date of the revision.

5 Make any changes you want and then click **Update** if the post already has been published (or **Save Draft** if the post has not been published).

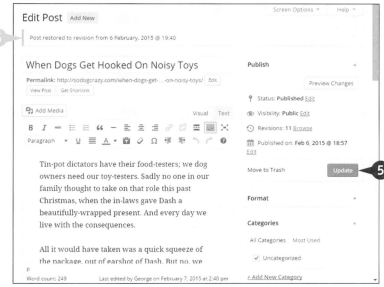

TIPS

What if I want only part of a revision to add to my current version?
Find the revision you want, but instead of clicking Restore, simply copy the text you want, click **Return to post editor**, and then paste the text into your current post.

I relied on WordPress automatically saving my post as I worked, but I see only one Autosave version in the list. How can I get an earlier Autosave version?
Unfortunately, you cannot. WordPress keeps only the most recent automatically saved version. Hence, you need to click **Save Draft** (or **Update Post**) as you work if you want to have access to older versions.

Import Posts from Existing Sites

If you have been writing a blog on platforms like Blogger or Tumblr and would like to import that material into a WordPress.com or a self-hosted WordPress.org site, WordPress provides tools to help you make the transition.

Another common scenario is to move from WordPress.com to a self-hosted site.

Import Posts from Existing Sites

Import Posts from a Non-WordPress Platform

Note: In this example, the move is from a Blogger account to a self-hosted WordPress site.

① Under Tools in the left admin menu, click **Import**.

The Import screen opens.

Note: WordPress.com offers many more choices of platforms from which to import, including Posterous, Storylane, GoDaddy Quick Blogcast, and more.

② Click **Blogger**.

On WordPress.org sites the import tools are not built in, so they must be loaded as needed.

A Blogger Importer window opens.

③ Click **Install Now**.

④ Click **Activate Plugin & Run Importer** on the next screen.

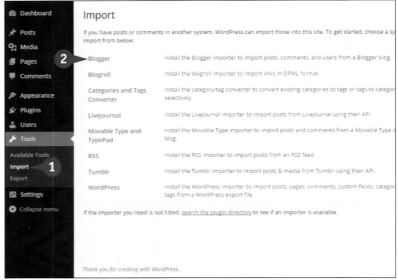

The Import Blogger screen opens.

5 Click **Authorize** to allow Google to send your Blogger data.

6 The Google Accounts window opens. If you are already logged in to Google, you can click **Grant access**. Otherwise, log in to Google first.

If authorization was successful, you are returned to the Import Blogger screen, which now shows all Blogger blogs associated with your Google account.

7 Click **Import** for the blog you want to import.

A The Posts and Comments columns indicate the progress of your import. If your previous blog was large, the import process may take a while.

8 When the import is complete, the boxes for posts and comments change color, and the Import button at the far right changes to Set Authors. Click **Set Authors**.

The Author Mapping screen opens.

9 Click ▼ to choose a WordPress user to associate with the Blogger username.

10 Click **Save Changes**.

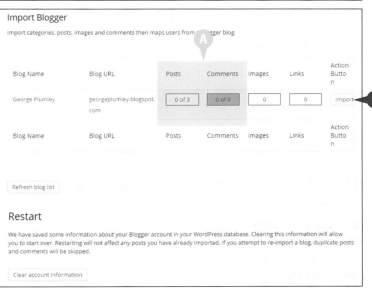

TIPS

I got a message saying the importer cannot authenticate my Blogger blog at Google. Is there anything to do?

You can go to www.google.com/support/blogger/bin/answer.py?hl=en&answer=97416. It explains how to export your blog, which creates a file you can save to your hard drive and then import to your WordPress blog.

My import was going okay and then stopped. What do I do?

Click **Clear account information**. It takes you back to the import panel. You can repeat the steps you took before, and WordPress will resume your import without duplicating posts.

continued ▶

T he process of moving from WordPress.com to a self-hosted site is very similar to importing content from Blogger and other platforms. On your WordPress.com site, you need to create an export file of your content.

Import Posts from Existing Sites (continued)

Import Posts from WordPress.com to a Self-Hosted Site

1 Click **Export** under Tools in the left admin menu.

A There is also a paid service for moving your site to a self-hosted version of WordPress, but if you already have a hosting account and WordPress installed, you do not need this.

2 Click **Export**.

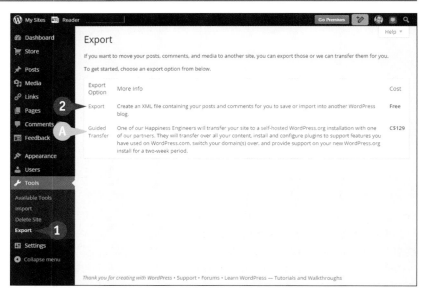

The Export screen opens.

3 Choose what parts of your content you want to export.

4 Click **Download Export File**.

5 Save the file to a location on your device where you can easily find it later.

6 Switch to the admin screen of your self-hosted WordPress site.

7 Click **Import** under Tools in the left admin menu. On the list of import tools, click **WordPress**.

8 A WordPress Importer window opens. Click **Install Now**, and then click **Activate Plugin & Run Importer** on the next screen.

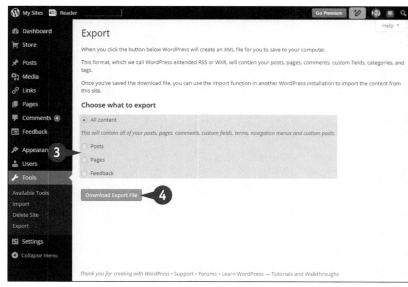

The Import WordPress screen opens.

9 Click **Choose File** and find the file you exported from WordPress.com.

10 Once the name of the file appears, click **Upload file and import**.

B The Import WordPress screen changes to the Assign Authors function.

11 You can assign any available WordPress user as the author of the imported content using the drop-down menu, or you can create a new user.

Note: If you create a new user, you will need to go to the created account afterwards and add email and other details, as well as change the role from the default Subscriber to Author or higher.

12 To import attachments such as images and documents, check the box for **Download and import file attachments** (☐ changes to ☑).

13 Click **Submit** to begin the import.

Why would I not leave my existing blog posts on WordPress.com and link them to my new self-hosted site?
Aside from having to log into two separate accounts, your domain name can only point to one location. Regularly maintained blog content is important for search engine rankings; you would be splitting that between the two sites.

I did not have my domain name pointing to WordPress.com. Will any existing links be broken if I move to a self-hosted site?
Yes, but WordPress.com offers a paid redirection service you can renew yearly. This works best if the pretty permalink structure on the new site matches the one used by WordPress.com.

CHAPTER 6

Creating Visual and Audio Content

Visual and audio content have become more and more important for websites, and WordPress makes working with images, video, and audio easy.

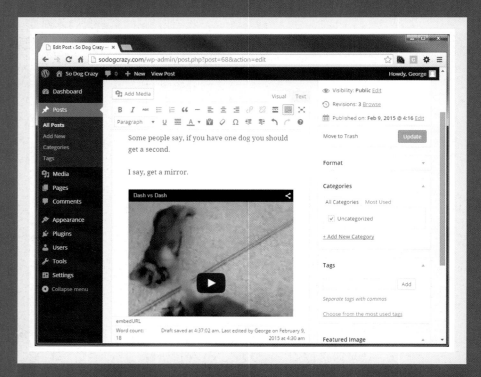

Think Visually about Content

Every month, the Internet becomes a more and more visual medium. The ability to instantly capture and upload images or video, and the bandwidth required to be able to view them on any device, has captured the attention of the world. That is why your content needs to be as visual as possible. Making it so may not be obvious at first, until you begin to think visually.

Capture Everything on Camera

The ability of smartphones to capture high-quality images, video, and audio makes the job of gathering material for your website a snap. The trick is remembering to do it. Fresh fruit just delivered to your restaurant? Good crowd at your event? Unusual cause of a flat tire? Get at least a few images and a bit of video. Even if you are not sure how it will be used — grab it!

One Image per Post or Page

Aim to have at least one image for every post or page you create. Do not worry about getting overly creative; think relevance. It is as simple as a box of fresh apples in an article about fresh ingredients for your restaurant, or a close-up of a dripping outdoor tap in an article about preparing your home for winter. Of course you have the option of adding more than one image, or even a video, where appropriate.

One of the pleasures of harvest season is having access to the freshest ingredients and this fall we're planning a lot of great dishes based on the fruits of the harvest.

Speaking of fruits, it's apple season, so that means apple pies and more great desserts. We've been fortunate to find a number of great growers in the area who supply us with a number of different apple species.

Put a Human Face on It

We all know — and studies confirm — that we respond more to human faces. When possible, and when appropriate, try to include faces in your images or videos. And use real people. Stock photo models come off as fake for most websites. Encourage testimonial providers to include a picture or even a video. And yes, puppies and kittens do well too, if it makes sense for the content.

Look for Visual WordPress Themes

With all your hard work finding imagery, make sure your WordPress theme is going to use them effectively too. You may control what goes in your content, but the theme controls the other elements on the page. For example, does the theme place a large version of a post's featured image at the top of the content? Does it use large thumbnails when listing posts?

Join the Infographics Revolution

Infographics are not new, just more sophisticated and, more importantly, easier to create. All it takes is a bit of imagination, and a free online image editing program, like Sumopaint.com, or even PowerPoint or Word to turn your statistics into a compelling visual. You can also use PowerPoint and Word as photo composition programs — mixing images, adding text, and so on.

Clear Text Is Worth a Thousand Pictures

Thinking visually is not just about images and video. Styling and laying out your text clearly helps the eye of the reader take in information. Can that paragraph be broken up into a list? Single-sentence paragraphs, used every once in a while, help create emphasis. Breaking up longer text with headings lets visitors scan more easily.

Dog Walking Services

Dogs love to go for walks. We all know what happens when we put on our shoes or coats, or accidently utter w-a-l-k. But work, health, or life in general sometimes keeps us from giving our best friends the walks we'd like to. That's where So Dog Crazy comes in (or rather, out).

We offer a number of options for making sure your dog is getting the exercise they need and deserve:

- Scheduled city walks (daily, weekly, custom)
- Country hikes
- Group or solo walking
- Longer-term boarding with walks

Prepare Images for Uploading

When you take the time to edit and resize images before you post them on your site, you ensure your images look their best and do not make your site load slowly.

Although WordPress has an image-editing tool, you will do better to prepare your images before uploading using image editors like Irfanview, GIMP, Picasa, or the do-it-all Adobe Photoshop. Your digital camera may provide a basic editing program, too.

Give Yourself Something to Work With

All the editing in the world cannot save a poor quality image. Lighting is one of the biggest problems for both images and video; position yourself or your subject for the best lighting possible. Framing your subject nicely, particularly for video, saves trying to fix it in the editor. And take photos or video at the highest quality possible. You can reduce size and quality in editing; you cannot increase them.

Crop to Focus Interest

Cropping is the term that editors use for trimming images. Use your editor's cropping tool to eliminate distracting activity, objects, or blank areas, or to zero-in on the item of particular interest. And save an unedited version of the photo — although your editor may do so automatically, in case you change your mind.

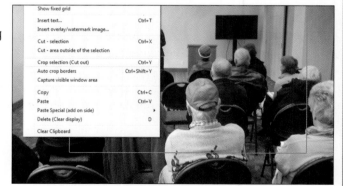

Adjust the Image

Take advantage of the editor's tools to eliminate "red eye" in flash photos, to straighten out sloping horizons, and to correct poorly rendered color, contrast, and other image flaws. You want people to see the image, not be put off by its shortcomings.

Resize the Image

The images that come out of the average digital camera or phone these days are at least 4 times larger than you need for the web. An image of 1,000 pixels in width essentially fills a screen; your camera generates images of 4,000 pixels or more. So resize the dimensions and save as a new image; never alter the original.

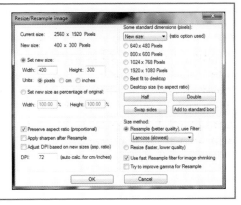

Save for Web

Whether you work in an image editor or a video program, always save your file for the web after fixing and resizing it. The Save for Web function (the name may vary) applies various types of compression to the file, making it as small as possible for faster loading in browsers. The editing program should advise you on the best settings, or you can search online.

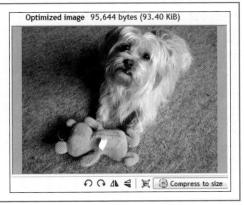

Choose the Right File Format

For photographs, the best file format to use is JPG (sometimes spelled JPEG). Do not use PNG because the file will be unnecessarily large. You want to use PNG or GIF for graphics, such as logos and icons. PNG is best for transparencies; GIF can handle animations. When it comes to video, it is best to export and save the file as an MP4. If your program does not save that format, free converters are available online that do.

```
EXE/DLL/CPL - Files
EXR - EXR Format
FPX - FlashPix Format
G3 - G3 FAX Format
GIF - Compuserve GIF
HDP/JXR/WDP - JPEG-XR/HD Photo
ICO/ICL - Windows Icons
ICS/IDS - Image Cytometry Standard Format
IFF/LBM - Amiga Interchange File Format
IMG - GEM Raster Format
JLS - JPEG-LS Format
JP2 - JPEG2000 Format
JPG/JPEG - JRG Files
JPM - JPM Format
KDC - Kodak Digital Camera Files
MED - MED/OctaMED Audio Format
MNG/JNG - Multiple Network Graphics
MP3/M3U - MPEG Audio Files
MOV - Apple QuickTime Movie
MPG/MPEG/DAT - MPEG Files
OGG - Ogg Vorbis Audio Format
PBM/PGM/PPM - Portable Bitmaps
PCD - Kodak Photo CD
PCX/DCX - Zsoft Paintbrush
```

Upload and Insert an Image to a Post

You can upload and insert images to a post or a page while you are writing, or at any time. The advantage of doing it while you write is so you do not forget to add the image or images later.

If you are not sure where you want to use an image, you can upload it to the media library for use later. That is covered in the section "Upload Images to the Media Library."

Upload and Insert an Image to a Post

1 From the Add New Post or Edit Post page, click in your post at the location where you want to insert your image.

2 Click **Add Media**.

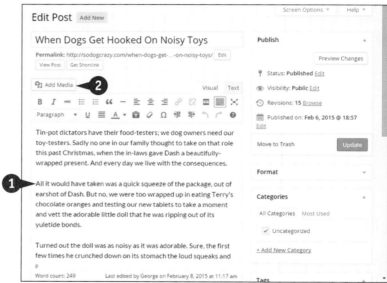

A The Media Uploader window opens on the Upload Files tab of Insert Media.

3 Click **Select Files** or drag an image from a folder on your computer to the upload window, and release the mouse button when the border of the drop-files area changes color.

The window switches to the Media Library tab; where the image thumbnail will eventually show, a bar indicating the upload progress appears.

B When the image has uploaded, it is outlined and displays a check mark.

4 Scroll down so you can see all the fields of attachment details.

5 Change the title to something descriptive. The default title is the image's filename.

6 Type alt text or alternate text to describe the image.

7 Choose the display settings: how you want the image aligned relative to the text, whether you want the image linked to anything, and finally the size of the image.

8 Click **Insert into post**.

The Media Uploader window closes.

C The Edit Post window displays the image at the cursor location.

9 Click **Save Draft** or **Update**, depending on whether the post is a new draft or an existing post, to save the change.

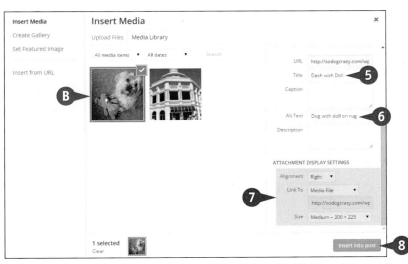

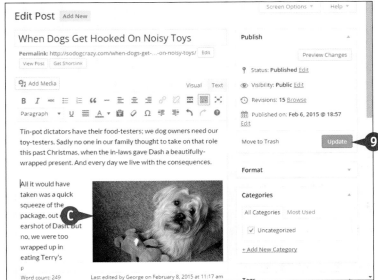

Work with Images in the Content Editor

After you have inserted an image into a post or page, you can easily make changes to various settings — alignment, position, size, and more — all from within the content editor.

Work with Images in the Content Editor

Edit Image Settings in the Content Editor

1 Click an image in the content editor; a small menu appears above the image.

A You can change the image alignment relative to the text.

B You can delete the image from the post by clicking ✖.

Note: The image is not deleted from WordPress and can still be found in the media library.

2 Click the pencil icon (✐).

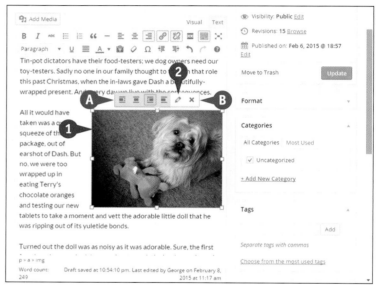

The Image Details window opens.

C You can edit the caption and the alternative text.

D You can access display settings: alignment, size, and whether the image links to anything.

E You can click the **Advanced Options ▼** to add CSS classes and more.

F You can click **Edit Original** to go to the WordPress image editor.

3 When you are finished making changes, click **Update**.

G To close the window without changing the image, you can click ✖.

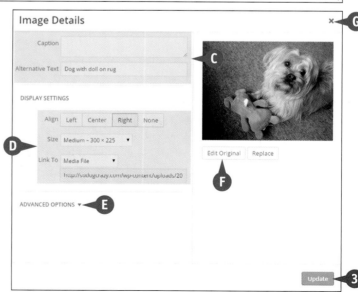

Move an Image

1 Click anywhere in the image, press and hold your left mouse button, and drag.

H A small transparent version of the image moves with you. If you cannot see the text cursor below the image, your mouse pointer also indicates where the image will be moved to.

2 When you reach the new position, let go of your mouse.

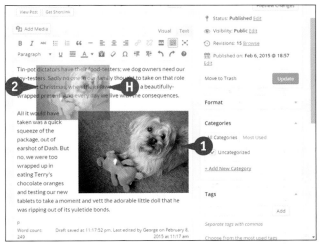

I The image appears in its new location. The alignment remains the same.

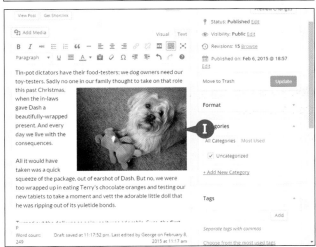

Resize Images in Real Time

Note: Although you can use the Image Details window to enter a custom width and height for your image, many people prefer to see what the change will look like in real time.

1 Drag one of the handles that appear after clicking anywhere in an image to resize.

J As you drag, the new-sized image appears as a transparency and a small box shows the dimensions.

When you stop dragging, the image is resized.

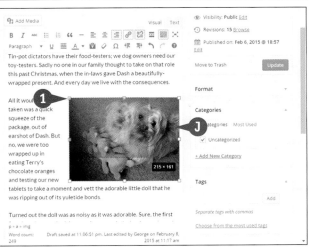

Upload Images to the Media Library

If you have images you think would be useful for your site, you can upload them without putting them into any particular post or page. They will simply remain in the media library until you need them.

You access the Upload New Media page by clicking **Add New** under Media on the left admin menu. You can also click **Media** on the New menu of the toolbar.

Upload Images to the Media Library

1 Click **Add New** under Media on the left admin menu.

The Upload New Media screen appears.

2 Click **Select Files** to open a window for browsing your device.

You can also drag files to the outlined box.

A browse window opens, enabling you to find files on your device.

3 Select one or more images to upload.

Note: To select multiple files, press `Ctrl` (`⌘` on a Mac) while clicking.

4 Click **Open** when you are finished selecting.

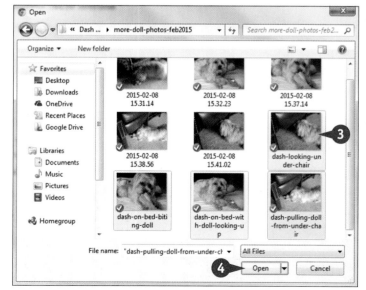

118

The browse window closes.

A A list of all images appears at the bottom of the Upload New Media screen, with a progress bar for each.

5 When all the files have uploaded, click **Library** under Media on the left admin menu.

B You can also edit any one of the uploaded images directly from this screen.

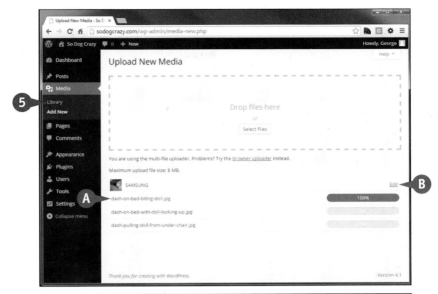

C You can see all the new images at the top of the Media Library listings.

Note: Depending on your viewing habits, the media library may be in Grid view — a series of thumbnails in rows and columns.

The images are now ready to use anywhere on your site.

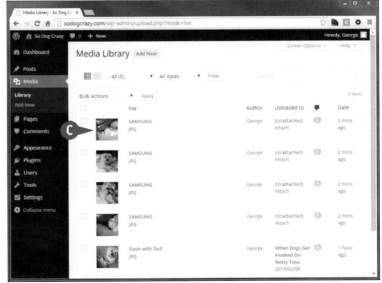

TIPS

Can I just upload images with my FTP client?
WordPress.com has no FTP access. Although you can upload media files this way on a self-hosted site, it is a bad idea. WordPress would have no record of the files and they would not show up in the media library.

I sometimes have one image that gets rejected by WordPress, whereas the others load fine. Why is that?
It could just be an upload error, so try again. If it still will not upload, the file itself may have been corrupted. Try resaving your image in your image editor and then uploading again.

Edit Images in WordPress

Although it is better to edit your images before uploading them to WordPress, some edits you can make from within WordPress. In particular, you can edit the thumbnail versions that WordPress automatically creates for each image uploaded.

You can find the Edit Image or Edit Original button in multiple locations: the Edit Media screen, the Media Uploader window, the Attachment Details window, and the Image Details window.

Edit Images in WordPress

Edit an Image

1 Click **Media** on the left admin menu and make sure you are in List mode rather than Grid mode.

2 Locate your image and click **Edit**.

The Edit Media screen opens.

3 Click **Edit Image**.

The Edit Media screen changes to show the image editing tools.

Ⓐ The button bar: Crop, Rotate, Flip, Undo, and Redo.

Ⓑ The Scale Image box.

Ⓒ The Image Crop box, where you can choose an aspect ratio or edit the selection box.

Ⓓ The Thumbnail Settings box, which displays the current thumbnail and allows you to choose which version or versions the changes will be applied to.

Re-Crop the Thumbnail

Note: Because of the way WordPress creates thumbnail versions of images, they may not always look good.

1 To begin, click the image and drag.

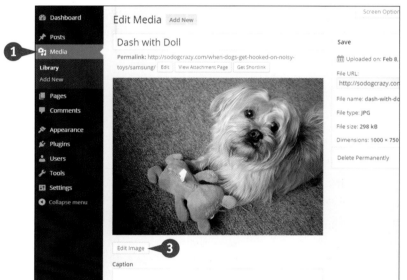

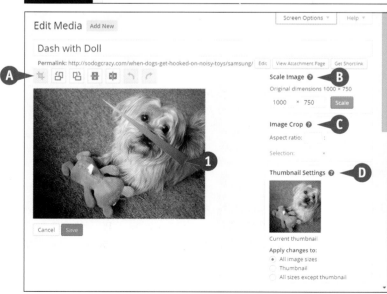

Dragging creates a box with dashed borders.

The image goes darker except for the area inside the box.

Ⓔ You can resize the box by clicking any edge and dragging. Position your cursor in the center of the box to drag it around the image.

The goal is to find the portion of the image you want as the thumbnail.

② When you are ready, click the **Crop** button (⌗), which is now active.

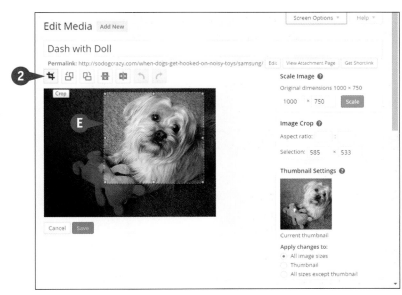

The image now changes to show only the area you selected.

Even if the image is the way you want it, do not click Save yet.

③ Click **Thumbnail** under Apply Changes To (○ changes to ⦿). You want the cropping to apply only to the thumbnail and no other size of the image.

④ Click **Save**.

The new thumbnail version will be visible under Thumbnail settings.

Note: You could also crop if you wanted to remove a portion of the image in all its versions — just be sure you correctly set Apply Changes To.

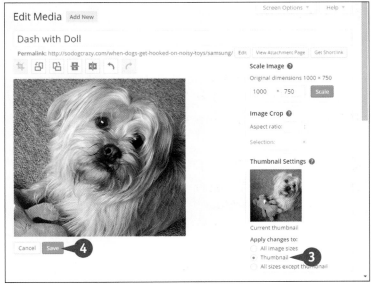

TIP

My theme creates additional image sizes. Why do I not see them as choices in the Image Editor?
There are plugins for WordPress.org sites which solve this by modifying the image editor or by creating their own image editing function.

continued ▶

Two other common image edits you can make through WordPress are: horizontally flipping an image and scaling the dimensions of the entire image.

Edit Images in WordPress (continued)

Horizontally Flip an Image

Note: Sometimes you find that an image would be better facing the opposite direction.

1. Click **Media** on the left admin menu and make sure you are in List mode rather than Grid mode.

2. Locate your image and click **Edit**.

   The Edit Media screen opens.

3. Click **Edit Image**.

4. Click the **Flip horizontally** button (🔃).

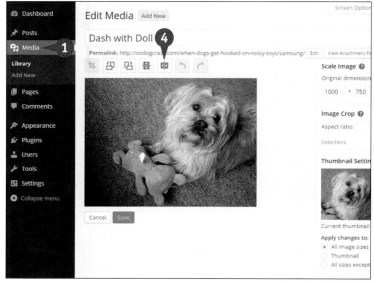

The image changes to face the other direction.

5. Choose which images this change should apply to (◯ changes to ⦿).

6. When you are satisfied with your settings, click **Save**.

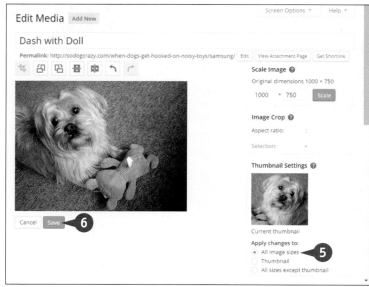

Scale an Image

Note: WordPress automatically creates smaller versions of every image you upload. If you need a smaller image, use one of those. The Scale Image function reduces the dimensions of the full-size version of your image.

1 Click **Media** on the left admin menu and make sure you are in List mode rather than Grid mode.

2 Locate your image and click **Edit**.

A On the Edit Media screen, the current full-size dimensions appear here.

3 Enter either a new width or new height. The other dimension is calculated automatically to keep the image proportions.

4 Click **Scale**.

The changes are applied. There is no Save required for this function.

B The original dimensions change to reflect the scaling.

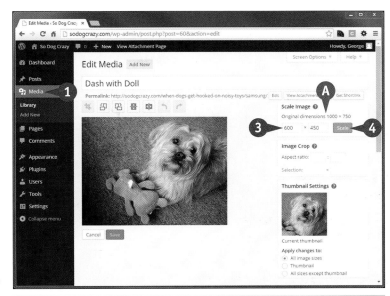

Restore Original Image

C When you make changes of any kind, except for cropping the thumbnail, the Restore Original Image box appears.

1 Click **Restore image** to discard any changes — in this case, the scaling of the image.

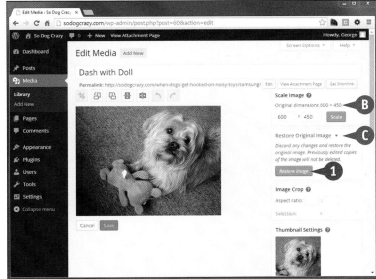

TIP

How can changes be restored, particularly if the original dimensions have been scaled?
WordPress always retains the original image you uploaded. Even scaling is actually being applied to a copy of the original image. The phrase "original dimensions" is a bit misleading after scaling, because those are now the dimensions of a copy of the original.

Understand Featured Images

WordPress posts and pages can be assigned a *featured image*, which is meant to be representative of the content. That image then gets used in various ways by themes.

Use of Featured Images Varies by Theme

Many themes use a small version of the featured image when listing posts. Others place the featured image at the top of the content area when viewing the full post. Some use the featured image as part of the Next and Previous links that may appear on posts. Featured images are sometimes used to replace the header image of the site. Check a theme's demo or documentation for an idea of how it would use a featured image.

The Lure Of A Fallen Tree

I always tell people Dash likes to climb trees. I don't mention the part about them having fallen over until absolutely necessary.

A Featured Image Is Not a Thumbnail Image

In WordPress coding, the technical name of featured images is *post thumbnail* (Ⓐ), so you sometimes hear them referred to that way. The confusion is compounded by the fact that featured

```
<article id="post-<?php the_ID(); ?>" <?php post_class(); ?>>
        <?php
                // Post thumbnail.
                twentyfifteen_post_thumbnail();
        ?>

        <header class="entry-header">
                <?php
                        if ( is_single() ) :
                                the_title( '<h1 class="entry-title">',
'</h1>' );
```

Ⓐ

images are often used as thumbnails. In fact, it is important to have a featured image whose original is large, in case a theme requires a large version in certain places.

Use Any Image Uploaded to WordPress

When choosing a featured image, you are not limited to images you have used within the post. You can upload an image specifically to be the featured image, or you can use any existing image from the media library. The key is that the image is representative of or related to the content of the post or page.

Set Featured Image

Upload Files   Media Library

Images   ▼   All dates   ▼

Add a Featured Image

Whether or not your current theme uses featured images, it is good to get in the habit of assigning one to every post or page you create. The process is as simple as uploading an image to WordPress or selecting an existing one from the media library.

You can find the Featured Image meta box on any individual post or page screen. If it is not visible, use the Screen Options panel to restore the box.

Add a Featured Image

① While writing or editing a post or page, click **Set featured image** in the Featured Image meta box.

The Media Uploader window opens, with only Set Featured Image as an option.

② Click an image from the media library.

Note: Alternatively, click the **Upload Files** tab and follow the steps in the section "Upload and Insert an Image to a Post."

Ⓐ The selected image appears in the Attachment Details section.

③ Click **Set featured image**.

The Media Uploader window closes.

Ⓑ The image you chose now appears in the Featured Image box.

Ⓒ The link has changed to Remove Featured Image. Click this and the image disappears and the link changes to Set Featured Image.

④ Save your changes to the post or page. Depending on its status, click **Update**, **Publish**, or **Save Draft**.

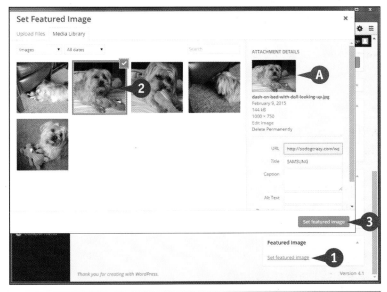

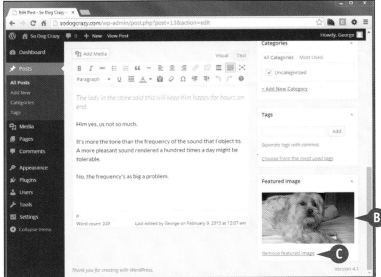

Insert an Image Gallery

The WordPress Image Gallery gives you a quick and easy way to display a set of photos or other images on your website. The gallery displays thumbnails of the images, and then you can click the individual images to view larger versions.

Insert an Image Gallery

1 Position your cursor in the content editor where you want the gallery to appear.

Note: Galleries cannot have text flowing around them, so your cursor needs to be on its own line.

Note: Commonly, galleries are placed at the end of a post or a page, but you can put them anywhere you want.

2 Click **Add Media**.

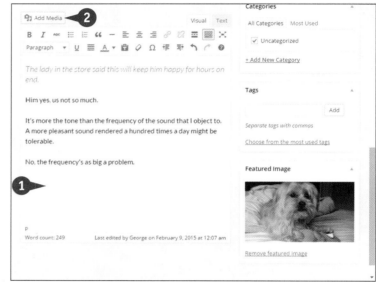

The Media Uploader window opens to the Create Gallery section.

If there are images in the media library, they appear by default. But you can upload images too.

3 Click each image you want. A check mark appears beside each.

A Small thumbnails of all selected images appear at the bottom of the screen. This is a helpful reminder when you have a lot of images to scroll through.

4 When you are ready, click **Create a new gallery**.

The Media Uploader window changes to Edit Gallery.

5 Click to remove images, drag them to rearrange the order, or add captions.

6 Click **Add to Gallery** to add more images.

7 Click the **Link To ▼** to determine what happens when visitors click an image: see just the full-sized image or see it on its attachment page.

8 Click **▼** and choose how many columns wide the gallery will be. This depends on the width of your content area and the image size you choose in step **10**.

9 Click **Random Order** (☐ changes to ☑) to have the order of images to vary.

10 Click **▼** and choose the size of the images displayed: thumbnail, medium, large, or full-size.

11 Click **Insert gallery** and return to the content editor.

In Visual mode, you will see the gallery images. In the example, you see what the gallery looks like live on the site.

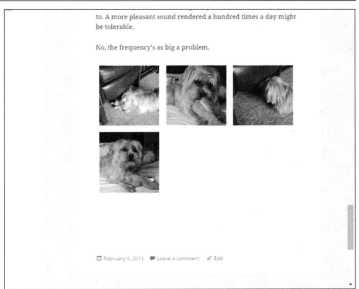

Why is it when I switch to Text mode, the gallery images are not there, just some code with square brackets?

This is called a *shortcode*, and it is how WordPress stores the information based on your choices in creating and editing a gallery. Be careful not to alter the shortcode, unless you know what you are doing, or you will break the gallery.

If I add a caption to an image in a gallery, will that caption appear anywhere else I might use that image?

Yes, but you can delete the caption in that other location without affecting the gallery caption.

Edit an Image Gallery

When you have created a WordPress gallery, you can edit it any time. That includes adding or removing images, and changing their order and sizing.

Edit an Image Gallery

① Click **Posts** or **Pages** on the left admin menu and locate the post or page with the gallery to be edited.

② Click **Edit** to open the post or page.

③ Click the **Visual** tab.

④ Click anywhere on the gallery images or the area around them, and a gray box appears, outlining the gallery area.

⑤ Click the pencil icon (✐) in the small menu that appears at the top of the gallery.

Ⓐ You can delete the gallery by clicking ✕.

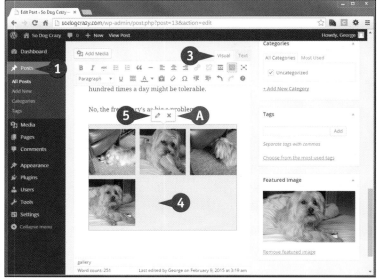

The Media Uploader window opens to display the Edit Gallery section.

The options here are the same as the ones described in the previous section, "Insert an Image Gallery."

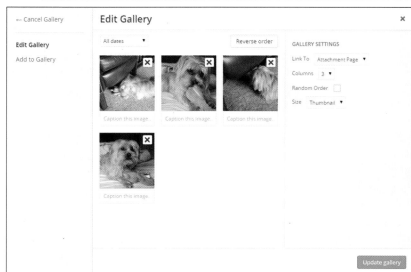

6 Click an image and drag it to change the order of images.

7 Click the **Columns ▼** to change the number of columns (2 in this example because of the size change in step **5**).

8 Click the **Size ▼** to change the image size (medium in this example).

9 Click **Update gallery**.

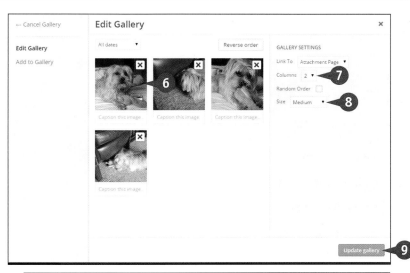

The new order, sizing, and columns are reflected in the content editor.

10 Click **Update** for the post or page.

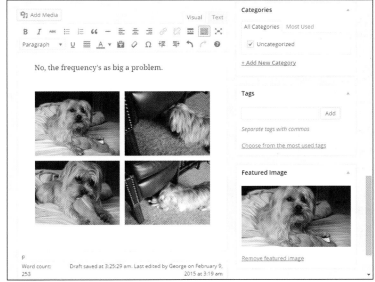

TIPS

What if I want to move a gallery to a different location within the post?

In Visual mode of the content editor, you can drag the gallery box around the content editor the same way you drag images. When you let go, the gallery appears in the new location.

I have done a lot of work setting up a large gallery. Do I need to set it all up again if I want to move it to a different post?

No. If you switch to Text mode, highlight the full shortcode of the gallery, cut it, and paste it into any other post or page.

Embed YouTube (and Other) Videos

If you have a YouTube channel or store videos on a major video sharing site, such as Vimeo, you can play your videos on any post or page. In fact, you can play any public video from YouTube or other sites.

Embed YouTube (and Other) Videos

Embed a Video

1 After you find the video you want to post on your site at YouTube.com, click **Share**. Along with the share icons, you see the URL for the video.

2 Click in the field and copy the URL.

3 Return to the tab or window with your post or page admin screen.

4 Paste the URL on its own separate line.

Note: You may not see the URL because WordPress immediately begins trying to load the video.

Note: If there is anything else on the line where you paste the URL, the embedding of the video will not work.

A A video player appears where you pasted the URL. Test the video by playing it right from the content editor.

5 Save your changes to the post or page. Depending on its status, click **Update**, **Publish**, or **Save Draft**.

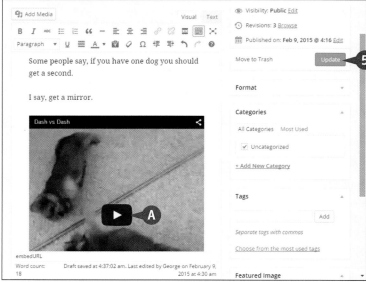

Control the Size of the Video

Note: WordPress tries to fill the content area with the video, but if you want to control the sizing, you can, using a *shortcode*.

① Click the **Text** tab in the content editor.

② Type the following shortcode:

```
[video src="http://the-url-to-
the-video.com" width="200"
height="150"]
```

The dimensions are in pixels, and you would use whatever values you want. This example is deliberately small to show the effect.

Note: This shortcode can also be used in situations when you need the video to be on the same line as other content.

③ Click the **Visual** tab.

Ⓑ Switching to Visual mode shows the new sizing of the video.

Note: This shortcode works with embeddable video links from third-party sites or any link to an MP4 video file.

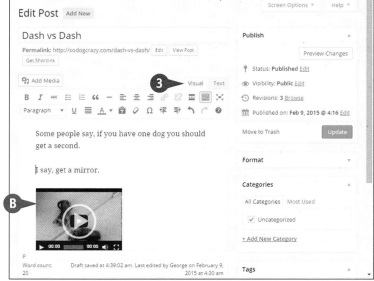

Do I have to pay for the video add-in to post YouTube videos with WordPress.com?

No, because you are posting a *link* to the video rather than hosting the video on your WordPress.com account.

What video sites does WordPress support for embedding players?

You can find the most current list at http://codex. wordpress.org/Embeds. This list includes not just video sites, but image, audio, document, and other types of sites as well.

Upload and Insert Video to a Post

While it is better to let YouTube or other video services store and serve your video files, there can be situations where you want to upload them to your site. On WordPress.com, you will need to buy the Premium upgrade to be able to upload video files.

Upload and Insert Video to a Post

Upload and Insert a Video File to a Post

1. Click **Add New** under Media on the left admin menu.

2. Click **Select Files** and upload your video file.

3. When the upload finishes, click the **Edit** link next to the filename.

   The Edit Media screen opens.

4. Copy the URL for the video.

5. Navigate to the post or page where you want to insert the video file.

6. Click the **Text** tab in the content editor.

7. Paste the URL on its own line in the content editor. This example uses Text mode, so no player appears.

8. Save your changes to the post or page. Depending on its status, click **Update**, **Publish**, or **Save Draft**.

Ⓐ WordPress automatically creates a player for your video file.

Ⓑ An embedded YouTube video has been left in this post to illustrate how the player for the uploaded file is equal in look and feel.

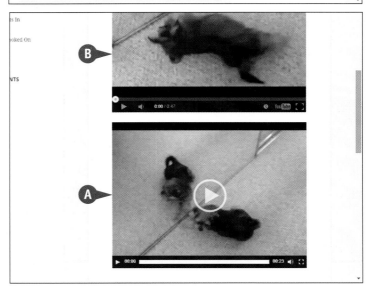

Add an Image to the Video Player

1 In an image editing program, create an image that the video player will display until play is started.

2 Click **Add New** under Media in the left admin menu, and upload the image to WordPress.

3 When the image finishes uploading, click **Edit**, and copy the URL for the image.

4 Click the **Text** tab in the content editor.

5 Type the following shortcode:

```
[video src="http://yoursite.
com/wp-content/uploads/year/
month.name-of-file.mp4"
poster="http://yoursite.com/
wp-content/uploads/year/
month/name-of-file"]
```

Note: Substitute the URLs for your video and image files.

6 Save your changes to the post or page. Depending on its status, click **Update**, **Publish**, or **Save Draft**.

C The image whose URL you placed in the shortcode now appears at the start of the video rather than the first frame of video.

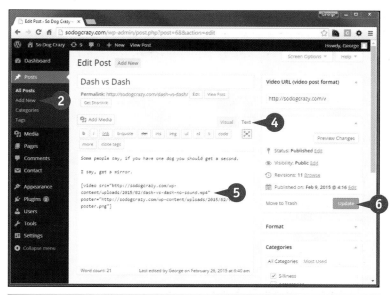

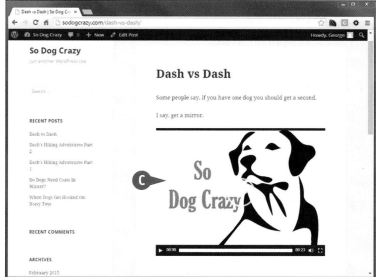

I do not want to use YouTube, and I cannot justify the cost of services like Vimeo or VideoPress. What alternatives are there?
Cloud storage like Amazon Web Services is very cost effective.

I have several videos that I want to show on one page, but visitors have to scroll so far to see the choices. Is there some other way to display them?
As soon as you have more than one video file in the media library, the Media Uploader window displays a Create Video Playlist link. You set it up much like you do an image gallery. You can also create Audio Playlists.

Upload and Insert Audio to a Post

Whether it is music, a recording of a teleseminar, a speech, or you reading a post, audio is a valuable but often overlooked type of content for your site. Like video files, you can embed audio from sharing sites, or simply paste a URL to any MP3 file, including ones you have uploaded to your site.

Upload and Insert Audio to a Post

Upload and Insert Your Own Audio to a Post

1 Click **Add New** under Media in the left admin menu.

2 Upload your MP3 file to WordPress.

Note: On WordPress.com, you need to buy an upgrade if you want to upload audio files. See http://en.support. wordpress.com/audio for the options.

3 When the upload finishes, click the **Edit** link next to the filename.

The Edit Media screen opens.

A An audio player appears at the top of the screen where you can test that your file is working.

4 Copy the URL for the audio file.

5 Navigate to the post or page where you want the audio to be played.

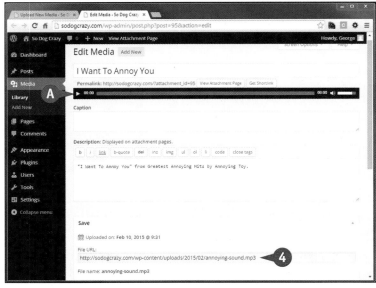

6 Click the **Visual** tab.

7 Paste the URL on its own line in the content editor.

Note: If there is anything else on the line where you paste the URL, then the audio player will not appear.

8 Click the Play button to make sure the audio works.

9 Save your changes to the post or page. Depending on its status, click **Update**, **Publish**, or **Save Draft**.

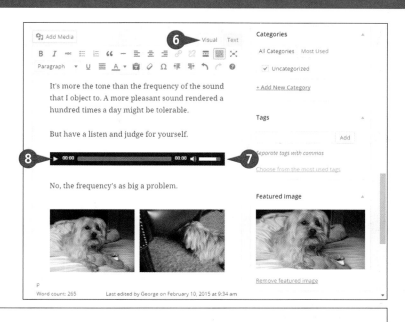

Upload and Insert Someone Else's Audio to a Post

1 Navigate to the website of the podcast you are interested in.

2 Check for permission to use podcasts on your site.

B If you want a particular episode, download the MP3 file and follow the instructions in the previous set of steps.

3 If the site has an embed code, copy and paste it into a widget, as described in the section "Display Social Feeds" in Chapter 11.

On this week's Dropout Nation Podcast, RiShawn Biddle considers the words of four contemporary champions for our children and discusses why systemic reform of public education as well as communities must begin with revolutionary love for every child.

You can listen to the Podcast at RiShawn Biddle Radio or download directly to your mobile or desktop device. Also, subscribe to the podcast series, and embed this podcast on your site. It is also available on iTunes, Blubrry, Stitcher, and PodBean.

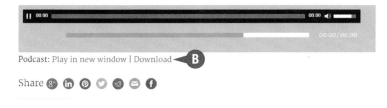

Podcast: Play in new window | Download ◄ **B**

Share

TIPS

Will the audio player work if I use a URL to an MP3 on another site?

Yes, any link to a file with the MP3 extension will work. But make sure you have permission to do so when the file is on someone else's site. And give credit to the other site.

Can I make music automatically play in the background?

It is not a good idea; many people object to that audio intrusion. Much better to let people choose to listen or not. The same is true of video.

CHAPTER 7

Organizing and Managing Your Site Content

A good-looking blog is all well and good, but in the end the content is king. You can improve your content's appeal with careful editing and attention to typography and organization.

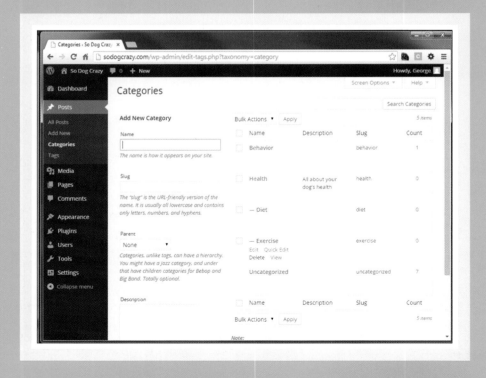

Understand Categories and Tags

ell-thought-out categories and tags provide a convenient way for readers to navigate your content. Think of them as another way for visitors to search your site. Although you can add categories and tags as you go along, doing a little planning will make them more useful.

Categories versus Tags

If you think of your site as a book, categories are the chapters and tags are the index terms. In other words, categories work best for bigger concepts, such as flowers, shrubs, and trees, whereas tags are very specific, like the name of a particular flower and so on. Also, every post must be assigned to at least one category, but tags are optional.

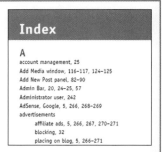

Categories and Subcategories

You have the option of creating subcategories, or *child* categories, for any category. For example, you may have a category *Flowers* with subcategories such as *Mixed Bouquets* and *Seasonal Bouquets*. Subcategories, in turn, can have their own subcategories. This is referred to as a *hierarchical* structure. Tags, on the other hand, are not hierarchical.

Why Use Tags?

Although tags are optional, they are useful because they provide another means to help and encourage readers to find content on your site. At the same time, they provide another means for search engines to index and rank your web pages. Imagine not having an index for a nonfiction book.

Default Category

If you do not specify a category when you create a post, WordPress assigns it to the default category, which initially is *Uncategorized*. One of your first tasks in setting up a site should be to rename this category to something useful; Google "uncategorized" to see how many WordPress users have not.

Uncategorized | - Republic Report
www.republicreport.org/category/**uncategorized**/ ▾
Charles Drevna, the top lobbyist for the refinery industry in America, likened companies that work with and fund environmental groups to "appeasers.

Outbrain | Uncategorized
www.outbrain.com/blog/category/**uncategorized** ▾ Outbrain ▾
Find out about **Uncategorized** on Outbrain's content marketing and discover Click to read interesting and informative articles about **Uncategorized**.

Uncategorized - Keep Talking Greece
www.keeptalkinggreece.com/category/**uncategorized**/ ▾
Feb 4, 2015 - Posted by keeptalkinggreece in Society, **Uncategorized**. tagge Minister for Public Order, Panousis, tear gas, two protests, unarmed ...

Custom Taxonomies

A *taxonomy* is the technical term in WordPress for a classification structure. Categories and tags are the default taxonomies for posts in WordPress, but themes, plugins, or your developer can create custom taxonomies. An e-commerce plugin, for example, could have a custom taxonomy called Product Categories.

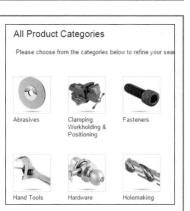

All Product Categories

Please choose from the categories below to refine your sear

Abrasives   Clamping Workholding & Positioning   Fasteners

Hand Tools   Hardware   Holemaking

Best Practices

There are no hard-and-fast rules for creating categories and tags. Flowers may be a category on one site, but a tag on another; it all depends on the content and the focus of the site. One helpful rule of thumb is to keep categories to a minimum (a clear overview) and have as many tags as you can think of (for digging deeper).

Browse by Categories:

Adapting & Adopting 7	FeaturedTextbook . 79	Stories _____ 3
Event Recap ____ 14	News _____ 55	Tutorials _____ 4
Events _____ 40	OpenStax ____ 2	Uncategorized ____ 17
Faculty Fellows ___ 16	PressBooks _____ 1	

Browse by Tags:

#fslt12 _____ 5	governance _____ 1	open textbooks ___ 41
#openeducationwk . 1	hackathon _____ 1	Open Textbooks Project ____ 4
adopting _____ 1	learning design ___ 2	Opening Education . 1
advocacy _____ 11	Librarians _____ 1	opening events ____ 1
authoring _____ 1	management ____ 1	otbsummit _____ 1

Add New Categories

The Categories screen lets you add new categories, but you also can add them while you add or edit posts. Either way, you add them to the same set of categories that help organize your content.

Add New Categories

Add a Category from the Categories Screen

1. Under Posts in the left admin menu, click **Categories**.

2. Type a name.

3. WordPress automatically creates a category slug using the name, but you can type one here.

Note: The Slug field does not appear on WordPress.com sites.

4. Type a description.

5. Scroll down and click **Add New Category**.

Ⓐ The screen refreshes and the category appears on the list at the right.

Add a Subcategory

1. Type a subcategory name.

2. If you want a slug other than the name, type it here.

3. Click the **Parent ▼** and choose the category you want as the parent of your subcategory.

4. Type a description.

5. Scroll down and click **Add New Category**.

The subcategory, preceded by a dash, appears under the parent category in the list at right on the Categories screen.

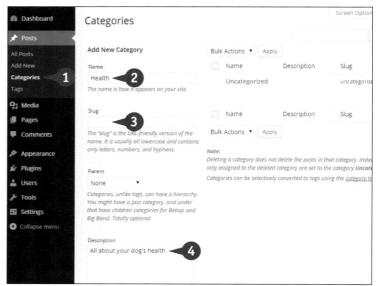

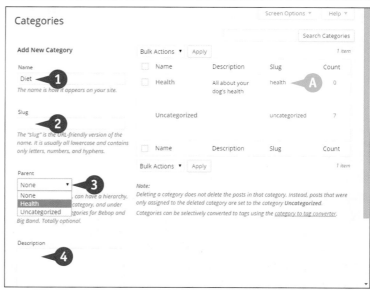

Add a Category from a Post Screen

1 On the New Post or Edit Post screen, click **Add New Category** at the bottom of the Categories meta box.

B A form for adding categories appears below the link.

2 Type the new category in the text field.

3 If the new category is a subcategory, click the **Parent Category ▼** and choose a category.

4 Click **Add New Category**.

C The new category appears in the Categories box as checked, meaning the post is assigned to it.

Note: Normally categories appear in alphabetical order, but when you assign a category to a post, it jumps to the top of the list. This makes it easier to see what categories you have assigned without having to scroll down the list.

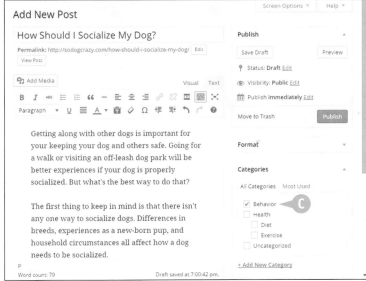

TIPS

Do category names need to be capitalized?
No, but it is the best way to write them. Category names get used in various ways on your website, and these should follow normal capitalization standards. The category slug, on the other hand, must be all lowercase, with hyphens rather than spaces.

Is it better to add categories as I add posts or do it all at once on the Categories screen?
When you first set up your site, it is better to create them on the Categories screen because it gives you a clear picture of the overall relationship between categories.

Manage Categories

Once you have created some categories, you can change their names, slugs, parent-child relationships, and delete them using the Categories screen. Remember that changing category slugs after your site is live breaks existing links to those categories.

If you want to add a category to multiple posts at one time, see the section "Bulk Edit Posts and Pages" later in this chapter.

Manage Categories

Quick Edit a Category Name

1. Under Posts in the left admin menu, click **Categories**.

2. Mouse over the category you want to edit to display a menu. The menu includes the Edit, Quick Edit, Delete, and View options.

3. Click **Quick Edit**.

4. In the Quick Edit area, type a new name.

5. Type a new slug.

6. Click **Update Category**.

   The new category name appears.

Change the Hierarchy of a Category

1. On the Categories screen, click a category name or the **Edit** menu item to display the Edit Category screen.

Ⓐ You can edit the Name, Slug, and Description from this screen. You can also make the category a child of another category.

2. Click the **Parent ▼** and choose the category you want to be the parent.

3. Click **Update**.

   The subcategory, preceded by a dash, appears under the parent category on the right-hand list of the Categories screen.

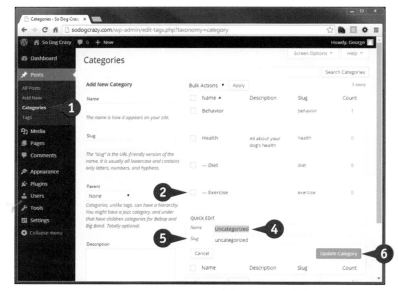

Delete a Category

1 Note the Count for the Stories category: 6. Stories is currently the default category for posts.

2 Mouse over the category you want to edit to display a menu.

3 Click **Delete**.

The category disappears from the list.

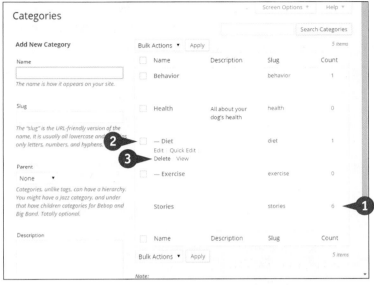

B The category disappears from the list.

4 Notice that the Count on the Stories category is now 7.

When you delete a category, any posts that were assigned only to that category are automatically assigned to the default category.

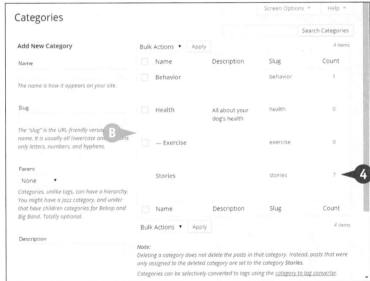

TIPS

How do I change the default category?

Click **Writing** under Settings in the left admin menu, and then choose the default category from the Default Post Category drop-down menu.

When I tried to change the name and slug of a category, WordPress said the slug is already in use, but it is not.

Slugs must be unique not only across all categories, but all tags as well or else you will end up with two URLs exactly the same. If the slug is not being used by any category, then it is being used by a tag. You need to change the tag's slug first if you want the category to have that slug.

Add New Tags

Like categories, new tags can be created from their own screen or from any post screen. You can also add new tags from the post's listing, but that is covered in the section "Quick Edit Posts and Pages" later in this chapter.

Because tags are for very specific items, it is hard to know in advance what tags you will need. It is easier to enter tags while working on a post, because that is where they first come up in your content.

Add New Tags

Add a Tag from the Add New Post or Edit Post Screens

Ⓐ When you are adding or editing a post, look for the Tags box at the bottom right. Typically you need to scroll to see it.

① Begin typing your tag into the field.

Note: Type fairly slowly to give WordPress time to search existing tags.

Ⓑ As you type, a box pops up revealing existing tags using the same letters.

If you see the tag you want on the list, click it to place it into the field.

If the tag you want is not on the list, continue typing in the field.

Usually you will be adding more than one tag to a post. Simply put a comma between each tag.

Ⓒ This link displays a list of the most used tags.

② Click **Add**.

Ⓓ The tag or tags appear below the Add Tags field with ⊗ next to each. If the tag is new, it will be added to the list on the Tags screen and be available to other posts.

③ Click **Update** or **Save Draft** or **Publish**, depending on the type of screen you are on.

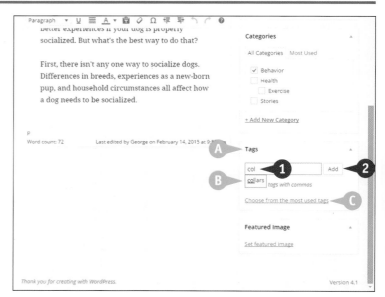

Delete Tags from a Post

1 Click **Posts** on the left admin menu and locate the relevant post.

2 Click **Edit**.

3 Mouse over ⊗ beside a tag until it turns red and then click.

The post is no longer assigned to that tag and the tag disappears from the Edit Post screen.

4 Click **Update** or **Save Draft** or **Publish**, depending on the status of the post or page.

Add New Tags from the Tags Screen

1 Under Posts in the left admin menu, click **Tags**.

2 Under Add New Tag on the left, type a name in the Name field.

3 WordPress automatically creates a tag slug using the name, but if you want a different slug, type it here.

Note: The Slug field does not appear on WordPress.com sites.

4 Type a description.

5 Scroll down and click **Add New Tag**.

The new tag is added to the listing on the right.

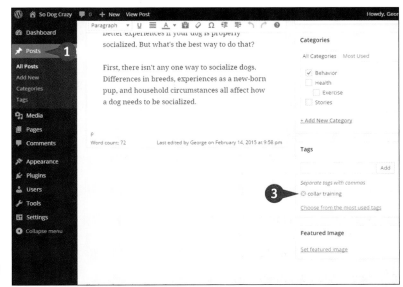

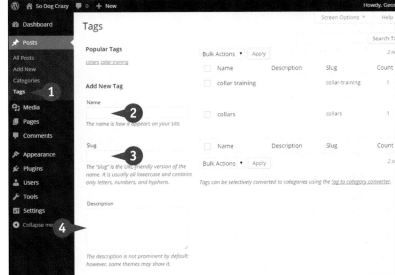

Why is it so important to enter tags slowly?

If you miss seeing the list of existing similar tags, you run the risk of entering a misspelled tag or a slightly different tag. That results in different tags, and the posts with those tags will be grouped separately. For example, WordPress treats three versions of "day care" differently if you type "daycare," "Day care," and "day care."

Can I capitalize tag names?

Yes, but a common convention is to capitalize only proper names: Colorado, Jane Doe, Purina, and so on. The important thing is to be consistent with whatever you decide to do. And of course tag slugs, like categories, need to be all lowercase.

Manage Tags

Whether it is adding a new tag, changing the name or slug of an existing tag, or deleting tags, you can manage it all from the Tags screen. Remember that changing tag slugs after your site is live breaks existing links to those tags.

If you want to add a tag to multiple posts at one time, see the section "Bulk Edit Posts and Pages," later in this chapter.

Manage Tags

Edit a Tag from the Tags Screen

1 Under Posts in the left admin menu, click **Tags**.

2 Mouse over the tag you want to edit to display a menu.

3 Click **Quick Edit**.

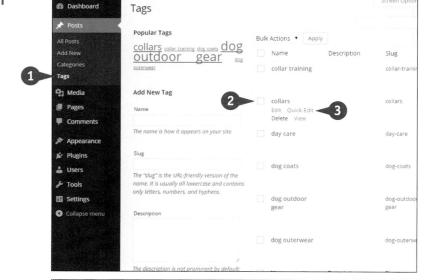

A The Quick Edit area appears.

4 Type a new name in the Name field.

5 Type a slug name. It must be changed as well. It can just be a lowercase version of the name or slightly different.

6 Click **Update Tag**.

The new tag name appears.

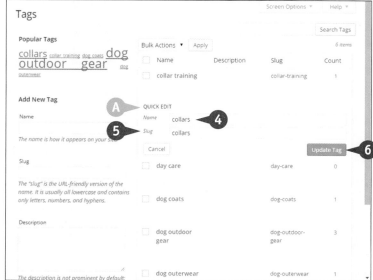

Deleting Multiple Tags Using Bulk Actions

① On the Tags screen, click the box beside each tag you want to delete (☐ changes to ☑).

② From the Bulk Actions dropdown at the top or bottom of the screen, click **Delete**.

③ Click **Apply**.

View All Posts Using a Particular Tag

① On the Tags screen, find the Count column for the tag of interest and click the number.

The Posts screen opens.

You now see all posts, three in this example, that have been assigned the tag you selected. This example was for "dog outdoor gear."

Ⓑ You can verify that all the posts share the particular tag by checking the Tags column.

Note: This same action can be taken for categories on the Categories screen.

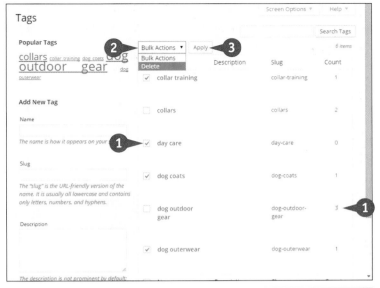

TIPS

I have not been entering descriptions for my categories or tags. Is that a problem?

Creating useful categories and tags is far more important than having a description for each of them. At the same time, many more themes these days display the description if you have one.

Do I need both categories and tags?

It is important that visitors and search engines be given as many ways as possible to find your content. Categories and tags do this in different ways, so both are vital. WordPress makes it so easy to work with them, there is no excuse not to take that little bit of extra time.

Convert Categories and Tags

If you imported your content to WordPress from another platform, you may find that all your old tags are now categories. Or maybe a tag has taken on more importance and should now be a category. Fortunately, WordPress has a tool that lets you convert categories to tags and vice versa.

Find the conversion tool by clicking the **Available Tools** link under Tools on the left admin menu. On WordPress.org sites, you can save a step by clicking the **Import** link under Tools.

Convert Categories and Tags

1 Under Tools in the left admin menu, click **Available Tools**.

2 Click **Categories and Tags Converter**.

On WordPress.com sites, the Convert Categories to Tags screen opens.

Note: WordPress.com users skip to step **6**.

On WordPress.org sites, the Import screen opens.

3 Click **Categories and Tags Converter**.

A plugin window opens.

4 Click **Install Now**.

5 After WordPress installs the plugin, click **Activate Plugin & Run Importer**.

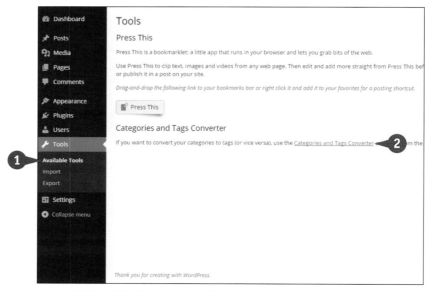

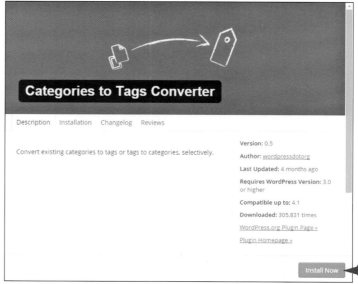

The Convert Categories (*n*) to Tags screen opens, where *n* represents the number of categories available to convert.

6 Click each category that you want to convert to a tag (☐ changes to ☑), or click **Check All** to convert all categories.

7 Click **Convert Categories to Tags**.

WordPress displays the progress and confirms the conversions.

8 Click **Tags to Categories** from the progress screen or the category conversion screen, which opens the Convert Tags (*n*) to Categories screen, with *n* as the available tags.

9 Click each tag that you want to convert to a category (☐ changes to ☑), or click **Check All** to convert all tags.

10 Click **Convert Tags to Categories**.

The tag is now a category. It will need to be edited and capitalized.

TIPS

What happens to the posts when I convert categories and tags?
They are still attached to the posts to which they were previously assigned, but as categories rather than tags, or vice versa. Because categories are required, though, if you changed all categories assigned to a particular post, the post automatically is assigned to the default category.

What happens if I convert a parent category to a tag but do not convert its child, or subcategory?
The subcategory becomes a top-level category.

Find Posts and Pages

As you add more and more content to your site — in particular, posts — finding the content you want to edit becomes a challenge. WordPress has a number of tools on its listings pages to make the task simpler.

Find Posts

A Filter by Status

Click a link to show all posts or only published, draft, pending, or trashed posts. The number of posts is shown in brackets. Note: This menu displays a status only if there are posts with that status.

B Filter by Date

Drop down the menu to choose a month and then click **Filter**.

C Filter by Category

Drop down the menu to choose a category and then click **Filter**.

D Search by Title

Type a term or terms and click **Search Posts**.

E Sort Listings

Click on column headings Title, Comments (🗨), or Date to sort the listings by the given parameter; toggles between ascending and descending order.

F Filter by Category

Click a category name to filter by that category.

G Filter by Tag

Click a tag name to filter by that tag.

H Filter by Author

Click an author's name to show only posts by that author.

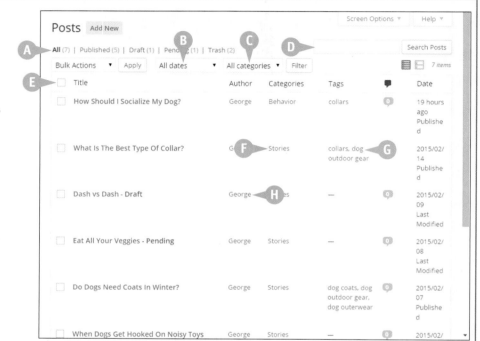

Find Pages

A Filter by Status

Click a link to show all pages or only published, draft, or trashed posts. The number of pages is shown in brackets. Note: This menu displays a status only if there are pages with that status.

B Filter by Date

Drop down the menu to choose a month and then click **Filter**.

C Search by Title

Type a term or terms and click **Search Pages**.

D Sort Listings

Click column headings Title, Comments (💬), or Date to sort the listings by the given parameter; toggles between ascending and descending order.

E Filter by Author

Click an author's name to show only pages by that author.

Use Screen Options

To display more than the default 20 listings, use the Screen Options link at the top right of both post and page listings to control the number of results shown at one time. You can also control which columns appear. WordPress.org sites may have more column choices depending on what plugins are installed, and there are plugins which allow even more control over what columns are shown.

Total Counts Explained

The Filter By status menu at the top shows the number of posts or pages with that status. However, trashed items are not counted on the All link, which is why the numbers do not always add up. Also, the Trash total will vary over time as trashed items are automatically deleted after 30 days.

Quick Edit Posts and Pages

When you are on post and page listings screens, WordPress makes it easy to edit certain elements without having to open the individual post or page.

The Quick Edit function is accessed by mousing over a particular post or page and clicking the **Quick Edit** link.

Quick Edit Posts

Ⓐ Edit the Title or Slug

Edit either the title of the post or its slug. Note: Changing the slug after publishing a post breaks existing links to that post.

Ⓑ Edit the Date

Edit the publication day, month, year, or time. If the post is already published, this affects the default order in which WordPress displays it. If the post is scheduled to publish, this changes that scheduled date.

Ⓒ Password Protect

Type a password here if you want the post to be visible only to those who know the password.

Ⓓ Assign Categories

Assign or unassign the post to available categories. You cannot add new categories from here.

Ⓔ Assign Tags

Assign or unassign the post to available tags. You can also add new tags here.

Ⓕ Allow Comments

Allow or disallow comments for this post.

Ⓖ Allow Pings

Allow or disallow pings for this post.

Ⓗ Change Status

Choose Published, Draft, or Pending Review from the drop-down menu.

Ⓘ Make the Post Sticky

Checking this box makes the post remain at the top of any post listings.

Ⓙ Update

Always remember to click **Update** when finished.

Quick Edit Pages

Ⓐ Edit the Title or Slug

Edit either the title of the page or its slug. Note: Changing the slug after publishing a page breaks existing links to that page.

Ⓑ Edit the Date

Edit the publication day, month, year, or time. If the page is scheduled to publish, this changes that scheduled date.

Ⓒ Password Protect

Type a password here if you want the page to be visible only to those who know the password.

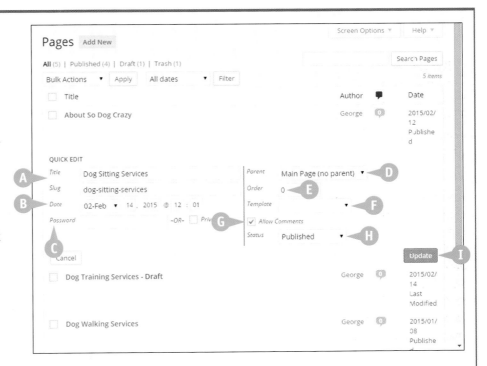

Ⓓ Assign a Parent

If you want the page to be the child or subpage of another, choose it from the dropdown.

Ⓔ Order

Override WordPress's default alphabetical ordering of pages.

Ⓕ Assign a Template

If your theme has page templates, you can choose from them using this drop-down menu.

Ⓖ Allow Comments

Allow or disallow comments for this page.

Ⓗ Change Status

Choose Published, Draft, or Pending Review from the drop-down menu.

Ⓘ Update

Always remember to click **Update** when finished.

Bulk Edit Posts and Pages

Sometimes you need to make the same change to multiple posts or pages at a time, such as adding posts to a category or changing pages to a new page template. The Bulk Edit function makes tasks like this a snap.

Bulk Edit Posts

Ⓐ Check Posts You Want to Edit

Check the box next to each post you want to edit, or if you want to select all posts, click the box in the column heading next to Title.

Ⓑ Choose Edit

From the Bulk Actions dropdown, choose **Edit** then click **Apply**.

Ⓒ Edit the List of Posts

All the posts you selected are shown with ⊗ beside each. Remove posts from the editing process by clicking ⊗.

Ⓓ Assign Categories

Assign the posts to available categories. You cannot remove posts from a category nor can you add new categories.

Ⓔ Assign Tags

Assign the posts to available tags. You can also add new tags here.

Ⓕ Change Author

Drop-down menu of all authors on the site.

Ⓖ Allow Comments

Allow or disallow comments.

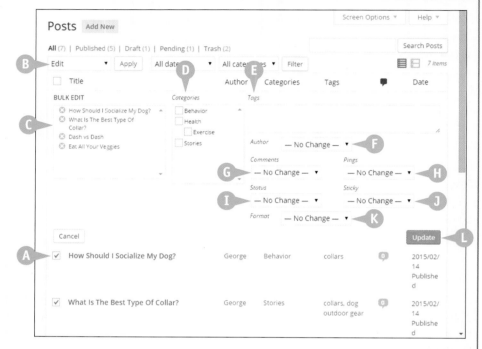

Ⓗ Allow Pings

Allow or disallow pings.

Ⓘ Change Status

Choose Published, Draft, or Pending Review from the drop-down menu.

Ⓙ Make Posts Sticky

Choose whether posts remain at the top of post listings.

Ⓚ Change Format

Choose from available post formats.

Ⓛ Update

Click **Update** when finished.

Bulk Edit Pages

Ⓐ Check Pages You Want to Edit

Check the box next to each page you want to edit, or if you want to select all pages, click the box in the column heading next to Title.

Ⓑ Choose Edit

From the Bulk Actions dropdown, choose **Edit** and then click **Apply**.

Ⓒ Edit the List of Pages

All the pages you selected are shown with ⊗ beside each. Remove pages from the editing process by clicking ⊗.

Ⓓ Change Author

Drop-down menu of all authors on the site.

Ⓔ Assign a Parent

If you want the pages to be children or subpages of another, choose it from the dropdown.

Ⓕ Assign a Template

If your theme has page templates, you can choose from them using this drop-down menu.

Ⓖ Allow Comments

Allow or disallow comments.

Ⓗ Change Status

Choose Published, Draft, or Pending Review from the drop-down menu.

Ⓘ Update

Always remember to click **Update** when finished.

CHAPTER 8

Using Widgets and Menus

After a web page's main content, the next most important elements visitors see are in sidebars and footers. WordPress widgets make it easy to manage these areas, whereas the WordPress menu system gives you full control over the navigation that helps visitors find what they need.

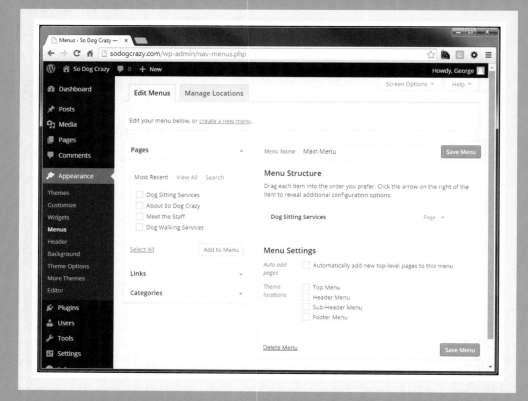

Understand Widgets and Widget Areas

A lot happens on websites outside of the main content area — in the header, footer, and sidebars. Whether you include a feed from your social media accounts, a sign-up form, or a search function for e-commerce, these features play an important role on your site, and in WordPress are performed by *widgets*.

Widgets

Think of widgets as individual apps that perform a specific function, such as displaying a list of your post categories or a countdown timer to a certain date. Usually the widget provides settings that allow you to customize it, such as choosing how to display categories or writing a message to go with a countdown timer. Widgets are easily added, removed, or rearranged through the WordPress interface.

Standard Widgets for WordPress.com Sites

WordPress.com sites come with more than 30 widgets, many of which connect to your social media accounts or other sites, like Flickr or Goodreads. Although new widgets are added to the system from time to time, you cannot add your own widgets.

Standard Widgets for WordPress.org Sites

WordPress.org sites come with fewer standard widgets, such as categories, recent comments, or custom menus. However, you can add as many widgets as you want using plugins, and many themes add their own widgets as well.

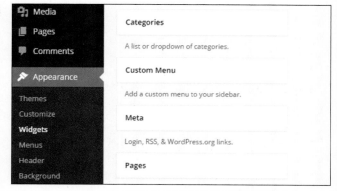

Widget Areas

A widget area is a location on your site where widgets can be placed. What widget areas you have is determined by your theme. On WordPress. com sites, this is usually limited to the sidebar or footer. On WordPress.org sites, themes may also have widget areas in the header, above or below the content area, or widget areas that appear only on certain pages.

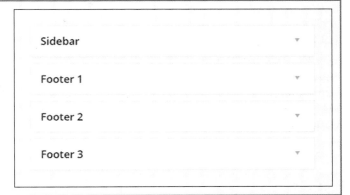

Custom Widget Areas

WordPress.org sites offer themes and plugins that allow you to create your own widget areas. If you get a developer to customize or create a theme, you can put widget areas wherever you want or have them restricted to whatever pages or sections of your site you want.

Restricting Widget Visibility

On WordPress.com sites, every widget can be set to appear only under certain circumstances: on specific pages or if a certain category is being viewed or to certain users. You can add the same functionality to WordPress.org sites using plugins. For example, you probably do not want testimonials in the sidebar to appear on the testimonials page.

Get to Know the Widgets Screens

You can manage widgets from two different locations in WordPress: the Widget screen and from the Widgets section of the Customizer. To access the Widgets screen, click **Widgets** under Appearance in the left admin menu. To access widgets in the Customizer screen, click **Customize** under Appearance and then click the arrow beside Widgets.

The Widgets Screen

A The left side of the screen contains all Available Widgets, listed in alphabetical order. On WordPress.org sites, what you see here varies depending on your theme and the plugins you have. Below this area, but not visible here, is the Inactive Widgets area, where you can store widgets with their settings saved.

B Individual widgets show as rectangular buttons that you drag over to one of the widget areas, or click one to see

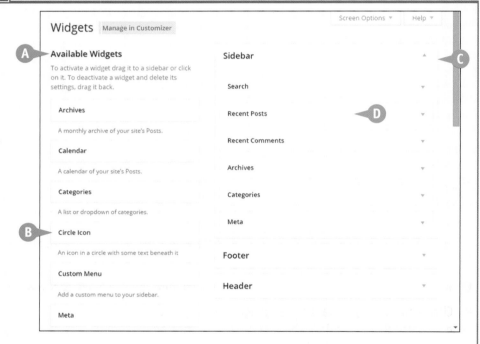

a list of widget areas you can add it to. A short description below each gives some details about what the widget does.

C The right side of the screen displays all available widget areas. Widgets are dragged or assigned to these areas. On WordPress.org sites, what areas you have vary depending on your theme and the plugins you have.

D When you arrive at the Widgets screen, WordPress automatically has the topmost widget area open. A widget area displays all its widgets vertically, and this is the order in which they are displayed on your site. Clicking a widget reveals its settings, and dragging a widget allows you to rearrange the order.

Widgets in the Customizer

Ⓐ The left side of the Customizer screen contains all available widget areas, and within them, the widgets that have been added. On WordPress.org sites, the widget areas vary depending on your theme and the plugins you have.

Ⓑ The right side of the screen displays a preview of your site, which you can navigate and view all pages. As you work with widgets, you see your changes in real time, but nothing affects your live site until you save.

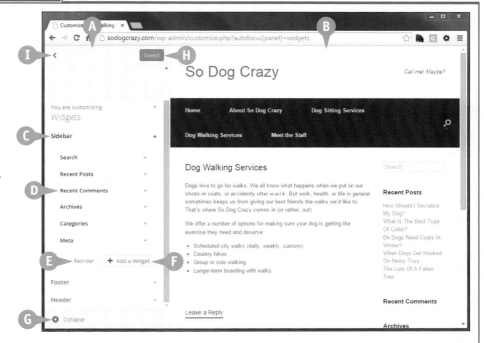

Ⓒ Widget areas toggle open and closed. When you arrive at the Widgets screen, WordPress automatically has the topmost widget area open.

Ⓓ Widgets are displayed in their widget areas, and you click a widget to reveal its configuration settings.

Ⓔ Click **Reorder** if you want to rearrange the widgets in a particular area. A widget area displays all its widgets vertically, and this is the order in which they are displayed on your site.

Ⓕ The Add a Widget button slides open a list of all available widgets. On WordPress.org sites, the available widgets vary depending on your theme and the plugins you have.

Ⓖ When the left side of the Customizer is not collapsed, the preview you get tends to be the mobile version of your theme. Click the **Collapse** link to collapse the widget areas and view your site in desktop format.

Ⓗ When you are finished, click the **Save and Publish** button. This makes all your changes live on the site. You remain on the Customizer screen and the button changes to Saved.

Ⓘ When you finish all changes, click ‹ to return to the primary Customizer screen. Clicking **Close** (✕) on that screen returns you to the regular WordPress admin screen.

Choose and Add Widgets

You can add or remove widgets any time from either the Widgets screen or the Customizer. This section covers the Widgets screen, but you can get the Customizer details in the section "Manage Widgets from the Customizer" later in this chapter.

Choose and Add Widgets

Add Widgets to a Widget Area

1 In the left admin menu, click **Widgets** under Appearance.

2 Click a widget in the list of available widgets.

The other widgets are grayed out and a list of widget areas appears.

3 Click the name of the widget area you want. The name is highlighted and a check mark appears.

4 Click **Add Widget**.

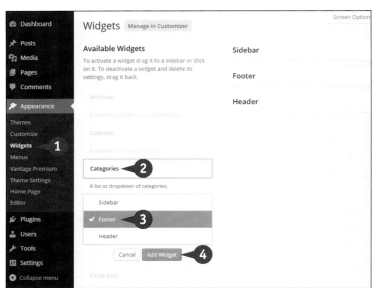

A The widget area opens and the widget settings appear.

Note: The widget is added to the bottom of any existing widgets. You can then drag it to change the order of its appearance.

5 Type a title for the widget.

6 Choose the settings ($\square$ changes to $\checkmark$).

Note: Widget settings vary widely. In a few cases there are not even any to choose.

7 Click **Save**.

A circular icon appears next to Save to indicate when the saving process is complete.

8 Click **Close**.

B You can also click the header of the widget to collapse it.

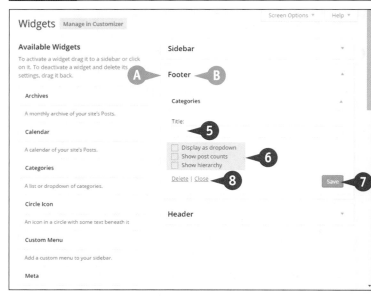

Drag Widgets to a Widget Area

1 Open the widget area where you want your widget to appear.

2 Click and drag the widget you want.

C A transparent copy of the widget moves with your mouse pointer.

D When the widget reaches the widget area, a box with a dotted line appears, indicating where your widget will be placed.

3 When the widget is in the location you want, release the mouse button.

Use Accessibility Mode

Note: If you have turned off JavaScript in your browser or if there is a problem with JavaScript, the Widgets screen will not work. You can, however, still work in accessibility mode.

1 Click **Screen Options**.

2 Click the **Enable accessibility mode** link at the top left.

E Available widgets on the left have Add links.

F Widgets in widget areas on the right have Edit links.

3 Click **Disable accessibility mode** to return to default widget behavior.

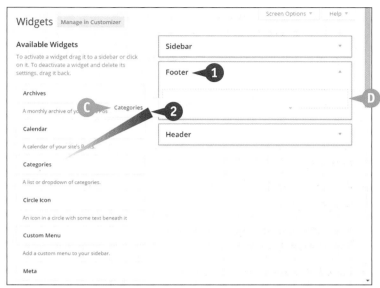

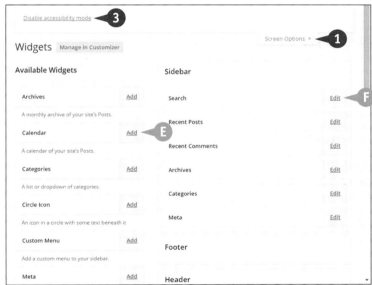

TIPS

The sidebar of my site displays some text, but there is nothing in the widget area. Why is that?
Some themes show default text to remind users that widgets need configuring and to show where the widgets will appear. As soon as you add one widget to the area, the sample text disappears.

Is there a way to know where Widget areas will appear?
Usually the area's name will give you some idea: Footer 2 or Left Sidebar. In addition, theme writers can add descriptive text which appears when you toggle the widget area open. If it is still not clear, insert a widget and see where it shows up.

Rearrange and Remove Widgets

Changing the order of widgets in a widget area is as easy as dragging and dropping. The same is true for deleting a particular widget.

Rearrange and Remove Widgets

Rearrange a Widget

1 Click and hold on the widget that you want to move.

2 Drag the widget to the position you want it to have in the widget area.

The widget becomes transparent as you drag it.

3 When a rectangle with a dotted line appears at the desired location, release the mouse button.

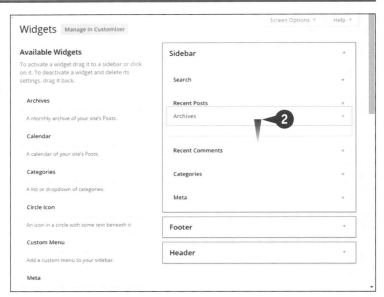

Ⓐ The widget appears in its new position in the widget area.

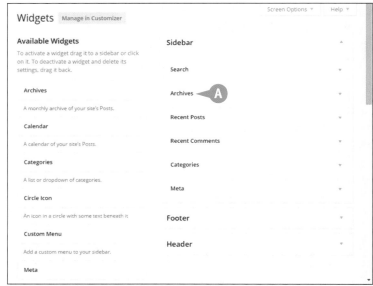

Remove a Widget without Retaining Its Settings

① Click a widget to open it, if it is not already.

② Click the **Delete** link at the bottom left.

The widget disappears and all settings are lost.

Note: You can also delete a widget by dragging it to Available Widgets. As you drag the widget, a Deactivate notice with the name of the widget appears beside the Available Widgets title.

Remove a Widget and Retain Its Settings

① Click the header area of Available Widgets to collapse that portion of the screen.

The Inactive Widgets area moves up.

② Drag the widget from the widget area over to Inactive Widgets.

③ Click the widget to open it and verify that your settings have been retained.

Note: If you want to use the widget again, you need to drag it to a widget area. The assign function does not work because the widget has settings.

TIPS

Can I drag a widget to a different widget area?
Yes, but make sure the destination widget area is already open. Just as with adding a widget, the dragging process does not automatically open a closed widget area.

Can I delete widget areas?
No. Simply removing all widgets from the area makes it disappear from a visitor's perspective, but you cannot delete the area on the Widgets screen. On WordPress.org sites, if the theme or a plugin makes it possible to create your own widget areas, then yes, you could delete any of the ones you create.

Manage Widgets from the Customizer

WordPress is adding more and more functions into its Customizer screen, and managing widgets is one of the most recent additions.

Find the Widgets customizer screen by going to Customize under Appearance in the left admin menu. WordPress.org sites also include a Manage in Customizer button on the Widgets screen.

Manage Widgets from the Customizer

Choose and Insert Widgets

1 In the left admin menu, click **Customize**.

Note: Once the Customizer screen opens, the left admin menu is gone. You can return to it by clicking < at the top left.

ⓐ A live preview of your site appears on the right side of the screen.

2 Click **Widgets** on the left side of the screen to open the Widget panel.

You can now see all widget areas on the left.

3 Click the widget area you want to manage.

ⓑ If you need to return to the main Customizer screen, click < .

ⓒ Whatever widgets are in the widget area are now displayed in order of appearance.

4 Click **Add a Widget**.

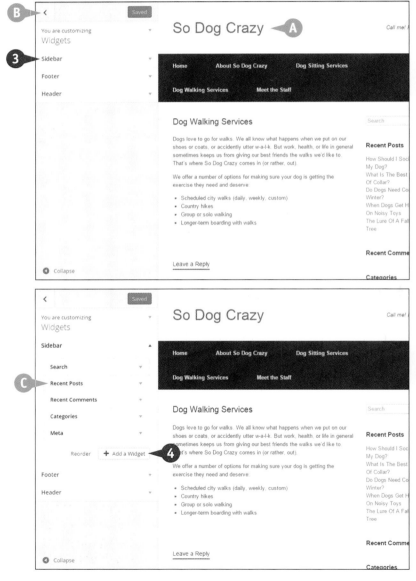

D A list of all available widgets appears.

You can click a widget to collapse the list; the open widget appears in the widget area, displaying its settings.

Note: There is no Save button on Customizer widgets. Any additions or changes are collectively saved by clicking **Save & Publish** at the top of the screen.

Reorder Widgets

1 Click the **Reorder** link located at the bottom of each widget area.

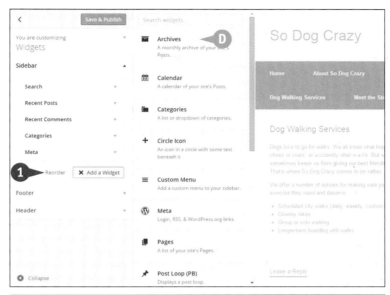

Each widget now displays three icons.

2 Click ⌃ or ⌄ to move one position.

3 If you want to move the widget to a different widget area, click the external icon (⤢).

4 A list of widget areas appears. Select the one you want and click **Move**.

5 When you finish reordering, click **Done**.

Note: You can also reorder widgets within a widget area by clicking and dragging.

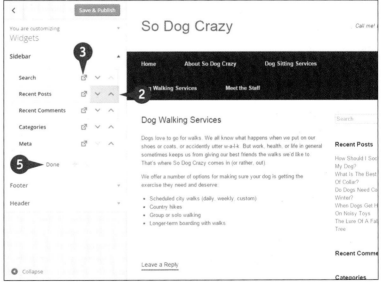

I clicked Reorder and successfully moved a widget, but now I cannot open it.

You have to click the **Done** link at the bottom of the widget area. That takes you out of reordering mode, at which point you can open widgets and configure them.

I added a widget using the customizer but it is not showing on the preview screen.

Because of screen size, sites in the customizer often display in mobile mode, pushing widgets far down the page. Another reason for not seeing a widget yet is because it requires configuring. And finally, the widget may be set to display on a web page you are not viewing.

Understand Menus and Menu Locations

Clear and comprehensive navigation is vital to any website. WordPress makes it easy to create menus that help your visitors find the content they need. And menu items are not restricted to pages; virtually any element in WordPress — posts, categories, tags, and more — can be on a menu.

Menus

A *menu* is a group of links to various elements of your WordPress site, which you can create, edit, and rearrange from the Menus screen. There are default elements to choose from, such as pages, posts, categories, and tags. On WordPress.org sites, you may have other elements such as products or events, depending on the plugins available for a particular theme. You can build as many different menus as you want in WordPress.

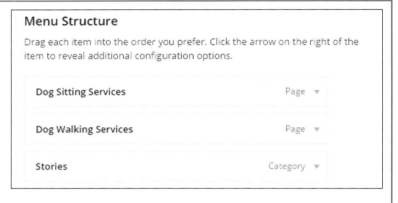

Menu Locations

A *menu location* is a designated area in a theme where you can place any menu you create. Virtually every theme has at least one menu location in the header area of the site. How many other menu locations there are — in the footer, say, or a secondary menu in the header — depends on the theme. On WordPress.org sites, you can customize theme code to include more menu locations.

Custom Menu Widget

Although themes determine what menu locations are available, you can, on any WordPress site, place a menu in any available widget area using the custom menu widget. For example, you might want a menu of all your categories in a sidebar, or if your theme does not include a footer menu location, simply drop a custom menu widget into a footer widget area.

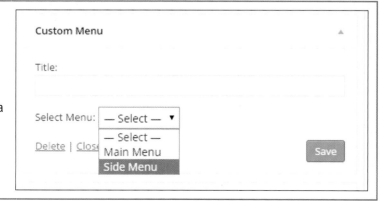

The Default Menu

To ensure there is some type of navigation for visitors, WordPress has a default menu that appears when you first set up a site. It automatically lists all WordPress pages in alphabetical order. The default menu disappears when you create and assign a menu to that location, and reappears if you ever delete your menu without replacing it.

Custom Links

In addition to adding any WordPress elements to a menu, you can create custom links. It could be a link to a special download file on your site, or it could be a link to a completely different site, such as a third-party shopping cart or another of your websites. Because all menu items can be targeted with CSS or even assigned their own classes, you could specially style a custom link to stand out from other menu items.

Know Your Limits

WordPress menus support multiple levels of dropdowns, which means they can get quite large. If you get beyond 60 or 70 items on a single menu, you could run into server security restrictions when trying to save such a large menu. You could ask your server to raise those restrictions, but a better plan is to rethink your menu. Could it be broken down into two menus or have separate menus for different areas of your site, with a simple main menu leading to each area?

Get to Know the Menus Screen

The WordPress menu system is a powerful tool for managing the navigation on your site. Every element of your content is a potential menu item, and the configuration possibilities are endless.

Get to Know the Menus Screen

Ⓐ Click **Menus** under Appearance on the left admin menu.

Ⓑ The Edit Menus tab displays the menu creation and editing panel.

Ⓒ The Manage Locations tab displays a set of dropdowns for managing the various menu locations created by your theme. Note: The Manage Locations tab appears only when you have created at least one menu, and not at all if your theme does not support menus or menu locations.

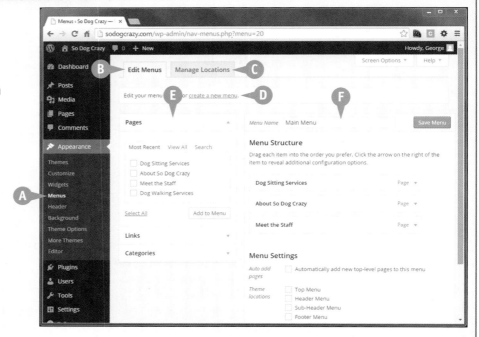

Ⓓ Click the **create a new menu** link to begin a new menu.

Ⓔ For the Edit Menus tab, the left side of the screen displays available menu items. What is shown here varies depending on your Screen Options settings, and on WordPress.org sites the available menu items also vary with themes and plugins.

Ⓕ For the Edit Menus tab, the right side of the screen displays all the settings of the menu being edited.

Tour the Dashboard

Ⓐ Click **Menus** under Appearance on the left admin menu.

Ⓑ The Manage Locations tab shows you which menus are assigned to which menu locations, and is one of the points where you can assign those locations.

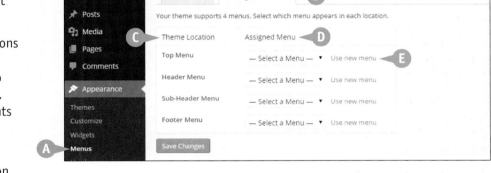

Ⓒ Every menu location provided by your theme is listed here.

Ⓓ The dropdown contains the names of all the menus you have created. From this you can assign a menu to a menu location. If a menu is already assigned, the dropdown says so.

Ⓔ The Use New Menu link allows you to create a new menu.

Ⓐ Click **Menus** under Appearance on the left admin menu.

Ⓑ The Edit Menus tab displays the menu creation and editing panel. When you are on the Edit Menus tab, WordPress by default does not show all available menu items. You can display them using Screen Options.

Ⓒ Clicking the **Screen Options** tab reveals the options for menus.

Ⓓ Clicking the **Show on screen** check boxes toggles the appearance of different menu items. On WordPress.org sites, the available menu items also vary with themes and plugins.

Create a Menu

You can create any number of menus in WordPress and assign any type and number of items to each. The easy-to-use interface helps keep you organized while you create navigation to help your visitors.

Create a Menu

1 In the left admin menu, click **Menus** under Appearance.

2 Click the **create a new menu** link.

Note: When you have no menus yet, the screen is ready to create a menu and everything remains grayed out until you click Create Menu.

3 Type a menu name. This is not displayed publicly, only to help you remember what the menu is for.

4 Click **Create Menu**.

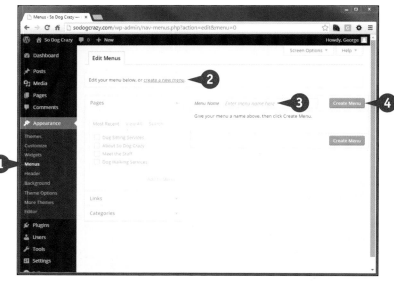

A You now see the Menu Settings and the Menu Structure areas.

B The menu items area now becomes active.

5 To add a page to the menu, click the box next to it (☐ changes to ☑).

6 Click **Add to Menu**.

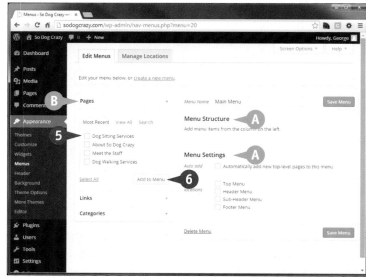

Ⓒ The page item you chose in step **5** now appears as a menu item under Menu Structure.

⑦ Click the Categories section of the menu items area to open its settings and close Pages.

⑧ Click the box beside the category you want to add to your menu (☐ changes to ☑).

⑨ Click **Add to Menu**.

Ⓓ The category you chose in step **8** now appears at the bottom of the list of items in the Menu Structure.

⑩ Click **Save Menu**.

TIPS

Under Menu Settings is a box for automatically adding pages to the menu. Should I check that box?
Sometimes, you will have WordPress pages that you do not want on your menu, such as thank you pages for people signing up to a mailing list. Leaving this box unchecked makes sure no pages are put on the menu without your approval.

When I look under Links in the menu items area, it is blank. What is this for?
You can add any sort of link to a WordPress menu. For example, if you have a store on a third-party site, you could have a Store link on your menu.

Reorder Menu Items

You can change the order of items on your menus in the same way you change the order of widgets: by dragging and dropping them. You can also have submenu items.

Reorder Menu Items

Reorder Menu Items

1 In the left admin menu, click **Menus** under Appearance.

2 Click and hold on the menu item you want to move and then drag it to the position you want.

3 When a rectangle with a dotted line appears at the desired location, release the mouse button.

The menu item appears in its new position.

Create a Submenu Item

1 In the left admin menu, click **Menus** under Appearance.

2 Click the menu item you want to appear as a dropdown and drag it below its parent menu item.

3 Keep dragging to the right until you see an indented dotted box. Now you can release your mouse button.

4 Click **Save Menu**.

A The submenu item now appears with a right indent and the words "sub item" next to its name.

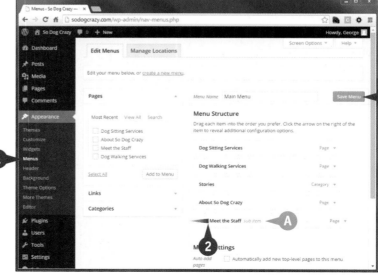

Assign a Menu Location

WordPress themes provide one or more menu locations to which you can assign any menu you create. There are two ways to assign locations from the Menus screen.

Assign a Menu Location

Assign a Location from Menu Settings

1 In the left admin menu, click **Menus** under Appearance.

2 While creating or editing a menu, click the box of a menu location in Menu Settings (☐ changes to ☑).

Note: WordPress tells you if a menu location is already assigned to another menu. You can assign the same menu to different locations.

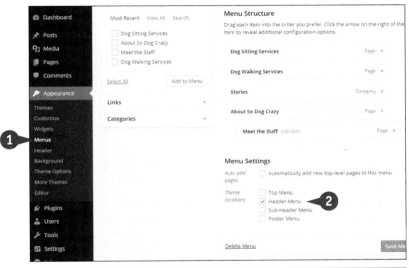

Assign a Menu from the Manage Locations Tab

1 In the left admin menu, click **Menus** under Appearance.

2 Click the **Manage Locations** tab.

3 Find the theme location you want to work with.

4 Click ▼ and select the menu you want to assign. If a menu is currently assigned, its name appears in the dropdown.

Note: The Edit link takes you to a currently assigned menu for editing.

5 If you want to create a new menu to assign here, click **Use new menu**.

6 Click **Save Changes**.

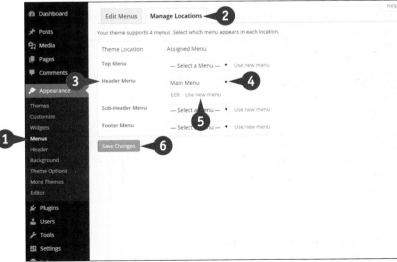

Edit and Delete Menu Items

The titles of pages and posts should be descriptive of the content, but that usually makes them too long for menus. WordPress makes it easy to edit the name that appears on the menu, as well as to edit other menu item parameters.

Edit and Delete Menu Items

Edit the Navigation Label

1 In the left admin menu, click **Menus** under Appearance.

2 Make sure you are editing the correct menu.

Note: If you have more than one menu, a dropdown appears below the Edit Menus tag, where you can select the correct menu.

3 Click the menu item you want to edit.

4 In the Navigation Label field, change the title of the menu item.

Note: This does not change the name of the item elsewhere on the site.

5 Click **Save Menu**.

6 Check that the menu item name has changed to match the navigation label setting.

A The original name of the menu item is always visible. This is also helpful to remember what the menu item is pointing to.

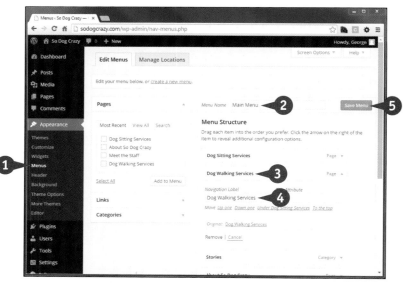

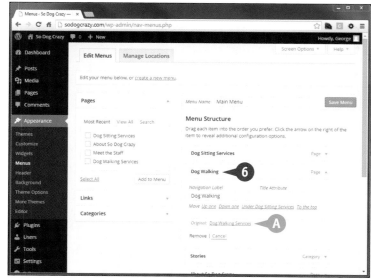

Edit Additional Elements of a Menu Item

1 While editing a menu, click **Screen Options** and then click check boxes under Show Advanced Menu Properties to reveal whichever menu item options you want, such as CSS Classes or Description.

2 Click **Open link in a new window/tab** (☐ changes to ☑) if you want the menu item to leave the current browser tab.

3 Assign custom CSS classes to menu items here.

4 Type a description of the menu item here. Some menus display this below the navigation label.

5 Scroll up or down and click **Save Menu**.

Move a Menu Item without Dragging

Note: If you have a lot of menu items, dragging one to a new position may be difficult. WordPress has links to speed the process.

1 Click a link, such as **Up one** or **To the top**, and the menu item moves.

Ⓑ You can delete a menu item by clicking **Remove** and scrolling up and clicking **Save Menu**.

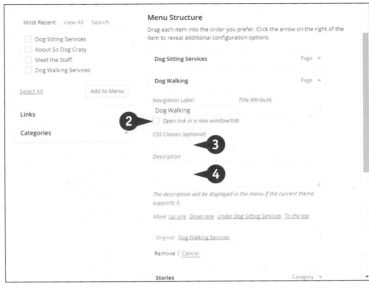

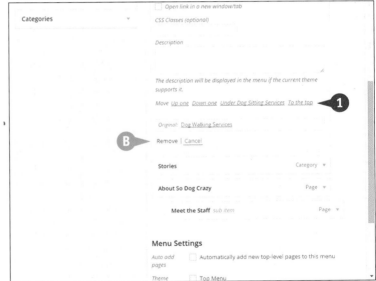

TIPS

I changed the navigation label for a menu item, but the original name of the page still appears on the menu.

Always remember to click **Save Menu** when you make any changes. WordPress displays the change on the Menus screen, but nothing is recorded in the database until you save the menu.

I changed the name of a page, but the menu item's navigation label did not.

Normally, the navigation label automatically updates if you change the name of the page, category, or whatever the menu item points to. However, if you created a custom navigation label, WordPress continues to display that until you manually change it.

Add a Custom Menu

You are not limited to displaying menus in the menu locations provided by your theme. Using the custom menu widget, you can display a menu in any available widget area.

Add a Custom Menu

1 In the left admin menu, click **Menus** under Appearance.

2 Click the **create a new menu** link and create a menu that you want to assign to a custom menu widget.

3 Type a name that helps you remember what this custom menu is for.

4 Do not assign the menu to any location.

5 Click **Save Menu**.

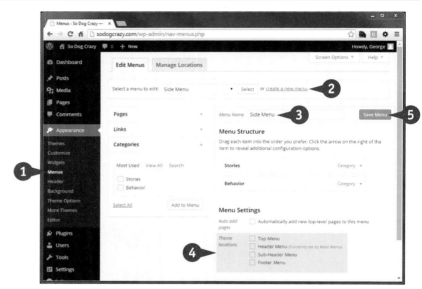

6 In the left admin menu, click **Widgets** under Appearance.

7 On the Widgets screen, click the **Custom Menu** widget under Available Widgets.

8 From the list of widget areas, select the one where you want your menu. The name is highlighted and a check mark appears beside it.

9 Click **Add Widget**.

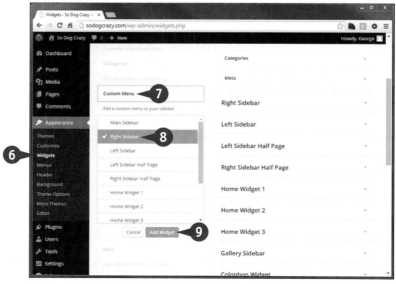

The Custom Menu widget opens in the widget area to which you assigned it.

10 Type a title for your menu.

11 Click the **Select Menu ▼** and choose the menu you created in steps **1** to **5**.

12 Click **Save**.

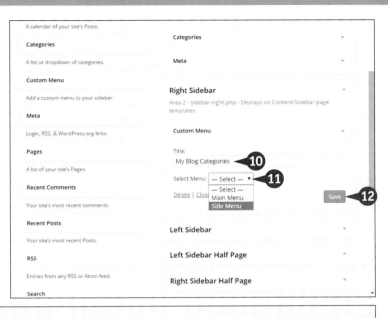

Ⓐ Confirm that the menu appears on the site in the location you placed it.

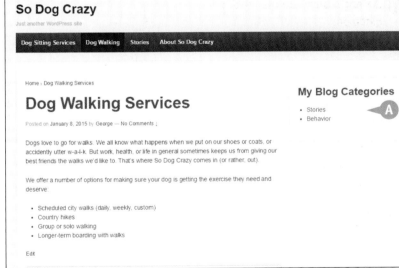

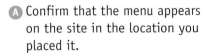

TIPS

I added a custom menu widget to a widget area, but I want it to appear only on certain pages.

On WordPress.com sites you can use the Visibility function next to a widget's Save button. On WordPress.org sites you need to install one of several plugins to provide this functionality.

Can I use the custom menu widget more than once in a widget area?

Yes, you can use it as many times as you want in as many widget areas as you want. Remember that a menu can be any set of links; for example, links to your restaurant's four menus in PDF format.

CHAPTER 9

Tweaking Your Theme

It is very rare for any theme to exactly match your design and functionality requirements. Fortunately, WordPress and its many themes offer ways to tweak the way things look and work. Beyond that, you can also customize themes as much as you want using CSS and PHP.

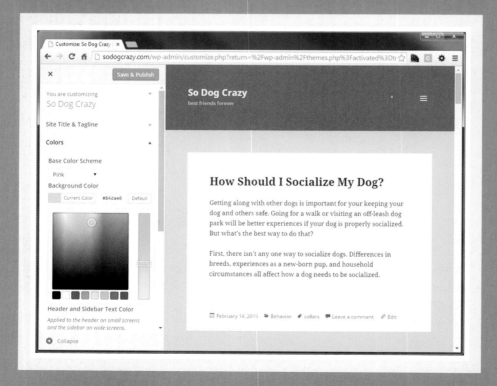

The Theme Customizer

Introduced in WordPress 3.4, the Theme Customizer interface is a way for theme developers to allow users to easily make changes using a consistent interface. Although WordPress has been adding more and more default elements to the Customizer, such as widget management, individual developers can use it any way they want, so there will be variations depending on the theme.

Theme Options

Prior to the introduction of the Theme Customizer, developers created their own interfaces for managing the look and functionality of sites. Typically called *theme options*, these interfaces continue to be important for many themes because they control far more than is included in the Customizer. The functionality and interface of theme options vary widely.

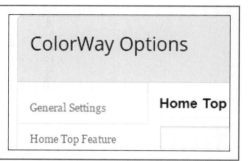

Custom CSS

Being able to override the styling of your theme using CSS is another option for those interested in learning even just a bit about this powerful design tool. On WordPress.org sites, some themes provide a custom CSS interface, but there are also plugins which add that functionality. On WordPress.com, custom CSS is a paid upgrade.

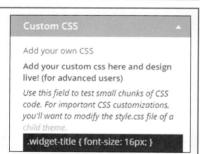

Child Themes

An even more powerful tool for customizing your theme is to create a *child theme*. It uses all the design and functionality of the parent, but looks first in the child theme folder to see if a file is present there. In other words, you can override absolutely any parent file, not just the CSS. You can also add new files, such as page templates or a template for a specific category.

This is a child theme of **Zerif Lite**.

Tags: Black, Gray, Red, White, One Column, Two Columns, Right Sidebar, Fixed Layout, Light, Front Page Posting, Full Width Template,

Get to Know the Theme Customizer

Learning to use WordPress's Theme Customizer is important, not only because it allows you to customize various aspects of your site's design and content, but because it works the same way no matter what theme you use. What you can customize varies by theme, but the interface is the same for all.

(A) Click **Customize** under Appearance on the left admin menu. The left admin menu disappears and is replaced with a list of options.

(B) A right arrow (>) on an option indicates a submenu of options.

(C) The preview pane displays your website, where you see in real time any changes you make. The live site is not changed until you click **Save & Publish**.

(D) The Collapse link hides the options pane temporarily to allow more space for the preview pane.

(E) Close (✕) allows you to exit the Theme Customizer. If you made changes but have not saved them, a reminder asks if you want to leave the screen or remain.

(A) What controls or inputs you get depend on the option that you open, such as **Colors** in this example. To close an option, either click its header again or open another option to close the first option automatically.

(B) Use the scroll bar to check if there are other controls for the option.

(C) In the preview pane, you see in real time any changes made using the various options.

(D) The live site is not changed until you click **Save & Publish**.

(E) If you are finished making changes, click **Close** (✕) to exit the Theme Customizer. If you made changes but forgot to save, a reminder asks if you want to leave the screen or remain.

Add a Logo

The most important way for business websites in particular to tweak their themes is to add their logo. Not all themes have a specific logo upload. Often there is only a header image upload, in which case the logo would need to be incorporated into that image.

This example uses the Hemingway Rewritten theme for WordPress.com or Hemingway for WordPress.org sites.

Add a Logo

1 Click **Customize** under Appearance in the left admin menu.

The Theme Customizer screen opens.

2 In the list of options at the left, click **Logo**. You can click anywhere in its box to reveal the controls.

A If no logo currently exists, this area will say No Image Selected.

3 Click **Select Image**.

A Select Image window opens, allowing you to choose from the media library or upload a new image.

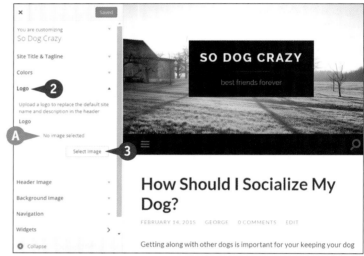

4 When you have selected the image, click **Choose Image**.

B Look for the image you selected to appear in the header.

C The logo also appears as a thumbnail in the Logo option area.

D A Change Image button appears, allowing you to replace the logo now or in the future.

E A Remove button appears.

5 To keep the changes and have them appear live on the site, click **Save & Publish**.

6 To exit, click **Close** (✖).

Add a Header Image

The use of header images varies widely between themes. In some cases, they display across the width of the header but inside of any margins. In others, the image is really a background that stretches the width of the browser window. In still others, the header image is used as a logo.

This example uses the Hemingway Rewritten theme for WordPress.com or Hemingway for WordPress.org sites.

Add a Header Image

1 Click **Customize** under Appearance in the left admin menu.

2 Click **Header Image**.

A The current header image appears here unless no custom header has been assigned.

B Previously uploaded images appear here. You can click to restore one.

C You can click **Randomize uploaded headers** to see one on each page load.

D Some themes provide one or more default images.

3 Click **Add new image**.

4 The Choose Image window opens, allowing you to choose from the media library or upload. Click **Select and Crop**.

5 In the Crop Image window, drag the crop box until you see the portion you want.

E You can skip cropping.

6 Click **Crop Image**.

Your header image appears in the preview pane.

7 Click **Save & Publish**.

8 Click **Close** (✕) to exit.

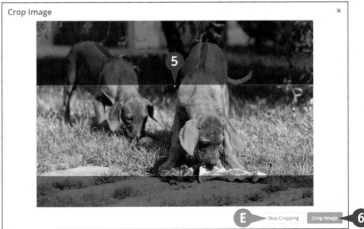

Change Color Scheme

Some themes offer predetermined color schemes to choose from. What exactly is controlled by the color scheme varies, but typically it will be headings, backgrounds, and links. The advantage of themes with this feature is that professional designers have chosen the colors, so you do not need to try and do your own matching.

This example uses the Twenty Fifteen theme for WordPress.com or WordPress.org sites.

Change Color Scheme

1 Click **Customize** under Appearance in the left admin menu.

2 Click **Colors** to reveal its controls.

Note: In this case, there are multiple controls under Colors, not just the Color Scheme. Some themes might separate those controls or use a slightly different naming convention.

3 Click ▼ and click a color scheme.

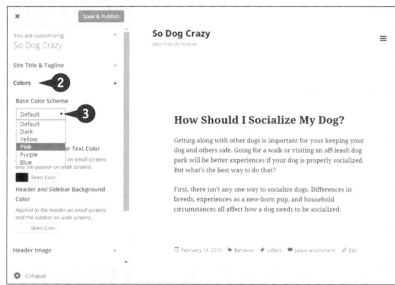

A The preview pane changes to show what your choice will look like on your site.

What changes color depends on your theme. In this case, the header area and the background for the content changed color.

B The changes also appear on the individual color controls.

Note: Some themes may not have these controls for individual elements of the color scheme.

4 To keep the changes, click **Save & Publish**.

5 Click **Close** (✕) to exit.

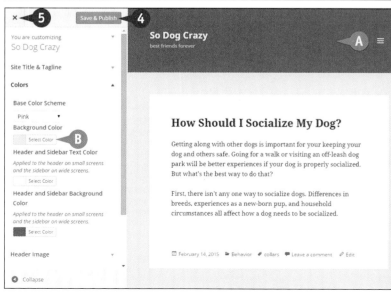

Change Background Color

Controlling the background color of a site is a common Customizer function among WordPress themes.

This example uses the Twenty Fifteen theme for WordPress.com or WordPress.org sites.

Change Background Color

1 Click **Customize** under Appearance in the left admin menu.

2 Click **Colors** to reveal its controls.

3 Under Background Color, click **Select Color**.

4 Use the various color picker controls to choose a color.

A As you move around the color picker, the current color appears here.

B The hexadecimal code of the current color appears here. You can also enter a code here for the color you want.

C The Default button restores the default background color of the theme.

D As you select from the color picker, the background color changes in the preview pane.

5 When you have got the background color you want, click **Save & Publish** to apply the changes to the live site.

6 Click **Close** (**✕**) to exit the Theme Customizer.

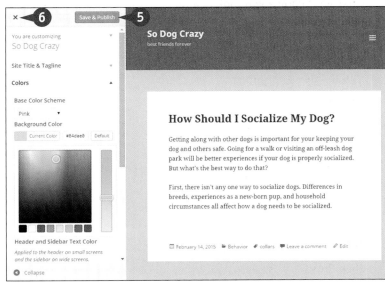

Change Text Color

Themes which allow you to change text color most commonly do so for linked text, but you may also be able to change heading colors and more.

This example uses the Hemingway Rewritten theme for WordPress.com or Hemingway for WordPress.org sites.

Change Text Color

1 Click **Customize** under Appearance in the left admin menu.

2 Click **Colors** to reveal its controls.

3 Under Accent Color, click **Select Color**.

Note: This particular theme uses the term Accent Color, but your theme may say Link Color or something else.

4 Navigate in the preview pane to a page where you can see one or more links.

5 Use the various color picker controls to choose a color.

A As you move around the color picker, the current color appears here.

B The hexadecimal code of the current color appears here. You can also enter a code here for the color you want.

C The Default button restores the default accent color of the theme.

6 When you have finished, click **Save & Publish** to apply the changes to the live site.

7 Click **Close** (✕) to exit.

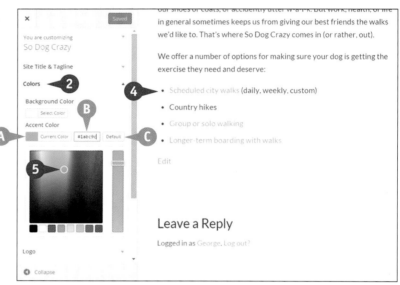

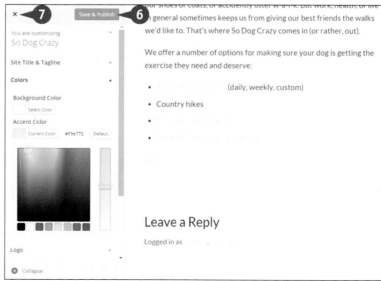

Add a Background Image

Many themes allow you to add a background image using the Customizer interface. Where and how much of the image appears depends on the design of the theme.

This example uses the Twenty Fifteen theme for WordPress.com or WordPress.org sites.

Add a Background Image

1 Click **Customize** under Appearance in the left admin menu.

2 Click **Background Image**.

Ⓐ The current background image appears here unless none has been assigned.

3 Click **Select Image**.

A Select Image window opens, allowing you to choose from the media library or upload.

4 Click **Choose Image**.

The image now appears in the background of your site in the preview panel.

Ⓑ The image also appears in the options area with two buttons: Remove and Change Image.

5 Choose how you want the background image to repeat (◯ changes to ⦿).

6 Choose how you want the background image positioned (◯ changes to ⦿).

7 Choose whether you want the background image to move as you scroll or stay fixed in place (◯ changes to ⦿).

8 Click **Save & Publish**.

9 Click **Close** (✖) to exit.

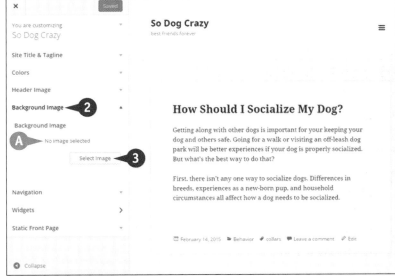

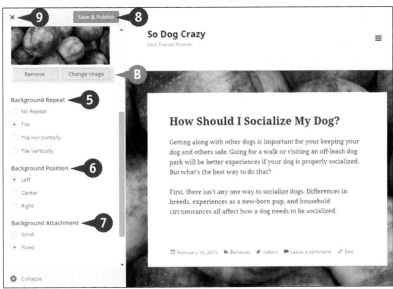

Get to Know Theme Options

Before the days of the WordPress Customizer, theme developers for WordPress.org sites began offering ways of customizing their themes and controlling elements of content through *theme options* screens. Not every theme has such a screen, but those that do vary widely in what is offered and in the design of the interface. Four examples are shown here.

Ⓐ Click **Theme Settings** under Appearance on the left admin menu. This example is from the Vantage theme, available in the WordPress.org theme directory.

Ⓑ The theme settings are divided up on a single page by the use of tabs.

Ⓒ This example shows the Blog settings available for this theme.

Ⓓ These controls affect the display of posts, sometimes on web pages that list posts or in other cases on individual posts.

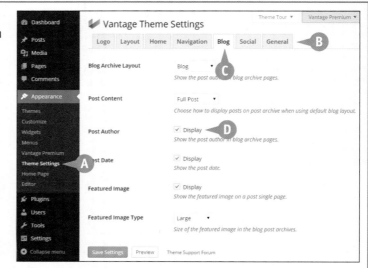

Ⓐ Click **Theme Options** under Appearance on the left admin menu. This example is from the Virtue theme, available in the WordPress.org theme directory.

Ⓑ The theme settings are divided up on a single page by the use of tabs displayed using vertically aligned tabs. Mouse over the icons to see their titles, such as Main Settings and Home Layout.

Ⓒ Click this button to display all settings in a single scrolling page instead of using the vertical tabs.

Ⓓ This example shows some of the miscellaneous settings available for this theme that affect the entire site.

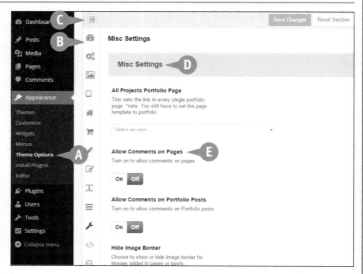

Ⓔ Some themes offer control of WordPress's settings, such as these controls for displaying comments.

A Click **Theme Options** under Appearance on the left admin menu. This example is from the AccessPress Lite theme, available in the WordPress. org theme directory.

B The theme settings are divided up on a single page by the use of tabs.

C This example shows some of the settings available for this theme that affect the entire site.

D Some themes manage the logo from here rather than with the Theme Customizer.

E This text appears in the header area. It is a good example of how theme options can control more than just design.

A Click **Chameleon Theme Options** under Appearance on the left admin menu. This example is from Chameleon, a paid theme from Elegant Themes.

B The ePanel interface may vary with some of the settings offered, but the look and feel is the same on all the company's themes.

C Many of the sections on the menu have their own tabbed content.

D The SEO settings are an example of themes going beyond the control of design.

E The Integration section allows you to add HTML code to various points on a web page, including the beginning and end of individual posts — something you would typically see under Widgets.

Use Post Formats

WordPress allows theme developers to display posts in a variety of ways using what are called *post formats*. There are nine possible formats designated by WordPress: aside, gallery, link, image, quote, status, video, audio, and chat. Although WordPress has suggested styling for each, it is really up to theme developers how, or even if, they use some or all of them.

This example uses the Hemingway Rewritten theme for WordPress.com or Hemingway for WordPress.org sites.

Use Post Formats

Ⓐ On the Add New Post or Edit Post screens, the Format meta box is located under the Publish meta box.

Note: If a theme does not support post formats, then no box appears.

❶ Click a format from the list of available post formats (◯ changes to ◉). This examples use a video post format.

Note: Themes show only the formats they support.

❷ Type the URL for your video.

Note: In this particular theme, the screen displays a custom meta box for the video URL. This is used only if the Video post format is chosen in step **1**. The theme displays the video at the top of the post.

❸ Click **Update**.

Ⓑ The post now displays a video icon in post listings.

Ⓒ Each post format has its own icon.

Note: Some themes display the post format publicly, with a link to display all other posts with that format.

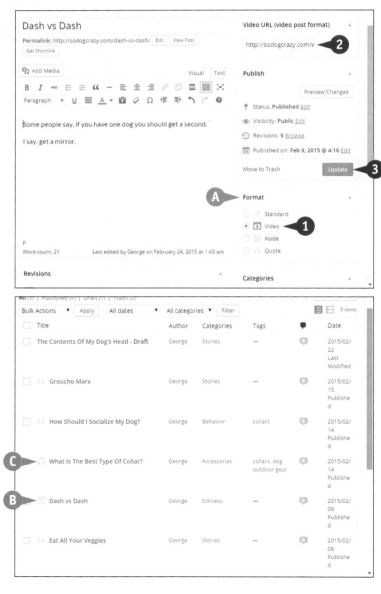

Use Page Templates

Whereas post formats control only the look of the post, *page templates* can control the look and layout of the entire web page. Some themes do not offer any page templates; others offer dozens. You can also have your own page templates created.

This example uses the Twenty Fifteen theme for WordPress.com or WordPress.org sites.

Use Page Templates

Note: For this theme, the default page template displays a sidebar on the right.

1 From the Pages screen, find the page you want and click **Edit**.

2 Locate the Page Attributes box on the right side of the screen.

3 Click the Template ▼ and choose the template you want. In this example, the theme has a full width template.

Note: If your theme only has a default page template, then the dropdown does not appear.

4 Click **Update**.

A The page now extends to the full width of the content area.

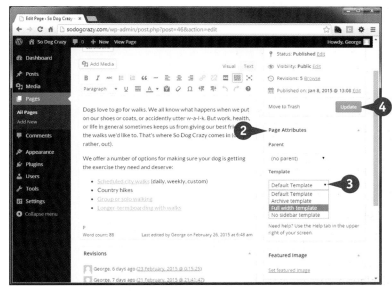

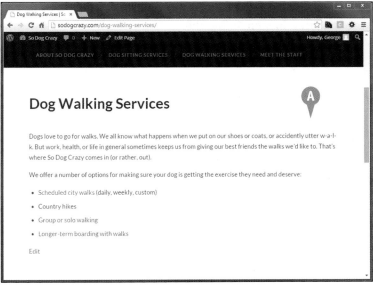

Make Your Site Mobile Friendly

It is vital that your website appear properly on any device. WordPress offers several options to make your site look good not just on desktops, but tablets and smartphones of all types.

Responsive Themes

A *responsive* web design is one that adjusts itself depending on the width of the screen displaying it. Most developers have been making their themes responsive since at least 2013, so plenty of choices are out there, both free and paid. If you are not sure if a theme is responsive, you can test it by making your web browser smaller and see whether the layout and images adjust accordingly.

Mobile Themes

If your theme is not responsive, there are options for displaying an alternative mobile-only theme. On WordPress.org sites, plugins are available that detect what device the user has and replaces the desktop theme with a separate mobile theme. In addition, some plugins allow you to have a separate menu and other options just for mobile users.

WordPress.com Mobile Options

For WordPress.com users, you have an option under Appearance for controlling what mobile users see. In most cases, the themes WordPress offers are responsive and the Mobile Options screen will tell you if your theme is or not. If it is not, you can turn on a generic, but good-looking mobile theme, as well as some controls affecting the appearance of the site.

Mobile Options

Mobile Theme

Awesome! Your theme, *Hemingway Rewritten*, is already deemed

Enable mobile theme   ○ Yes ● No

Update

Image Optimization

Image optimization has always been important for fast-loading sites, but for mobile it is even more crucial. Make sure you have sized your dimensions to no more than 1,000 pixels on the longest side and remember to Save For Web, using the compression settings to get the file size as low as possible.

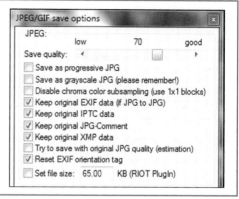

Make Existing Themes Responsive

For WordPress.org sites, if your theme is not mobile-friendly and you are very attached to it, you can have it modified to be responsive. However, keep in mind that HTML has changed greatly in the last couple of years, so it is not just your CSS you would need to update. It might be less costly to take a responsive theme and modify it to match your current design.

More than Just Design

For WordPress.org sites, being mobile-friendly is not just about design. For example, a smartphone user may not have the time or patience to wade through your 60-page site. Showing only key pages to mobile users is one way to be mobile-friendly. Similarly, a lengthy page that reads well on desktop could be trimmed to a couple of paragraphs for mobile users. These examples of *adaptive content* can be handled by plugins or with the help of your web designer.

Understand CSS

CSS, which stands for Cascading Style Sheets, defines how your browser should display HTML elements, such as paragraphs or headings. Every WordPress theme has at least one stylesheet, although some have stylesheets for specific parts of design, such as colors or layout.

How CSS Works

In the early days of HTML, a few attributes were added to HTML tags, which allowed developers to control the look of the element. But that was limited and cumbersome. CSS was created to keep formatting separate and let HTML focus on what it was intended for: defining content. CSS is applied to HTML using *rules*, which are commonly contained in *stylesheets* separate from the HTML.

```
style.css?ver=4.1.1 ×
1383 }
1384
1385 .widget_calendar td,
1386 .widget_calendar th {
1387     line-height: 2.3333;
1388     text-align: center;
1389     padding: 0;
1390 }
1391
1392 .widget_calendar caption {
1393     font-family: "Noto Serif", serif;
1394     font-weight: 700;
1395     margin: 0 0 1.6em;
1396     letter-spacing: 0.04em;
1397     text-transform: uppercase;
1398 }
1399
```

CSS Rules

The first part of a CSS rule is the *selector*, which can be an HTML element, or a class or id which has been applied to an HTML element. The second part of a CSS rule is the *declaration*, which defines how you want the element to look. In the CSS rule body `{background-color: beige;}`, body is the selector and `{background-color: beige;}` is the declaration. If a selector has several declarations, it is efficient to group them in a *rule set*, instead of repeating the selector over and over.
Similarly, several selectors, separated by commas, can belong to a single rule or rule set.

```
body { background-color: beige; }
body {
    background-color: beige;
    padding: 10px;
}
```

CSS Declarations

CSS declarations consist of a *property - value* pair, where *property* (Ⓐ) is the aspect of the element you want to define, and *value* (Ⓑ) is the definition. In the previous example, `background-color` is the property, and `beige` is the value. To save on declarations, sometimes you see multiple values under a single declaration, such as `{border: 1px solid black;}`, instead of specifying the thickness, style, and color of the border separately.

Ⓐ   Ⓑ

`{ border-width: 1px; }`

`{ border-style: solid; }`

`{ border-color: black; }`

`{ border: 1px solid black; }`

Media Queries for Mobile

Responsive designs rely on a feature of CSS called *media queries*. These are conditional sections of CSS triggered by the parameters of the media query, most commonly the width of the browser. If you specify a maximum browser width of 500 pixels, the CSS rules within that media query will apply only for browser windows with a width of that many pixels or less.

```
@media (max-width: 500px) {


    body { font-size: 15px; }

    /* Header ------------------
```

The Growing Power of CSS

With each new generation of CSS, the control over design greatly increases. Transforming elements on the page, such as making images appear at an angle, or animating elements, such as having an element slide out from the side of the browser window, are some of the more recent additions to the CSS repertoire. Google doodles often show off cutting-edge CSS capabilities.

What Is The Best Type Of Collar?

Learn More about CSS

Whether you just want to feel comfortable making a few changes or you want to truly learn CSS, there are hundreds of free and paid tutorials online. Some excellent starting points are: http://learn.shayhowe.com or www.w3schools.com. Another excellent site which is free but requires registration is http://www.codecademy.com/en/tracks/web.

CSS Margin

« Previous   Watch video of this tutorial   N

The CSS margin properties define the space around elements.

Margin

The margin clears an area around an element (outside the border). not have a background color, and is completely transparent.

Experiment with Your Site's CSS

If you are interested in learning about CSS or are ready to try some changes, you can experiment in your browser without affecting the actual site. Because CSS is applied at the browser level, you can literally interrupt the process and apply your own CSS to see what it does.

To view your page's CSS, most browsers today have a function called Inspect Element, or you can add extensions to your browser with different versions of the same function.

Experiment with Your Site's CSS

Use Chrome to Work with CSS

1 Position your mouse pointer over any element on the page and right-click.

2 Click **Inspect element**.

Note: The name may vary.

A developer pane opens across the bottom of the browser, while still displaying the page above.

A The left portion of the new pane shows the HTML for your page.

B The right portion shows the CSS rules governing whatever you chose using Inspect Element.

3 Mouse over the highlighted element in the HTML area.

C The element is now highlighted on the web page, with variously colored regions. Here the lighter color is the bottom margin.

Note: You can mouse over any element in the HTML and it will be highlighted, although you may have to scroll to see it.

4 Click any element in the HTML portion of the developer pane.

D Its CSS opens on the right.

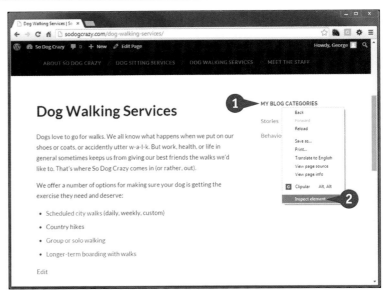

Test a New Font Size

1 In the CSS portion of the developer pane, next to font-size, double-click the value; it becomes editable.

2 Increase the value.

E The size of the element's font changes.

Note: These changes are only in your browser, not on the site itself.

Move the Sidebar

1 Click the HTML element that contains the main content; in this case, `div class="content left"`.

F The content area is highlighted.

2 Locate the rule that was putting the content area on the left of the sidebar. In this case it is the `float` property of the class `left`, so double-click the value until it becomes editable.

3 Change the value from `left` to `right`.

G The sidebar switches places with the content area.

Note: It can take some time to figure out what rule or rules needs to be changed, and often a new rule is required in order to properly target the element. If you just changed the `left` class, all elements with that class would be floating right.

TIPS

I am having trouble finding the rule on the right side of the developer pane.
Often, multiple rules are involved, but keep in mind that the most influential rules are closer to the top of the list.

This developer pane is a bit hard to work with.
On virtually all browsers, the developer pane is easily configured. You can change the width and height of each section — so you could make the CSS portion wider. Or even better, detach the pane from the browser and make it as large as you want, say, on another screen.

Modify Your Site's CSS

If you are comfortable working with CSS or you have a web designer, you can modify the styles of your theme in two simple ways.

On WordPress.com, the ability to edit a theme's CSS is a paid upgrade.

Modify Your Site's CSS

Use a Theme's Custom CSS

1. Click **Theme Options** under Appearance in the left admin menu.

   The Theme Options screen opens.

2. Locate the Custom CSS area. In this case, it is in its own section, but in other themes, it could be with other settings.

3. In the text area, type or paste your CSS rules.

4. Click **Save Changes**.

5. In your browser, refresh your website for the change to take effect.

6. Right-click anywhere and select **View Source**.

7. Look for the closing `</head>` tag fairly near the top of the page.

   Ⓐ Your custom CSS should be just above that closing tag.

Note: The reason it needs to be in that location is so it will override any other stylesheet. If your theme is not putting the custom CSS there, you can use a plugin that will.

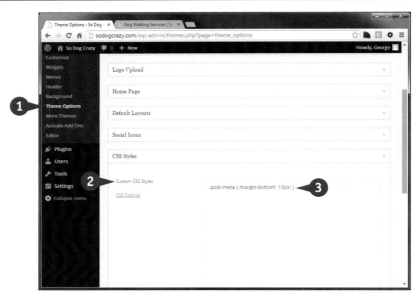

Use a Custom CSS Plugin on WordPress.org Sites

Note: This example uses a plugin called Lazyest Stylesheet.

1 Install and activate the plugin.

2 Click **Lazyest Stylesheet** under Appearance in the left admin menu.

3 In the text area, after the initial comment area, type your CSS rule.

4 Click **Save Changes**.

5 In your browser, refresh your website for the change to take effect.

6 Right-click anywhere and select **View Source**.

7 Look for the closing `</head>` tag fairly near the top of the page.

Ⓑ A link to the plugin's stylesheet is in the correct place.

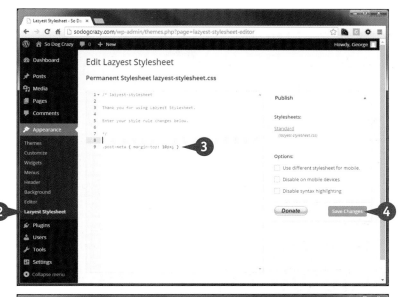

TIPS

How is a theme's custom.css file different from the two options mentioned here?

The `custom.css` file is an alternative to these methods. The file can be downloaded via FTP, edited using a plain-text editor and then uploaded again. It will not be overwritten when updating your theme.

My new CSS rule is correct, yet the change does not show on my site.

Likely this is a caching issue. Hold **Shift** while clicking your browser's Refresh button. If you have a caching plugin, click its **Refresh Now** button. Your host may also be caching, so try waiting a while.

Understand Child Themes

I f you are thinking of modifying more than just a few CSS rules, a child theme could be a better option. A *child theme* allows you to change virtually anything about another theme, not just the CSS.

Child themes are possible only on WordPress.org sites.

The Parent-Child Relationship

The relationship between a parent theme and a child theme is much like the human one: The parents do all the work and the child looks cute. A child theme is typically used to modify or provide the entire design of the site. In fact, the only file a child theme must contain is a stylesheet. What WordPress does is look for a *template file* in the child theme, and if it does not find it, goes to the parent theme.

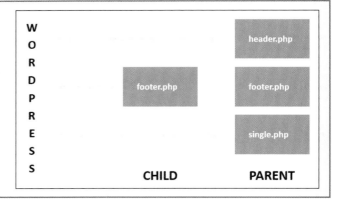

WordPress Template Hierarchy

The relationship of child and parent files is part of a broader relationship called the *template hierarchy*. If WordPress does not find a particular file, it looks for the next one in the hierarchy, and so on, until it comes to index.php. For example, if you want to make one category look different from the others, simply name the template file category-thename.php, and WordPress will use that instead of the category.php file.

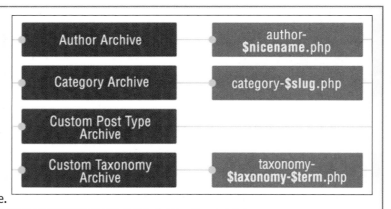

Change as Much as You Want

The important advantage of a child theme over simply customizing some CSS is that it allows you to change as much of the parent theme as you want. You could have additional page templates, a different footer area, custom layouts for category listings, and much more. You could activate WordPress functions that the parent theme does not have, or deactivate ones it has. You could also add menu locations or widget areas.

attribution.txt	948	01/27/14 00:0
author-box.php	1 KB	01/27/14 00:0
author.php	2 KB	01/27/14 00:0
category.php	1 KB	01/27/14 00:0
changelog.txt	1 KB	01/27/14 00:0
comments.php	4 KB	01/27/14 00:0
content-none.php	579	01/27/14 00:0
content-page.php	705	01/27/14 00:0
content-single.php	2 KB	01/27/14 00:0
content.php	2 KB	01/27/14 00:0
footer.php	1 KB	01/27/14 00:0
functions.php	33 KB	01/27/14 00:0
header.php	4 KB	01/27/14 00:0
index.php	1 KB	01/27/14 00:0

Add a Child to Any Theme

You do not have to look for themes that have child themes already — you can make a child theme for any theme. A theme requires no special coding for it to have a child theme. However, because a child theme does not have a complete set of template files, you cannot make a child theme for a child theme.

Circle LITE   NuvioLiquid Gr...

HeatMap AdAp...   GeneratePress

Theme Frameworks

When a theme developer makes various child themes for a single parent theme, it is referred to as a *theme framework*. Parent themes in this case tend to look very minimalist; the children do all the design work. One of the advantages of a theme framework is that you have to learn the backend only once, because all the children function the same way. And because child themes can themselves be tweaked, you customize the look as much as you want while having a consistent administrative interface.

THEMATIC, A WORDPRESS THEME FRAMEWORK

Thematic is a free, open-source, highly extensible, search-engine optimized WordPress Theme Framework featuring 13 widget-ready areas, grid-based layout samples, styling for popular plugins, and a whole community behind it. It's perfect

When to Create a Plugin Instead

There may be some functions you want a child theme to perform that are better suited to a plugin. The question to ask yourself is: Would I want this functionality if the theme was deactivated? If so, then that functionality should be generated by a plugin. Widgets are a good example. If you customize a child theme to create a widget, you would likely want that widget even without the child or parent theme; so have it generated by a plugin instead.

Programming Your Plugin

Now, it's time to make your Plugin actually do something. This sect describes how to accomplish several tasks your Plugin will need to

WordPress Plugin Hooks

Many WordPress Plugins accomplish their goals by connecting to d work is that at various times while WordPress is running, WordPres

CHAPTER 10

Adding Functionality with Plugins

One of the key advantages of a WordPress.org site is the ability to add whatever functionality you need through the use of plugins. These mini-programs do everything from adding your logo to the login page to running complete shopping carts.

Understand Plugins

You are probably familiar with the idea of downloading apps to make your smartphones and tablets more useful. Plugins do the same for WordPress.

What Is a Plugin?

Plugins are pieces of software that use the functions of WordPress and add many of their own to provide functionality that WordPress itself does not have. A plugin could consist of a single file or it could be comprised of dozens or even hundreds of files. What they all share is the ability to hook into the WordPress code and become a part of WordPress; they literally plug in.

WordPress SEO by Yoast

Install Now | More Details

Improve your WordPress SEO: Write better content and have a fully optimized WordPress site using Yoast's WordPress SEO plugin.

By Team Yoast

The Importance of Unplugging

Being able to unplug or deactivate is another very important feature of plugins. If you no longer need the functionality, you can unplug. If there are problems, you can unplug. If a better plugin comes along, you can unplug. Even if a new plugin completely crashed your site, you could unplug it by deleting it from the server, and your site would be up and running again.

Lightbox Plus Colorbox

Deactivate | Edit

Lightbox Plus Colorbox implement lightbox image overlay tool for Wor Colorbox was created by Jack Moor Powered and is licensed under the

The Importance of Choice

There are more than 36,000 plugins in the WordPress.org directory, such as Jetpack, and there are thousands more plugins you can buy elsewhere. So not only do you have choices, you have a lot of them for a lot of different functions. If the self-hosted version of WordPress had to have every function possible built into it, not only would it be monstrously huge and inefficient, but users would be limited to the functionality provided.

Jetpack by WordPress.com

Your WordPress, Streamlined.

By: automattic, alternatekev, Andy Skelton, Andy Peatling, Andrew Ozz, and others

★★★★☆ (517)   **Last Updated:** 2 weeks ago

1+ million active installs   **Compatible up to:** 4.1.1

Why No Plugins on WordPress.com?

On a single WordPress installation, the potential exists for two plugins to clash with each other or a new plugin to clash with WordPress itself. Imagine multiplying that potential by the millions of users on WordPress.com, and you can see why it is impossible for administrators to allow individual users to add their own plugins.

Millions of users

We welcome 50,000 new sites every day. From small business sites, artist portfolios, and blogs, to giant media organizations like TIME and CNN.

Free versus Paid

There are paid plugins that do not work well and have poor support. There are free plugins that have been working for years and offer great support. The fact is, paying for a plugin is no guarantee of quality or of getting your issues resolved. You just need to do your homework when it comes to choosing plugins. With paid plugins, make sure they have a money-back guarantee. And if a free plugin has a Donate button, please support the authors.

Popular Files

Weekly Top Sellers

Visual Composer: Pag...
★ ★ ★ ★ ★
1100 Sales | $28

Slider Revolution Res...
★ ★ ★ ★ ★
599 Sales | $18

Ultimate Addons for V...
★ ★ ★ ★ ★
322 Sales | $17

Make Your Own

Having a plugin custom made for your needs is a great way to have the functionality you want, along with all the advantages discussed here. Another advantage of having a custom plugin is that you might be able to use it over and over again if you need more websites. Depending on your needs, it does not have to be very costly to hire a developer to make your plugin.

Programming Your Plugin

Now, it's time to make your Plugin actually do something. Th describes how to accomplish several tasks your Plugin will n

WordPress Plugin Hooks

Many WordPress Plugins accomplish their goals by connecti work is that at various times while WordPress is running, Wo that time, and if so, the functions are run. These functions m

Find Plugins

Although tens of thousands of plugins are available through the WordPress Plugins Directory, searching for them is easy, either through the administration area of your installation or directly at WordPress.org.

Find Plugins

Find Plugins via the Add Plugins Screen

1 Click **Add New** under Plugins on the left admin menu.

Ⓐ Each plugin appears in a separate box with a brief description and a few details, along with an Install Now button and a link to show additional details.

Ⓑ A search menu has links for Featured, Popular, Recommended, and Favorites.

Note: Favorites works only if you are registered and are logged in to WordPress.org.

2 Type a name of a plugin or a keyword and click **Enter** to search.

The results appear.

Ⓒ The total number of search results appears here.

Ⓓ Over 30 results, a page navigation appears.

3 Click **More Details** to view the full listing.

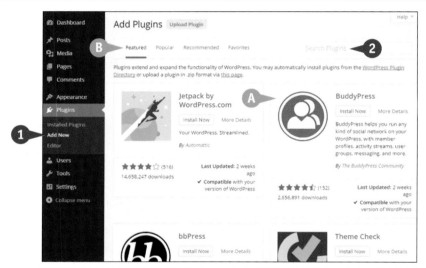

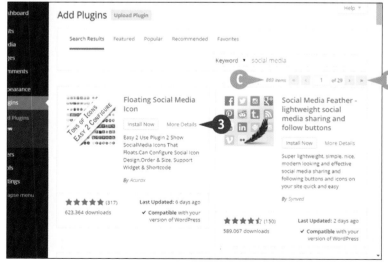

A window opens showing plugin details.

E Tabs displays information.

F The sidebar contains details such as Version, Author, and Last Updated.

G A link to the full listing on WordPress.org and a link to the plugin's home page appear here.

H If you want this plugin, click **Install Now**.

4 Click **Close** (🗙) to close the window and continue your search.

Find Plugins via the WordPress. org Directory

1 In your browser, go to https:// wordpress.org/plugins.

I The search menu has links for Featured, Popular, Favorites, and Beta Testing.

Note: Beta plugins are being considered for inclusion in WordPress. Do not test on live sites.

J If you register at WordPress. org, you can keep a favorites list.

2 Type the name of a plugin or a keyword and click Enter to search.

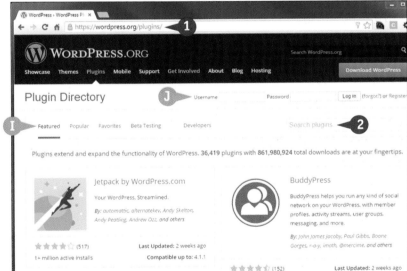

TIP

Is it any better to search from the Add Plugins screen rather than WordPress.org?
The Add Plugins screen is simply an interface to the WordPress Plugin Directory, so the information is exactly the same. However, when you search from the Directory itself, you can access the support forums.

Choose Plugins Wisely

With over 36,000 plugins in the WordPress Plugin Directory, searching usually turns up dozens if not hundreds of choices. Knowing which one or ones to try is not easy. However, there are some guidelines that can help you pick the most likely candidates.

Choose Plugins Wisely

Browse Plugins

1 In your browser, go to https://wordpress.org/plugins.

2 Type a search term. In this example, the search is for *lightbox*.

3 Scroll to view the first few results.

4 For each of the results whose titles and short descriptions meet or come close to meeting your needs, compare the star ratings and the number of active installs.

5 Click the title of each of the promising results to view their details.

Ⓐ In addition to Description, the tabs along the top can include the following: Installation, FAQ, Screenshots, Other Notes, Changelog, Stats, Support, Reviews, and Developers.

6 Check that your version of WordPress meets the minimum required version.

Note: The Compatible Up To version should be as new as possible, but do not worry if it is not the latest version. The newer the Last Updated date the better.

7 Check the breakdown of the star ratings.

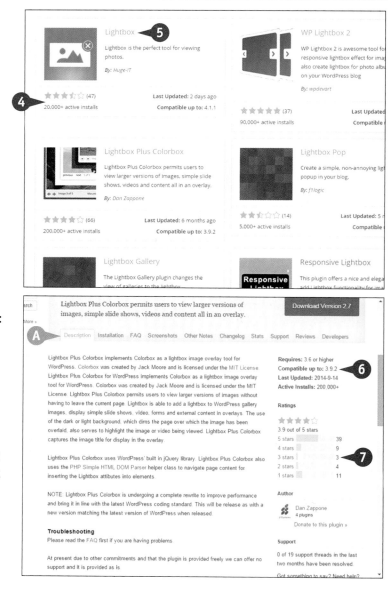

210

This image shows the star ratings for the top five results of the search for "lightbox."

8 In the breakdown of the star ratings, pay particular attention to the number of 5 stars and 1 stars.

9 Now, take into account the number of active installs.

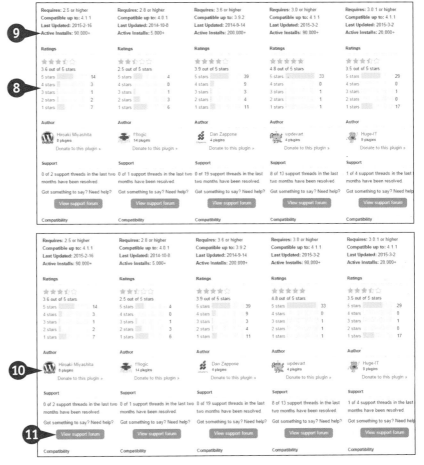

This image shows the author and support links for the top five results of the search for *lightbox*.

10 Check and compare the number of plugins by the author or authors.

Clicking the author's name takes you to a list of all his or her plugins so you can see how well rated the others are.

11 Click **View support forum** to see all related entries from the WordPress support forums.

Sometimes I see a statistic for downloads. How is that different from active installs?
Downloads includes downloading updates, and downloaded plugins no longer in use. Both have their uses, but active installs can be handier for deciding if the plugin continues to be well-used.

What is the Compatibility function?
It shows how many people say a version of a plugin is working with a particular version of WordPress. It is always worth checking, although often there are not enough reports to generate an answer.

continued ▶

Reading what others have to say about a plugin, in the support forums or on the web, is invaluable. And after you have made a choice, it is good to check whether the plugin is using too many resources and slowing down your site.

Choose Plugins Wisely (continued)

12 Always check the sticky threads at the top of the support forum.

13 Checking the freshness and volume of threads can alert you to issues; for example, not much activity for several months and then numerous threads in the last week.

14 As you look through the topics, notice that they are a mix of problems, how-to questions, and feature requests. Read threads that suggest the plugin is broken. Some are server-specific; others turn out to be user error, so reading the full thread is important.

Use Search Engines for Research

1 Type the phrase "disallowed plugins wordpress" in a search engine.

2 Look through the search results and see if your plugin appears on any lists of plugins banned by hosting companies.

Note: Most lists are clear about why they disallow certain plugins. It could simply be that the plugin clashes with a service provided by the host, such as caching or backing up.

3 Search for your plugin's name along with "problems" or "reviews."

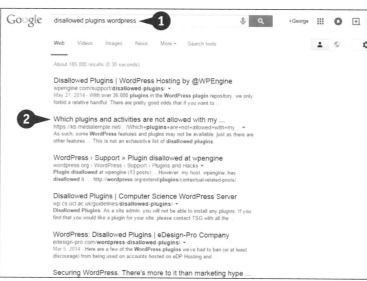

Use Plugin Performance Profiler

Note: You can monitor whether a plugin is adding a lot to the load time of your site.

1 Install and activate the P3 - Plugin Performance Profiler from the WordPress Plugin Directory.

2 Click **P3 Plugin Profiler** under Tools on the left admin menu.

Ⓐ The total number of active plugins is shown.

Ⓑ Any previous reports are listed here.

3 Click **Start Scan**.

A window opens with buttons for Auto Scan or Manual Scan.

4 Click **Auto Scan**.

A progress bar appears during the scan.

5 Click **View Report**.

The window closes and the profiler screen is refreshed.

Ⓒ The total load time for all plugins.

Ⓓ The percentage of the page load time taken up by all plugins.

Ⓔ The number of times the database was accessed by all plugins.

6 Look for your plugin in the color-coded pie chart.

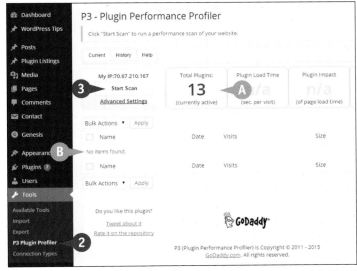

P3 (Plugin Performance Profiler) is Copyright © 2011 - 2015
GoDaddy.com. All rights reserved.

TIPS

A lot of plugins say that 0 issues have been resolved in the last two months. Should I be worried?

No. The only concern would be if questions never get answered or major issues go unresolved over time. The authors of these plugins are doing this for free, and sometimes they cannot answer everyone quickly.

Some plugins have a warning that they have not been updated in over two years. Should I be worried?

Although some plugins can work for years because changes in WordPress do not affect them, this warning is good reason to check active installs and recent forum posts, or better still, look for a newer plugin.

Install and Activate Plugins

After you know the plugin you want from the WordPress Plugin Directory, installing it is as simple as clicking a button. If you have downloaded a file for a paid plugin, there is a simple installation process for that too. And if you are comfortable with FTP programs, this can all be done directly on the server. After installation it takes just one click to activate your plugin.

Install and Activate Plugins

Install and Activate a Plugin from the Add Plugins Screen

1 Click **Add New** under Plugins on the left admin menu.

The Add Plugins screen opens.

2 After you have found your chosen plugin, click **Install Now**.

The progress of the installation is shown on a new screen.

3 After *Successfully installed* appears on the Installing Plugin screen, click **Activate Plugin**.

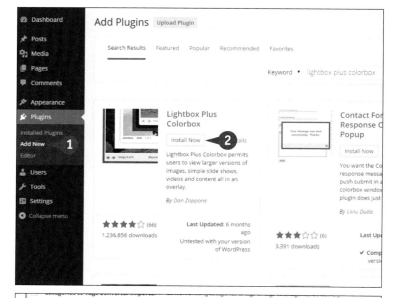

A The Plugins screen appears, which confirms the activation and lists the new plugin.

4 Look for a Settings link in the listing, or you may have to search through the left admin menu.

Use the Upload Plugin Function

1 Click **Add New** under Plugins on the left admin menu.

2 At the top of the Add Plugins screen, click **Upload Plugin**.

B Plugin files must be in .zip format.

3 Click **Choose File**.

4 Locate the file on your device and choose it.

C The chosen file's name appears.

5 Click **Install Now**.

Use FTP to Install a Plugin

1 Unzip the plugin's file.

2 Using an FTP program, log in to your server and navigate to the `plugins` directory within the `wp-contents` directory.

3 In the device pane of the FTP program, navigate to where you stored the unzipped plugin. Highlight the plugin folder.

4 Click the **Upload** icon (⇨) or drag the folder over.

5 After uploading, return to Installed Plugins in WordPress and you will see the plugin. Click **Activate**.

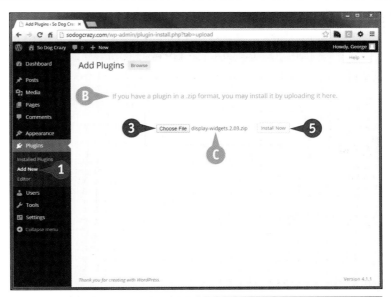

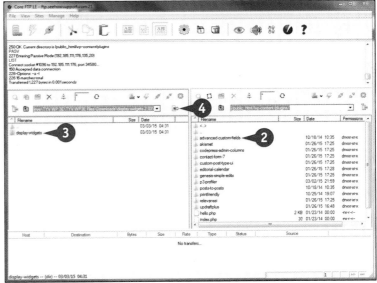

TIPS

I activated a plugin and there was no Settings link, nor did I see anything on the left admin menu.

What a plugin does after activation varies widely. Try looking under Settings or under one of the other menu items. Some plugins have no settings or any location at all — they simply take an action, like creating a widget or altering the way WordPress works.

When I activated a plugin I got an error. What should I do?

You need to deactivate the plugin — see the next section, "Deactivate and Delete Plugins." If you cannot access your admin screens, you need to use FTP to delete the files for the plugin.

Deactivate and Delete Plugins

Deactivating a plugin is the technical term for unplugging it, and that is an important feature of plugins. If you no longer need the plugin or it potentially causes problems, you want to be able to remove it easily and quickly. Deactivation means the plugin is still on your server, so if you will never need it again or it really was causing problems, then it is time to delete.

Deactivate and Delete Plugins

Deactivate a Plugin

1 Click **Installed Plugins** under Plugins on the left admin menu.

2 Click **Deactivate** for the plugin.

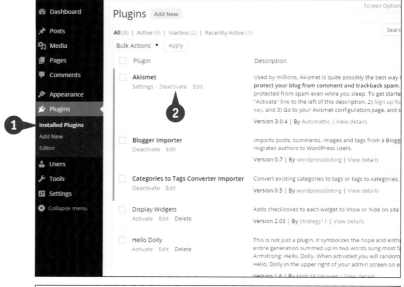

The Plugins screen refreshes.

3 Look for the Plugin Deactivated message to confirm that the action took place.

A The background color of the plugin has changed, the Deactivate link is gone, and a Delete link now appears.

B You can also deactivate multiple plugins. Click the box beside each plugin for which you want to take an action (☐ changes to ☑).

C Click ▼ and choose Activate, Deactivate, Update, or Delete from the menu.

D Click **Apply**.

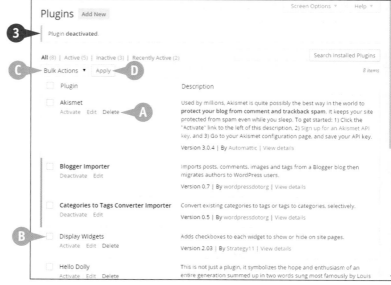

Delete a Plugin

1 After deactivating a plugin, look for and click **Delete**.

The Delete Plugin screen appears.

2 Review a list of all plugins to be deleted.

E WordPress notifies you if the particular plugin also has data which will be deleted.

F You can click this link if you want to review a list of all files to be deleted.

3 Click **Yes** to delete all files and data.

G You can click **No** to return to the Plugins screen.

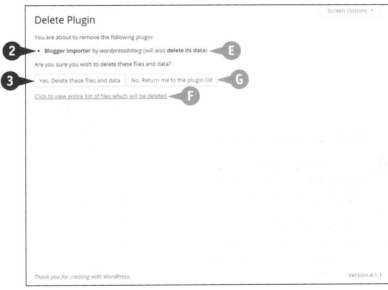

TIPS

Do I need to delete a plugin if I deactivate it?
It is better not to leave a lot of deactivated plugins in place — WordPress still has to take a bit of time to process all of them. Sometimes there may be a plugin that you use only once in a while, so it can be handy to leave it deactivated instead of having to install and activate it each time you want to use it.

Is there a limit to how many plugins I can have?
The only limit is how much they slow down your site. And of course the more plugins you have, the greater the chance of conflicts. A good rule of thumb is to minimize plugins as much as you can while still having the site that your visitors need.

Add a Contact Form

Setting up forms in WordPress is made easy by using a plugin. In this example, you see how simple it is to add a contact form using the form-building plugin Contact Form 7. It can create as many forms as you need, however complex they might be.

Add a Contact Form

Create a Contact Form

1 Install and activate Contact Form 7 from the WordPress Plugin Directory.

Note: See the section "Install and Activate Plugins" for more information.

2 Click **Add New** under Contact on the left admin menu.

The Add New Contact Form screen appears.

3 To use the default language, English, click **Add New**.

Ⓐ Alternatively, click ▼ to select a different language.

Ⓑ Click **Add New**.

A new form screen opens.

4 Type a title for the form. Only you will see this, so make it something that reminds you what it is for.

Ⓒ On the left side of the screen is the HTML for the form, with the shortcodes that create the form fields. Contact Form 7 populates it with a basic form to start.

5 Click the **Generate Tag** ▼ to create various types of form fields.

6 Select **Text Field**.

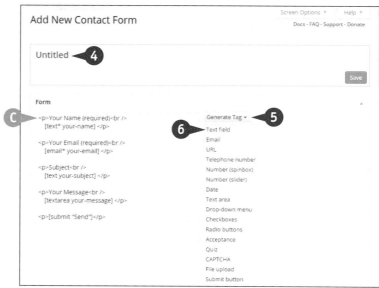

D The Generate Tag area opens. Depending on the form element, the settings in this area will differ.

7 Fill in all the settings you want for the form elements.

8 When finished, copy this shortcode for pasting into the HTML box on the left.

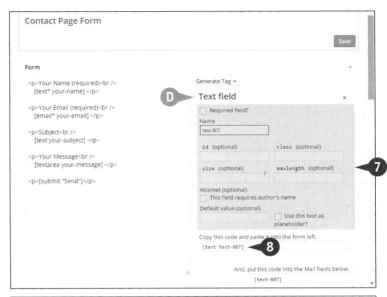

9 After typing any accompanying text or HTML, paste in the shortcode you copied in step **8**.

10 Copy the second shortcode — it displays the value entered in the form.

11 Scroll down the page until you see the Message Body box.

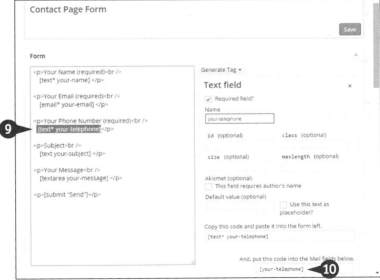

continued ▶

Add a Contact Form (continued)

Having finished the form itself, you must now configure the settings for sending the form as an email.

Add a Contact Form (continued)

Ⓐ The message body is what will appear in the email that comes to you with the form values filled out by visitors.

Contact Form 7 has put in the corresponding shortcodes to its default HTML.

⑫ Type a title for the new field you created, and then paste in the shortcode you copied from above.

Ⓑ On the left side of the Mail area are the settings for the email.

Ⓒ The To address is taken from your administrative email.

You can change this to whatever you want; you can send to multiple emails by separating them by commas.

Ⓓ The From address must have an email with your domain name.

Ⓔ In the Additional Headers field, the plugin places the shortcode for the sender's email, so you can reply in your mail program.

⑬ Scroll to the top of the screen.

⑭ Click **Save.**

⑮ Copy the form's shortcode.

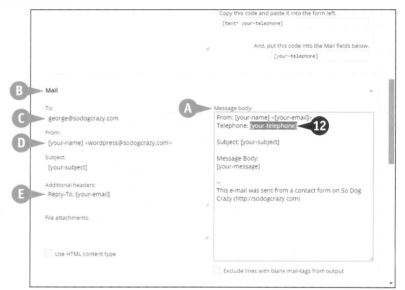

Put the Contact Form on a Page

1 Click **Add New** under Pages on the left admin menu.

2 Give the page a title.

3 Type whatever text you want to appear before the form.

4 Paste in the form's shortcode.

5 Click **Publish**.

6 Once the success message shows the page is published, click **View Page.**

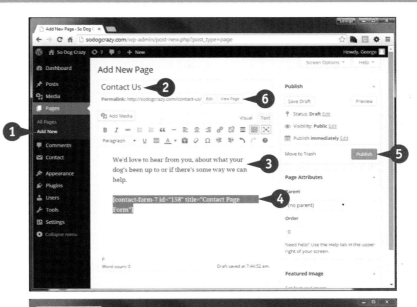

The contact form appears on your page and is ready to use.

7 Try sending yourself an email. Watch for the green verification message to say the message was sent.

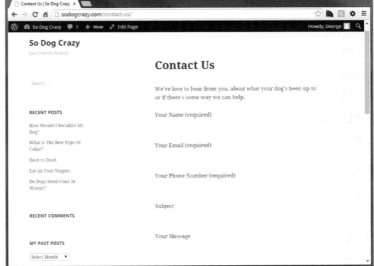

TIP

Could I use this form in another location on my site as well?

You could paste the same shortcode into another page, but it would be better to use the duplicate function and give the other form a new name. In addition, you would change the wording of the message or the subject line, so you could identify which form a person was sending from.

Control the Display of Widgets

By default, WordPress displays widgets on all pages where the widget area appears. However, plugins can add the ability to control individual pages where a widget should display. In this example, you see how the plugin Display Widgets functions when installed and activated.

Control the Display of Widgets

1 Install and activate Display Widgets from the WordPress Plugin Directory.

Note: See the section "Install and Activate Plugins" for more information.

2 Check the Display Widgets listing for any Settings link. In this case there is none, nor is there any link on the left admin menu.

3 Click **Widget**s under Appearance on the left admin menu.

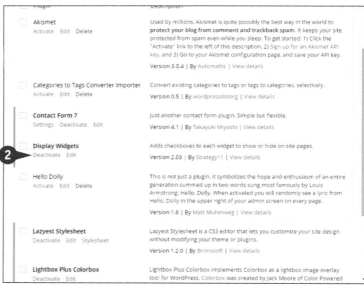

4 Click a widget to reveal its settings.

Ⓐ A new section appears at the bottom of every widget, allowing you to restrict how it displays.

5 Click ▼ and choose whether the widget will be shown or hidden when a page is checked.

6 Click the pages where you want the display rule to be applied (☐ changes to ☑). In this case, the Recent Posts widget should not appear on the Dog Walking Services page.

7 Click **Save.**

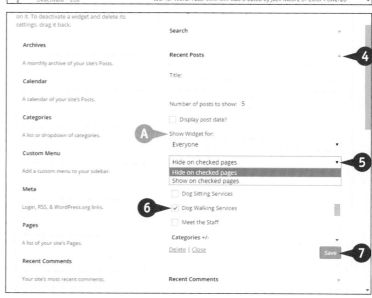

Ⓑ On every other page, the Recent Posts widget continues to appear.

Ⓒ On the Dog Walking Services page, however, Recent Posts is now hidden.

TIPS

If I deactivate or delete the Display Widgets plugin, will the widgets show up again everywhere?

Yes. You do not even have to reset the affected widgets before deactivating — the settings just go away. All plugins work this way. They only affect WordPress while they are active.

How would you know where to look for the Display Widget controls?

If there is no immediately obvious place to look for a plugin's settings or controls, you can check its documentation; many plugins also have screenshots on their listing at the Plugins Directory. Or sometimes you just have to look around. Typically the plugin's function gives a clue where to look; in this case, somewhere in Widgets.

Use the Jetpack Plugin

Jetpack is actually a collection of plugins which you install like a single plugin. You can then deactivate or activate various functions — over 30 at the time of writing. Some of its features are run through the WordPress.com servers, which is why you need an account there to activate the plugin as a whole. Jetpack is made by the company that runs WordPress.org and WordPress.com: Automattic.

Use the Jetpack Plugin

Install and Activate Jetpack

1 Install and activate Jetpack from the WordPress Plugin Directory.

Note: See the section "Install and Activate Plugins" for more information.

Ⓐ After activating Jetpack, a large notification banner appears at the top of the Plugins page.

2 Click **Connect to WordPress.com**.

Note: You need a WordPress.com account to activate many of the features of Jetpack. If you do not already have an account, you can register for one, which is free.

3 Type your WordPress.com username and password.

Ⓑ If you do not have an account, a link to register appears here.

4 Click **Authorize Jetpack**.

Note: Here is a list of Jetpack modules not shown in the screenshot accompanying the next set of steps: Markdown, Mobile Theme, Monitor, Notifications, Omnisearch, Photon, Post by Email, Publicize, Related Posts, Sharing, Shortcode Embeds, Site Icon, Site Verification, Spelling and Grammar, Subscriptions, Tiled Galleries, VideoPress, WP.me Shortlinks, Widget Visibility, WordPress.com Stats, and VaultPress.

Configure Jetpack Modules

1 Click **Settings** under Jetpack on the left admin menu.

C A list of modules appears on the left. The colored modules are active and many are active by default.

Note: Although the term *module* is used, each one performs functions which are equivalent to a plugin.

D Filters for displaying modules appear on the right. There are many options for filtering, including by topic.

2 Mouse over a module for links to configure or activate/deactivate.

E The All My Sites function is not just for all your WordPress.com sites, but any Jetpack-enabled self-hosted sites.

F You can add, edit, or delete posts or pages.

G You can activate or deactivate any plugin on any site where you have Jetpack.

H You can click a particular plugin and WordPress shows on which sites it is installed, with controls to activate/ deactivate the plugin or turn autoupdates off or on.

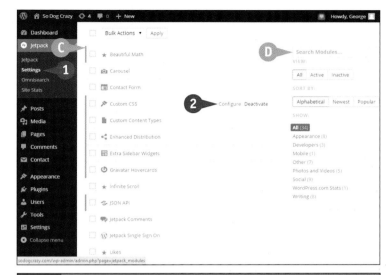

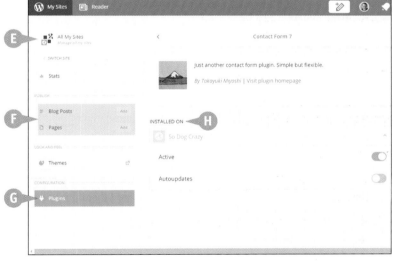

Will the size of the Jetpack plugin slow down my site?
Each module of Jetpack essentially is its own plugin, so the more you use, the more you are going to see some slowing. Whether it is faster or slower than having the equivalent number of individual plugins is debated in the WordPress community. You need to monitor your site speed whether you use Jetpack or individual plugins.

One of my self-hosted sites, with Jetpack activated, does not show up in the site dashboard of WordPress.com.
Double-check that the JSON API module is activated, and on its configuration screen, make sure the Allow Management option is checked.

Consider These Admin Plugins

Being able to customize and add to the WordPress administrative functions is a huge advantage to running your own WordPress site. These lists are meant as a starting point, to give you an idea of the possibilities involved with using plugins.

Backups

Scheduling regular backups for your site is absolutely crucial. If you want to automatically save both database and files to third-party services like Amazon S3, try BackWPup Free – WordPress Backup Plugin or UpdraftPlus Backup and Restoration. If you download backups to a hard drive, you can use BackUpWordPress. If you only need your database emailed to you, you could use WP-DB-Backup.

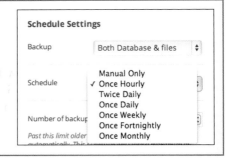

Security

Apart from taking your own precautions, plugins can help make your WordPress installation more secure. Some offer a full set of tools, such as iThemes Security (formerly Better WP Security) or Wordfence Security. Or you can use individual plugins to provide specific kinds of security, such as Force Strong Passwords, which requires users to follow WordPress guidelines, or Login LockDown, which blocks hackers after a set number of failed logins.

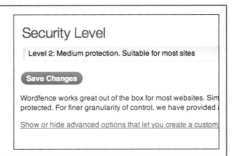

Administration Screens

To control almost all aspects of admin screens, try Adminimize. If you want to control what is seen on various listings screens, there is Admin Columns. For customizing just the toolbar at the top of admin screens, look into Custom Admin Bar. And if you want to expand the capabilities of the content editor button bar, there is TinyMCE Advanced.

Images

How fast images load is important, so plugins such as EWWW Image Optimizer are useful for optimizing images after they have been uploaded to WordPress. There are also plugins such as Imsanity to resize images with large dimensions, even as you are uploading them. When you switch themes or add plugins, they may have custom thumbnail sizes. A plugin like Regenerate Thumbnails makes all existing thumbnails conform to the new dimensions, whereas Post Thumbnail Editor lets you edit any custom thumbnail sizes that WordPress's editor does not address.

Content Layout

When you need more complex layouts for the content area of your site, such as columns or tabbed content, several options are available. The latest trend is toward drag-and-drop interfaces, such as Page Builder by SiteOrigin, but using WordPress shortcodes has been a dependable route for many years: Shortcodes Ultimate is a popular choice. If you need only tables, Websimon Tables is an example of using a separate interface, whereas MCE Table Buttons adds table functionality to the button bar of the content editor.

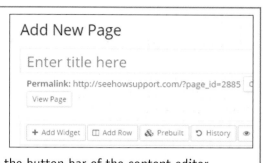

Comments

If you want to combat spam comments, Akismet is the system that powers WordPress.com but it does cost money for noncommercial sites. Many free alternatives exist, such as Antispam Bee or Anti-spam. These plugins also work on spam from any forms you may have on your site. It is also possible with plugins to bypass or supplement WordPress's comment system, such as using Disqus Comment System or Facebook Comments.

Design

Overriding the design of your theme is possible using various types of plugins. If you want to change the typography, plugins such as Easy Google Fonts give you that control. If you are comfortable using CSS, a plugin such as Lazyest Stylesheet creates a custom stylesheet that overrides theme and plugin styling. And if you want even greater control using child themes, plugins such as Child Themify automate the process of setting up the right file.

Caching

If you want to serve visitors fast-loading HTML pages, caching plugins take your dynamic WordPress pages and make them static. Even the plugins that have a one-click setup contain settings that can mess up your site, so proceed with caution. For maximum control and sites with complex caching needs, there is W3 Total Cache. WP Super Cache and ZenCache (formerly Quick Cache) are two other popular caching choices.

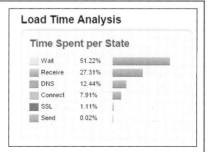

Consider These Content Plugins

Every site has different needs for its visitors, and plugins allow each site owner to add the functionality his or her visitors require. Here are just a few suggestions in some common content categories.

Social Media

Connecting your site to your social media is crucial. In all three areas — following, sharing, and displaying feeds — there are hundreds of plugins available. For following, Simple Social Icons is an example, whereas for sharing, have a look at Simple Share Buttons Adder. Showing a feed from a social media account is as simple as searching the name of the service; Easy Twitter Feed Widget Plugin is an example. And for plugins that have follow and share functions, try Shareaholic or Social Media Feather.

Sliders and Galleries

Sliders are handy way of presenting information and attracting interest on a home page. Meta Slider offers a choice of several different sliders in a single plugin. When it comes to image galleries, plugins such as Lightbox Plus Colorbox allow you to have pop-up lightbox and slideshow effects for WordPress galleries. For custom galleries, there are dozens of well-rated plugins to choose from — it is a matter of design taste — but one you could try is Photo Gallery. If you need heavy-duty image organization and administration, there is NextGEN Gallery.

Forms

Most sites need at least a contact form, and there are many plugins that offer easy ways to set one up, such as Contact Form. If you need more complex forms, such as application forms or booking forms, try plugins like Fast Secure Contact Form or Contact Form 7. If you want to have drag-and-drop form building capability, there are plugins such as Ninja Forms.

Maps

Whether you want to display your business location or the location of all your members, maps are a powerful visual tool. Integrating with Google Maps is the most common method, and there are many plugins to help make that simpler, such as MapPress Easy Google Maps or Comprehensive Google Map Plugin. You can also put a map in a sidebar, footer, and so on, using Google Maps Widget. But Google is not your only choice; check out OSM - OpenStreetMap or Leaflet Maps Marker (Google Maps, OpenStreetMap, Bing Maps).

Events

Listing events and displaying them effectively is a complex task, made easy with plugins. For handling a lot of events, plugins such as The Events Calendar or Events Manager have event categories, widgets, and more. These and other plugins can often tie in with selling tickets to events through e-commerce plugins or third-party services such as Eventbrite. If you want to use your Google Calendar for your website event listings, try Google Calendar Events.

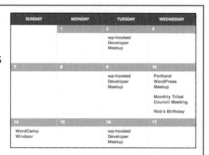

Membership Sites

Membership does have its rewards, and these plugins allow you to restrict some or all of your content to members only. If you do not need to collect money through your website, Members is a great choice. If you do need to integrate with PayPal or other payment gateways, Paid Memberships Pro or s2Member Framework keep track of renewal dates and more.

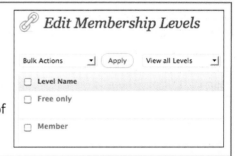

E-Commerce

Whether you just need to accept payments for two or three different services or you have hundreds of products to sell, there are plugins to help out. For basic PayPal buttons, there is WP Easy Paypal Payment Accept. If you need a shopping cart without complex product, shipping, or

tax variations, try WordPress Simple Paypal Shopping Cart. Full-fledged shopping cart systems include WooCommerce or WP eCommerce. There are also specialized e-commerce plugins, such as Easy Digital Downloads or PayPal Donations.

CHAPTER 11

Making Your Site Social

Interaction with visitors has always been crucial to website owners, but the rise of social media and easy mailing-list-management tools has expanded the possibilities enormously.

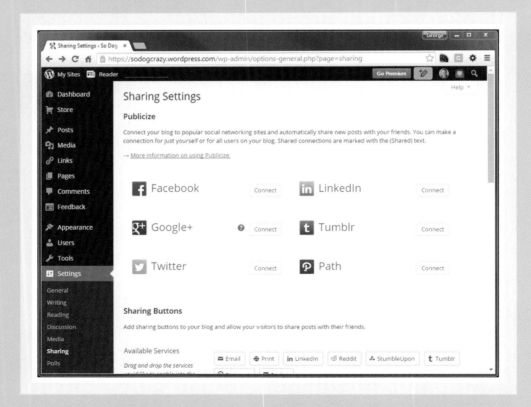

Understand How to Make a Site Social

There are many different ways in which owners can make their sites social, and WordPress accommodates them all while making the technical aspects straightforward.

Connecting with Social Media

Whether you want to provide links to your social media accounts, or enable visitors to share what they have found on your site with their social media friends, it is vital that your site be able to connect in as many ways as possible with social media.

in breeds, experiences as a ne

circumstances all affect how

It's only fair to share...

Your Website as the Hub of Social Activity

You can easily get caught up with particular social media and lose sight of your website's role. As much as possible, everything you do on the web should begin and end with your website. Got something fun to share? Put it on your website and link your social media to that post. Those viewing your social media accounts should always know that you have a website and that it has the final word on your online presence.

Socialize Where Your Audience Socializes

There are literally thousands of social media sites on the web. Even if you consider only the top ten, it is very hard to participate well on all of them, nor do you need to. Go where your audience is. That might be Twitter and LinkedIn, or it could be Facebook and a niche social media site for your field. Do a great job on the social media sites that matter instead of spreading yourself too thin and being ineffective.

GENERAL NETWORKING: AIM Pages Badoo Bebo CyWorld Ea Friendster Grono Hi5 iBritz LiveJournal Lovento Multiply MySp Netlog Orkut Passado Plaxo Skyrock Tagged Tribe Trig Windov

HEALTH/MEDICAL: DailyStrength DrConnected Health Ranke recovery Sermo – Doctors Walker Tracker Who is Sick?

KIDS: imbee KidLinks

INTERNET MARKETING: Gooruze PlugIM Sphinn

Do Not Forget about Email

Social media may get all the attention, but working quietly and effectively away from the spotlight is the email list. Receiving an email from a trusted source is a more personal experience and a very powerful one. Alongside your social media strategy you need a mailing list strategy. What you use the list for will vary greatly: Authors emailing about a new book, stores sending out specials, or plumbers sending out reminders about seasonal issues are just a few examples.

Make Your Mailing List as Diverse as Your Audience

Even with a focused mailing list of interested visitors, there will always be groups within that list: by gender, by how recently they signed up, by the circumstances of the sign-up (website versus trade show), by which incentive they signed up for, and so on. The more you can segment your list — and people can be in more than one segment — the more likely you can deliver an effective message based on the segment's needs.

Comments as Conversations

Comments have long been a staple of website blogs, but do not take them for granted. View each comment as part of a conversation that you help to foster by replying to each comment in some way. And listen to those comments. They help to shape what you do on your site and in your business because they are like votes for good topics or suggestions for new topics.

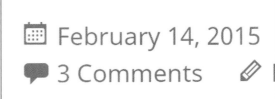

Testimonials as Social Proof

You can get so caught up in the rush to be liked on social media that you forget the classic way to show that you are liked: testimonials. Useful and heartfelt testimonials have always and continue to be a powerful tool in proving that you are trustworthy and helpful. WordPress.org sites have dozens of plugins to help with testimonials; but even if you are manually inserting them into pages, solicit testimonials and display them.

WHAT CLIENTS SAY...

"We've noticed how much better Rover's behavior is after consistently getting walked. You've saved our shoes in more ways than one. Thanks!"

– D and M Parkinson,
Haysville

Let Visitors Share Your Content

One of the most powerful features of social media is *sharing*. All of us love to let our friends know about something new, and Share buttons on a website enable us to instantly and easily tell everyone in our circles about what we have found.

Let Visitors Share Your Content

Share on WordPress.com and Sites Using Jetpack

1. Click **Sharing** under Settings in the left admin menu.

2. Scroll down to Sharing Buttons.

A. Available Services appear here as buttons.

B. Enabled Services appear here.

3. Drag a service from Available to Enabled.

C. This area shows a preview of how the buttons will appear.

D. Services dragged here become part of a single Share button.

4. Click ▼ to change the style of buttons, the group label, and whether links open in a new window.

E. Check boxes for locations where you want the buttons to appear.

5. If you use Twitter, type your username here.

F. Only WordPress.com sites display these three settings for Likes, Reblogging, and Comment Likes.

6. Click **Save Changes**.

On the site, Share buttons appear at the end of content.

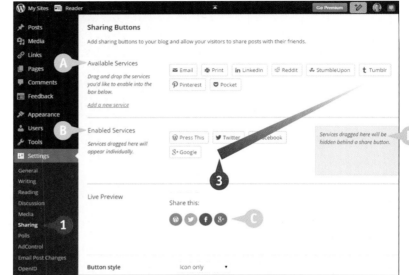

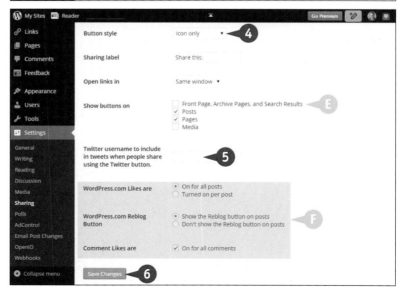

Use a Share Plugin on WordPress.org Sites

1 Install and activate the plugin Simple Share Buttons Adder.

Note: See Chapter 10 for more about plugins.

2 Click **Share Buttons** under Settings on the left admin menu.

3 Under Basic Settings, choose where buttons will appear, either before or after the content.

4 Type text to accompany the buttons.

5 Click the **Image Set** ▼ and select the style.

G The left column of buttons shows available services.

H The right column shows the services you have selected.

6 Drag a button from Available to Selected.

7 Scroll down and click **Save All Changes**.

I The Share buttons appear on your site in the locations specified.

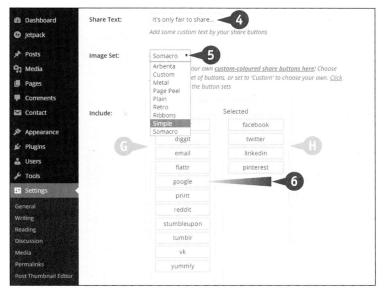

There is a social media site I want to make available for sharing, but it is not shown as available. Can I add services?

For WordPress.com and Jetpack sites, an Add Service link is available. Some plugins allow that, so you would need to check the features.

Can I turn off sharing on a per-post basis?

WordPress.com and Jetpack sites have a meta box on each post or page where you can turn off Likes, Sharing, or both. There are plugins for which individual control is available, but you would need to check the features or try out the plugin to be sure.

Following, joining; whatever you call it, visitors need to know where they can be part of your social media circles. Follow buttons provide those links. This section explains some ways you can place them on your WordPress site.

Add Follow Buttons

Use a Plugin on WordPress.org Sites

1 Install and activate the plugin Simple Social Icons.

Note: See Chapter 10 for more about plugins.

2 Click **Widgets** under Appearance on the left admin menu.

3 Locate the widget and click it.

4 Click the widget area where you want your Follow buttons to appear.

5 Click **Add Widget**.

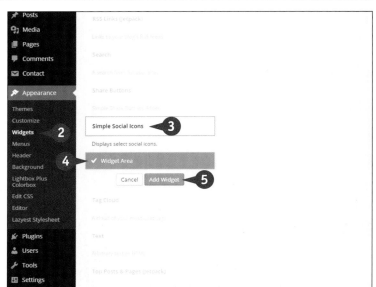

The widget settings appear.

6 Type a title to accompany the icons.

7 Adjust the size, border radius, and alignment of the icons here.

Note: Border radius sets the rounding of the corners. Set it to 50 px to make circles.

8 Change the font and background colors of the buttons as well as the hover colors here.

Note: There is no color picker; you enter a hexadecimal value. Colorexplorer.com is one place to pick a color, or consult your theme's CSS.

9 For each service that you want to display, type the full URL to your account.

10 Scroll down and click **Save**.

Ⓐ The follow icons appear where you placed them in the widget area.

Note: All the icons use the same color scheme. You can target individual icons to change their color using CSS. For more information on CSS, see Chapter 9.

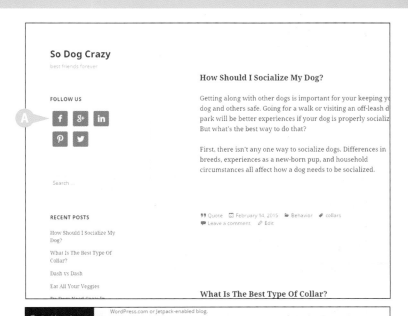

Use a Widget on WordPress.com Sites

❶ Click **Widgets** under Appearance on the left admin menu.

Ⓑ Look for widgets that allow visitors to follow you on services like Facebook or Twitter.

Note: In the case of Twitter and other services, a feed also appears along with the ability to follow.

Ⓒ A widget is available here that allows visitors to follow your WordPress.com site.

Note: See Chapter 8 for more about widgets.

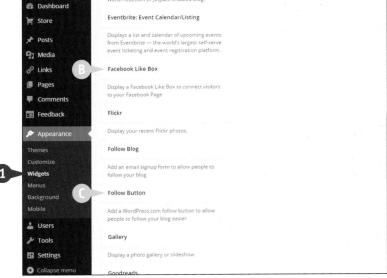

What if I want to have my own custom follow icons?
Most WordPress.org social media plugins allow you to add your own icons, but double-check before committing to a plugin.

WordPress.com does not have a follow widget for the social media site I am a part of. Is there anything I can do?
In the next section, "Display Social Feeds," you see how to paste HTML from a social media site into a Text widget to display an activity feed. You can add a Follow button using the same method.

Display Social Feeds

I n some circumstances you may want to share the feed from one of your social media accounts with your website visitors. This section discusses some ways you can do that using WordPress. And keep in mind that the same can be done with other people's feeds — for example, an organization you are involved with.

Display Social Feeds

Use a Plugin on WordPress.org Sites

1 Click **Add New** under Plugins on the left admin menu.

2 Search for "social media feeds" or a particular social media site you are interested in.

A There are plugins that display the feed of a specific social media site, like Instagram.

B Some plugins allow you to choose from several social media sites, and others combine several feeds into a single display.

Note: See Chapter 10 for more about plugins.

Use a Widget on WordPress.com Sites

1 Click **Widgets** under Appearance on the left admin menu.

C Look for widgets that display a feed from a social media site, such as Goodreads.

D Instagram is another example of a feed you can display.

Note: See Chapter 8 for more about widgets.

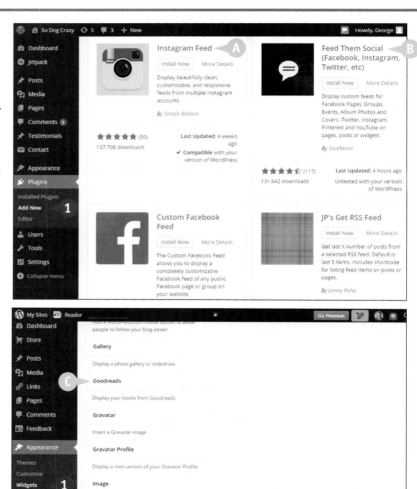

Manually Add a Feed Using HTML

1 Log in to your account. The example is from Twitter.

2 Locate your account settings and click **Widgets** or **Promotion** or whatever link leads to creating feeds.

3 Choose the source of the feed. In this example, you display your own timeline.

E Options appear on the left side of the screen for how your feed will display.

F On the right side you see a preview.

4 Click **Create widget**.

5 A box with HTML appears below the preview. Copy all the HTML.

6 Click **Widgets** under Appearance on the left admin menu.

7 Add a Text widget where you want the feed to appear.

Note: See Chapter 8 for more about widgets.

8 In the text area of the widget, paste the HTML from step **5**.

9 Click **Save**.

The feed appears on your site.

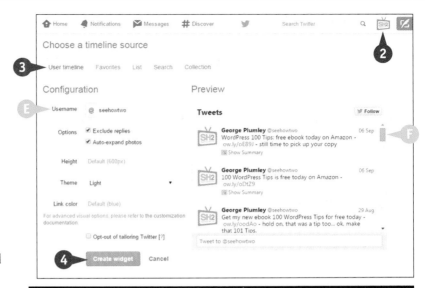

 TIP

The feed from my social media account appeared fine on my site, but now it is gone.
If you are using a plugin, remove the widget that produces the feed and replace it with a Text widget containing the HTML for the feed, as shown above. If you were already using HTML, try generating new code, because the feed may have changed.

Publicize Posts on Social Media

osting to social media about something new on your website is one of the most important parts of a social media strategy. But that can be time consuming and therefore is seldom done in our busy schedules. The publicize function at WordPress.com, or the same functionality provided by a plugin, allows you to publish and promote at the same time.

Publicize Posts on Social Media

Use the Publicize Function on WordPress.com and Jetpack-enabled Sites

1 Click **Sharing** under Settings on the left admin menu.

2 Choose a social media site to which you want to post content and click **Connect**.

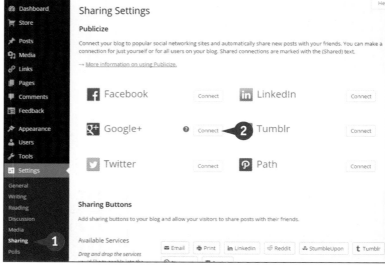

If you are not already logged into the social media site, you are first asked to log in.

A Depending on the site, you are asked to grant various permissions for WordPress to access your account. Some of these permissions may have settings you can edit.

3 Click **Accept**.

B When you add a new post, you see your social media site listed under Publicize in the Publish meta box.

C If you want to add a custom message to the posting on your social media account, you can type it here too.

If you have connected to more than one social media site, they all appear here with check boxes. You can choose not to post to a particular social site.

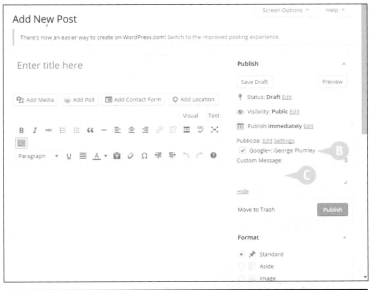

Use a Plugin on WordPress.org Sites

1 Click **Add New** under Plugins on the left admin menu.

2 Search for "post social networks" or the name of a particular social media site.

D Some plugins allow you to publish to multiple social media sites.

E Other plugins are for publishing to particular social media sites.

Note: See Chapter 10 for more about plugins.

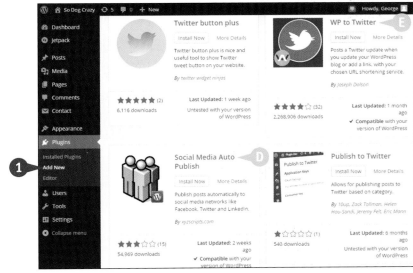

To connect to Facebook it says I need to create an app. How do I do that?
You should be given instructions for completing that process. Pay close attention, though: Creating an app is not complicated, but you need to follow every step. Also, the process for creating apps has changed several times, so make sure your plugin is up to date.

Can I add a social media site to the list of possible connections?
Not on WordPress.com or Jetpack sites. There may be plugins which allow you to do that, but you would need to check the available features. Also, check the site in question — it may provide instructions.

Understand Mailing Lists

aving website visitors join a mailing list means that you can stay in touch with them even when they are not visiting. Those who sign up for your list should occupy a very important place in your marketing strategy — they have told you they are interested in what you do and have let you into their email program.

What Is a Mailing List?

A website *mailing list* is a set of email addresses and possibly other information you collect using a form on your site or other locations, such as Facebook pages. A *mailing list manager* is a service or program that collects the emails and enables you to send out messages to all subscribers.

Why Not Use My Email Program?

There are three key reasons: Your email program cannot collect and verify sign-ups automatically; it cannot track responses, bounce-backs, or other important data; and your email program sends email through a normal server — which limits emails to about 200 per hour — rather than a specialized email server. On top of that, your email program does not have the drag-and-drop email design tools that a mailing list manager has.

Why Not Use a Plugin?

Although plugins exist for WordPress.org sites that manage a mailing list, and many people are using them, they usually cannot match the features of third-party services — plus you still have the potential problems of sending emails from your hosting account. In addition, running an effective mailing list requires a complex plugin and, the more complex, the more potential for problems. Let a third party manage the software side of things.

93 Subscribers	45.3% Opens	21.2% Clicks
231 Subscribers	26.7% Opens	6.1% Clicks

Do I Need to Offer an Incentive?

Whatever form it takes, visitors need a reason for joining your mailing list, and a bonus for signing up helps. It could be information in the form of a PDF, it could be access to a video, or it may be a discount on a product or service. Of course, being on the list needs to be of value too, but a valuable incentive helps to build initial trust with subscribers.

What If I Do Not Want to Send to Everyone?

A mailing list manager should offer some way of segmenting your list and send only to one or more segments at a time. Some of the segmenting will be built in: Send only to those who did not click on a link in the previous mailing. Some of the segmenting is up to you: Group everyone who signed up to the mailing list from a recent webinar.

Tips-Home	★★
Tips-Home	★★
Tips-100 Beginner WordPress Tips	★★
Tips-Video Tour Of Our Navigation System	★★

What Do I Send to My List?

Whatever is useful to your subscribers: tips, special offers, downloadable items, and links to important information. Remember, they have allowed you to send them emails and you do not want to break that trust by sending them useless information. Keeping in mind that you should segment your list — or have separate lists, depending on the provider — what you send to one segment may differ from what you send to another.

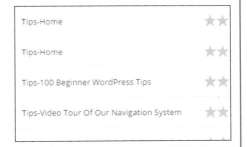

How Often Should I Send?

We have all subscribed to a list, only to discover that we are getting messages every other day or worse. Of course it depends on what your subscribers are expecting or what you are sending, but even great material can be annoying if it is arriving too often. At the other end of the spectrum, make sure you are emailing at least once a month or people tend to forget they are on your list — and some will even report it as spam.

Don't Spam Your Customers!: How Often Should You Send Marketing Emails?

Offer Email Subscriptions

Even if someone is not interested right now in being on your mailing list or receiving your newsletter, he or she may well be interested in knowing when you have updated your website. An email subscription allows people to keep up with your latest posts, without having to remember to return to your site.

Offer Email Subscriptions

Use the Subscription Function on WordPress.com and Jetpack-enabled Sites

Note: Steps **1** and **2** display a Follow tab at the bottom right of every web page.

1 Click **Reading** under Settings on the left admin menu.

2 Under Follower Settings, click the box (☐ changes to ☑) under Logged Out Users to make the tab appear.

Note: Steps **3** to **10** allow you to use a widget for the sign-up form.

3 Click **Widgets** under Appearance on the left admin menu.

4 Click the Follow Blog widget.

5 Click the widget area you want.

6 Click **Add Widget**.

The widget opens to display its settings.

7 Change the default wording of various elements here.

8 Change the sign-up button text here.

9 Click this option to display the total number of followers (☐ changes to ☑).

10 Click **Save**.

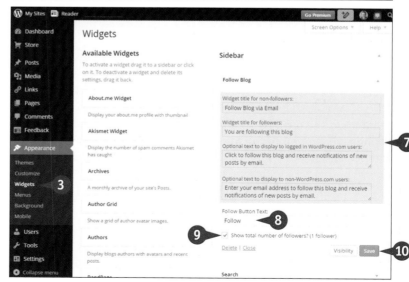

A The form now appears in the widget area, asking for the visitor's email address.

B If you use the Follow tab method from steps **1** and **2**, this is what visitors see when they click the tab.

Use a Mailing List Manager for WordPress.org Sites without Jetpack

1 Log in to your mail list account.

2 Look for an option called something like RSS to Email, or RSS Feed to Subscription or Blog Subscription.

3 Type the URL for your RSS feed. With self-hosted WordPress, adding/feed to the end of your site URL or a category URL produces an RSS feed.

4 Choose how often new content will be emailed to subscribers.

5 Choose the days of the week when emails can be sent.

After you finish setting up the mailing, it will work automatically as new content is posted.

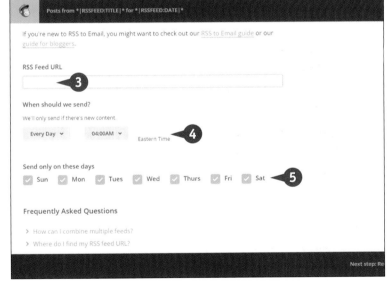

TIPS

I do not have a mailing list manager or Jetpack. Are there any other subscription options?

Services such as Feedly.com or Feedburner are available and free to use. They give you some code to put in a Text widget to produce a Subscribe button. Also, anyone who has an RSS reader can pick up the RSS feed generated automatically by WordPress.

How often should I set my service to send out emails?

When you have a choice, it is best to have the emails sent out no more than once a week, in particular if you blog frequently. You do not typically want an email going out every time you post.

Add a Mailing List Manager

The technical aspects of running a useful mailing list are enormous. Automating the sign-up process, tracking clicks within emails, segmenting the list according to past behavior, or simply keeping track of bounced emails — this is not something your email program can handle or something you should be trying to run on your server. Third-party mailing list managers do the heavy lifting; you just communicate with your list members. Integration with your WordPress site can be as simple as copying and pasting.

Add a Mailing List Manager

Manually Add a Sign-up Form

1. Log in to your mailing list manager.

2. Look for a link to Embedded Forms or Website Forms or a similar name.

3. Choose **Signup Form**.

4. Choose the type of form you want.

5. Type the form title.

Ⓐ Your changes appear in a preview.

6. Choose whether to show only required fields.

7. Click any other options you may be offered.

8. Copy the HTML from this box to use on your site.

9. Click **Widgets** under Appearance on the left admin menu.

10. Add a Text widget where you want the feed to appear.

Note: See Chapter 8 for more about widgets.

11. In the text area of the widget, paste the HTML.

Note: If the form already has a title, leave the widget title blank.

12. Click **Save**.

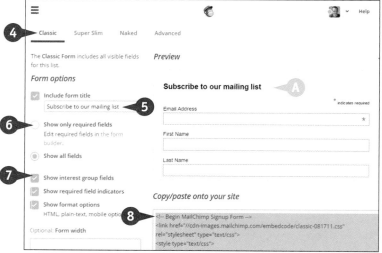

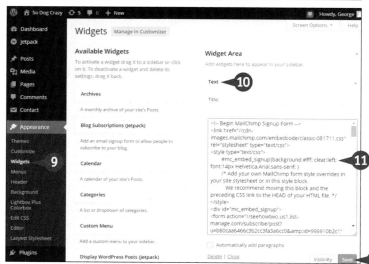

B The mailing list sign-up form appears in the sidebar.

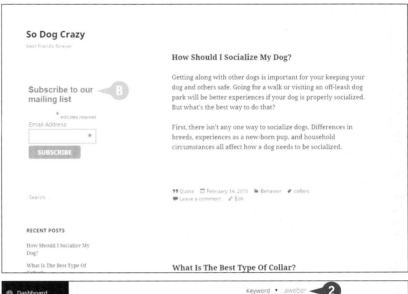

Use a Plugin to Integrate a Sign-up Form

Note: Although adding a sign-up form manually is easy, a plugin for a WordPress.org site can make it even easier, or offer additional tools for design or integration.

1 Click **Add New** under Plugins on the left admin menu.

2 Search by the name of your mailing list manager. There are plugins for Aweber, Mailchimp, Constant Contact, and many other providers.

3 Install and activate the plugin and follow its instructions.

Note: See Chapter 10 for more about plugins.

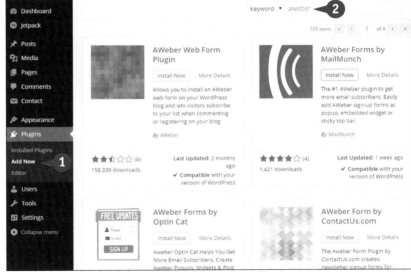

TIPS

The form I pasted into a Text widget does not look good with my site. What can I do?

The form maker provided by your mailing list manager may offer more customization tools, so check that first. If not, see if it has a version with no styling so that the form will pick up the styles of your theme.

I tried a plugin for my mailing list manager but it cannot connect.

Check that you have properly pasted in any secret key or API key provided by your mailing list manager. If that still does not work, make sure your plugin is up to date or try another plugin.

Understand Comments

Good communication is at the heart of any relationship, and comments are a great way to communicate with visitors. WordPress has an excellent commenting system built in. It is up to you to use it to your advantage.

Allow Comments?

The first thing you need to decide is whether you want to accept comments at all. If so, then you need to decide where. The most common place is on blog posts, but perhaps not on all of them; comments on posts about events are great, but not necessarily on posts about press releases, for example. You also may have individual WordPress pages that could benefit from comments.

Leave a Reply

Logged in as George. Log out?

COMMENT

Reply to Comments

Someone making a comment on your site represents a potential conversation. Even if someone is just making an observation, it is good to respond, even if just to agree. It shows you are listening. Other kinds of comments lead to expanding on the topic of the post or taking it in a new direction. You do not need to reply to every comment if your site is very busy, but then busy is good.

Angelica Crane

March 4, 2015 at 9:08 am   ✎ Edit

From the time they're a puppy, I let my dogs, and I think that helps socialize th

REPLY

Threaded Comments

By default WordPress comes with threaded comments turned on, which is good. Being able to read responses to a comment right there rather than having to jump back and forth in the stream of comments is a huge boost for creating conversations.

Special Uses for Comments

The comment system in WordPress does not always have to be used for comments. You could use it as a way of gathering testimonials or as a kind of trouble-ticket system or for gathering user-submitted stories. And you could use it differently for different areas of your site. Whatever kind of communication you want to have publicly with your audience, the comment system may be a great tool.

Submit Your Story

Logged in as George. Log out?

NO MORE THAN 500 WORDS PLEASE

Comment Spam

Unfortunately, opening your site to comments also opens it to spammers. In fact, even without turning on comments it is possible to get spammed, so you will want some form of spam protection. WordPress.com sites are automatically covered, whereas WordPress.org sites have many options through plugins. Typically this protection covers more than just comments, such as a contact form or a registration form.

SAY GOODBYE TO
COMMENT SPAM

Third-Party Comments

Although WordPress has a great built-in comment system, there are also third-party servers, such as Disqus. Not only do they provide a comment system for you, but they have become social networks where visitors share comments and interact with one another through their individual feeds, which means comments about you can extend beyond your site.

**Always free,
works everywhere**

Disqus is easy to add to any type of website.

Choose Comment Settings

Wordress's default settings for comments do a good job of balancing between comment settings that are too lax and ones that are too restrictive. Knowing how those settings work and possible ways to adjust them is important to an effective and hopefully busy comment environment on your site. This section talks about the key discussion settings instead of trying to explain them all.

Find comment settings by clicking **Discussion** under Settings on the left admin menu.

WordPress.com and WordPress.org Settings

A Default Article Settings

The setting to allow people to post comments on new articles is turned on by default, which means comments will appear on all posts or pages. A note reminds you that you can override this setting on individual posts or pages.

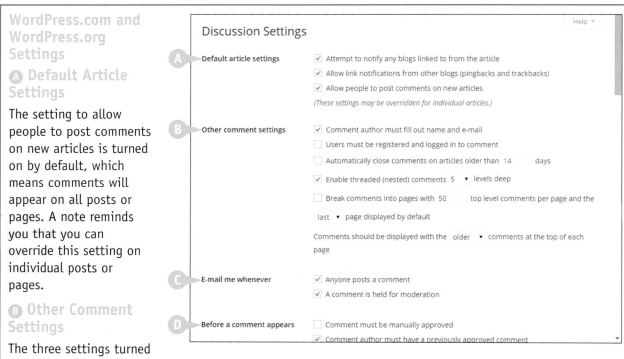

B Other Comment Settings

The three settings turned on by default are:
Comment authors must fill out their name and email, threaded comments are enabled, and the order of comments is set to oldest first. Those are best left as is; the first helps manage spam, and the second two are for readability.

C E-Mail Me Whenever

By default, the administrator will receive an email whenever anyone posts a comment or when one is held for moderation. Unless comments are extremely busy, it is good to leave this turned on.

D Before a Comment Appears

By default, comments are automatically approved if the author has had one comment approved manually. The other setting, which is turned off, would require every comment to be manually approved.

More WordPress.com and WordPress.org Settings

Ⓐ Comment Moderation

Because a lot of spam is filled with links, the default setting is to hold a comment for moderation (even if the author has been approved before) if it contains two or more links. There is also a box for triggers to hold a comment for moderation if the listed words appear in the content, name, URL, email, or IP address.

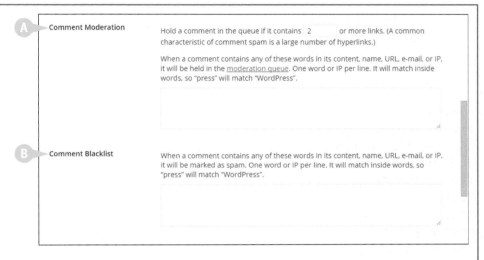

Ⓑ Comment Blacklist

Similar to the moderation box, but in this case, matched words cause the comment to be marked as spam.

WordPress.com Additional Settings

Ⓐ Follow Comments

By default, WordPress.com creates a button on the comment form allowing visitors to follow the comments for that post or page.

Ⓑ Follow Blog

By default, WordPress.com creates a button on the comment form allowing visitors to follow the site as a whole.

Moderate Comments

N o site should have a completely open comment policy; that is, where a comment from anyone is automatically published on your site. The previous section "Choose Comment Settings" makes it clear how important some form of moderation is required. Here you learn about how to do the moderating.

Moderate Comments

Moderate an Individual Comment

Note: WordPress notifies you in a number of ways that comments need moderation.

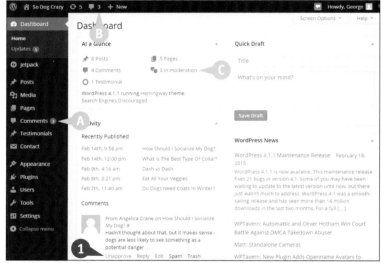

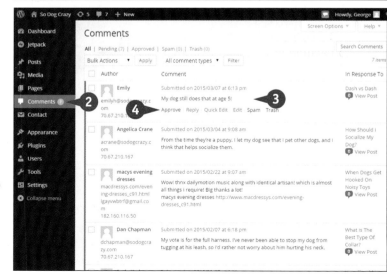

A Watch for the circle icon next to Comments on the left admin menu.

B Watch for a number next to the dialog icon in the toolbar menu.

C On the Dashboard under At a Glance, a notice of comments awaiting moderation appears.

1 Click **Approve** to moderate the most recent comments appearing on the Dashboard.

Note: The wording of the link changes to Unapprove.

2 Click **Comments** on the left admin menu.

All comments awaiting moderation have a light orange background.

3 Mouse over a comment to reveal a menu.

4 Click **Approve** to make the comment go public.

Moderate Multiple Comments

1 Click **Comments** on the left admin menu.

2 Click the **Pending** link to show only comments awaiting moderation.

3 Click the box beside each comment you want to approve (☐ changes to ☑).

Note: If you want to approve them all, check the box in the header row to select all.

4 Click ▼ and choose **Approve**.

5 Click **Apply**.

All chosen comments are approved.

Ⓓ The success message at the top of the screen shows how many comments were approved.

Ⓔ All approved comments now show a gray background. Mouse over any of the comments you approved and you can click **Unapprove** to return it to pending or moderation status again.

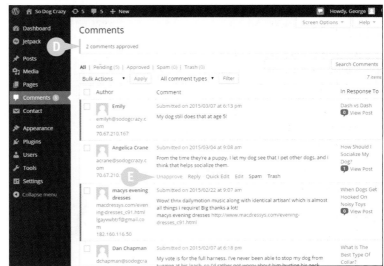

TIPS

What do I do about the email I got asking me to moderate a comment?

Just click the appropriate link to approve the comment, delete it, or "spam it." Or, you can click the fourth link, which takes you to the Edit Comment screen.

Someone I approved at one time is now sending emails that I have to manually remove as inappropriate. Is there something I can do?

You can unapprove the first comment that you manually approved and then mark it and the other comments as spam. That puts his or her email address on the spam list. You could also put the email address on the Comment Blacklist if emails are still getting through.

Edit Comments

Editing comments lets you correct typos, tone down rhetoric, or make comments conform to a particular comment policy. Editing often is a nicer alternative to approving or deleting troublesome comments.

Edit a Comment

Note: There are several points from which you can edit a comment in WordPress.

From the Comments Screen

1 Click **Comments** on the left admin menu.

2 Mouse over the comment you want to edit and click the **Edit** link.

From the Posts Screen

1 Open a post and scroll down past the content editor where you see all comments relating to that post.

2 Mouse over the comment you want to edit and click the **Edit** link.

From Your Blog

1 While you are logged on to your blog, click **Edit** next to the published comment you want to change.

Edit a Comment

Note: All three Edit links described in the previous steps lead to an Edit Comment screen.

1 Edit the author's information here.

2 Change the status of the comment here (○ changes to ◉).

3 Edit the date the comment was posted here.

4 Edit the content of the post using the HTML editor box.

5 Click **Update**.

Use Quick Edit to Edit a Comment

Note: If you need to change only the content of a comment, the steps that follow are a faster way of doing it.

1 Mouse over the comment and click **Quick Edit**.

2 Make any changes you want, including spelling, grammar, and HTML formatting, in the HTML editing box.

3 Click **Update Comment** when you are done.

The changes are saved, and the Quick Edit pane closes.

Deal with Comment Spam

The less time spent worrying about or dealing with spammers, the better. That is why it is important you have a tool in place to do the worrying and the dealing. WordPress.com has a built-in system called Akismet, which is highly effective. It is also available as a plugin to any WordPress.org site, though it does cost money for commercial sites. Other effective plugins are also available.

Deal with Comment Spam

Access Comments

1 Click **Comments** on the left admin menu.

A Spotting spam comments is generally pretty easy. They often have crazy names and long email addresses filled with advertising terms, and the comments rarely make any sense or are simplistically complimentary — they **love** your site.

2 Mouse over the comment you want to mark as spam and from the menu that appears, click the **Spam** link.

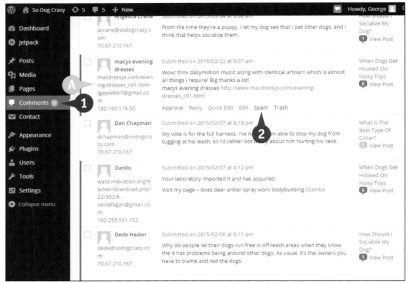

Mark Multiple Comments as Spam

1 Click **Comments** on the left admin menu.

2 Click **Pending** to show only comments awaiting moderation.

3 Click the box beside each comment you want to mark as spam (☐ changes to ☑).

4 Click ▼ and choose **Mark as Spam**.

5 Click **Apply**.

All chosen comments are marked as spam and are moved to the spam screen.

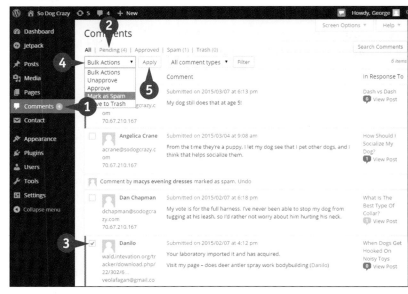

Understand the Spam Comments Screen

1 Click **Comments** on the left admin menu.

2 Click **Spam** to show only comments marked as spam.

3 Mouse over a particular comment and you can unmark it as spam or you can delete it permanently.

Note: You can use the Bulk Actions function to take these actions for several or all of the spam comments.

Anti-Spam Plugins for WordPress.org Sites

1 Click **Plugins** on the left admin menu.

B The Akismet anti-spam service, run by WordPress.com, is available as a plugin that comes installed with WordPress. To activate it, you need to sign up with Akismet or have a WordPress.com account. It is free for personal sites, but there is a small monthly fee for commercial sites.

C Two other anti-spam plugins have been installed here to illustrate some of the alternatives to Akismet — there are many others. Click **Add New** under Plugins and search for "anti-spam."

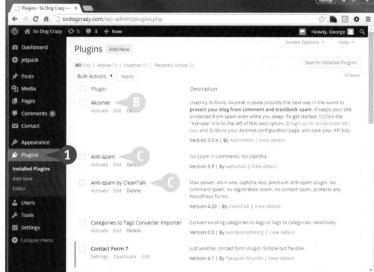

What if a spam plugin wrongly identifies a comment as spam?

When you first set up your site, it can be helpful to look through your spam comments to make sure WordPress.com or your plugin is not catching legitimate email. Once you're confident about the process you will not feel the need to check.

Why not just click Trash when a spam comment shows up in the Comments panel?

Clicking **Trash** rather than **Spam** does not let Akismet learn what senders and IP addresses are generating spam comments. The information Akismet gathers is shared across the network, which is part of what makes it so effective.

Display Testimonials

Building trust is one of the most important goals of any website, and quality testimonials do exactly that. One method is to create a category of posts for testimonials, but for WordPress.org sites there are plugins that give you even more control over how individual testimonials can be displayed throughout your site.

Display Testimonials

Testimonials in Existing Pages and Posts

1. Click **Posts** or **Pages** on the left admin menu to find the post or page where you want to place your testimonial.

2. Click **Edit** to edit the post or page.

3. Type the testimonial text where you want it to appear in the content editor.

4. Highlight the testimonial and click the **Block Quote** button (").

Ⓐ Your testimonial is styled by your theme.

Input Testimonials as Individual Posts

1. Click **Add New** under Posts on the left admin menu.

2. Type the name of the person who gave the testimonial.

3. Type the testimonial in the content editor.

Ⓑ If your theme supports the Quote format, you could assign that to the post.

4. Assign the post to the Testimonials category (☐ changes to ☑).

Note: If the category does not exist, see the section "Add New Categories" in Chapter 7.

5. Click **Publish**.

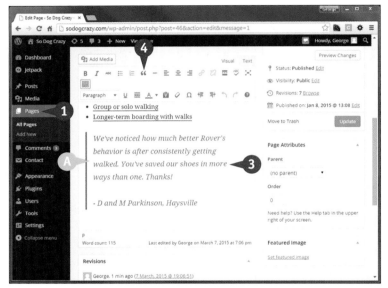

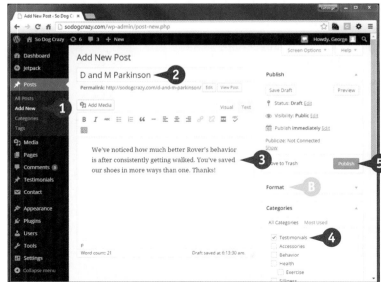

Use a Testimonials Plugin on WordPress.org Sites

1 Install and activate the Testimonials Widget plugin.

Note: See Chapter 10 for more about plugins.

2 Click **Add New** under Testimonials on the left admin menu.

3 Type the name of the person who gave the testimonial.

4 Type the testimonial.

5 Type information such as location, company, URL, and email in the Testimonial Data meta box.

C You can categorize the testimonial (☐ changes to ☑).

6 Click **Publish**.

7 Click **Widgets** under Appearance on the left admin menu.

8 Add the Testimonials Slider widget to the widget area you want.

9 Type a title to appear above the testimonials.

10 Go through all the settings for this widget, such as how many testimonials to revolve, and how long to display each.

11 Scroll down and click **Save**.

The Testimonial Slider appears in the widget area of your blog.

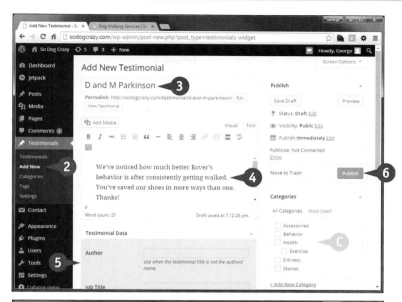

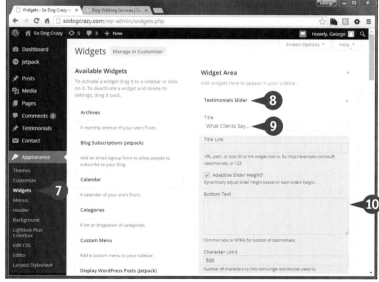

TIP

Can I display all testimonials on a single page?

Most testimonials plugins include shortcodes that allow you to display the testimonials in a number of ways, including a complete list on a single page. You can also display individual testimonials within a post or a page.

CHAPTER 12

Managing Your WordPress Site

Whether you are tracking site statistics or making your site search-engine friendly, there are many ways you can make it easier to manage your WordPress site.

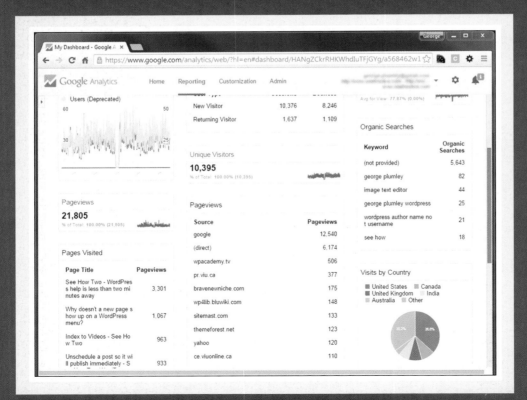

Change What Your Front Page Displays

By default, WordPress displays your latest posts on the home page, but you can change that by using a WordPress setting. Or on WordPress.org sites, your theme may have a particular way of handling content on the front page.

Change What Your Front Page Displays

For WordPress.com and WordPress.org Sites

1. Add a new page with the content you want to appear on the front page, and publish the page.

Note: See Chapter 5 to add a new page.

2. Click **Add New** under Pages on the left admin menu.

3. Type the title for your blog.

4. Leave the content editor blank.

Note: Any content you place in here will not be shown. This is a placeholder page only.

5. Click **Publish**.

6. Click **Reading** under Settings on the left admin menu.

7. For Front Page Displays, click the **A static page** option (○ changes to ◉).

8. Click the **Front page** ▼ and select the page you created as your home page — in this case, Home.

9. Click **Save Changes**.

Now, when visitors arrive at your domain name, the front page displays the contents of the Home page. And all blog posts will appear on the Posts or Blog page.

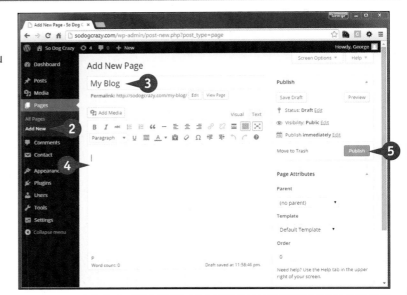

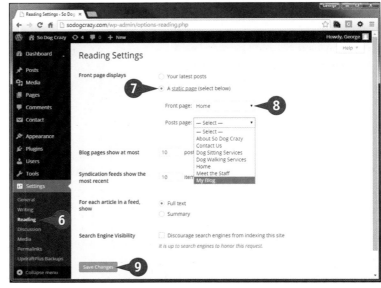

For WordPress.org Sites

Note: Some themes on WordPress.org sites operate in a third way: by controlling the front page through Theme Options or Widgets or a combination of the two.

A The top portion of the default home page for the theme Accesspress contains images from a slider.

B The text and featured image of one of the site's posts.

C The events section is a list of the latest posts from one of the site's categories.

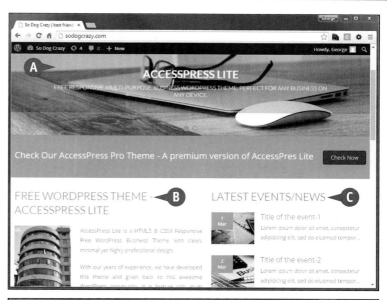

1 Click **Theme Options** under Appearance on the left admin menu.

2 Click the layout of the top portion of the home page (○ changes to ⦿).

3 Click ▼ and choose the content of any post to appear as the welcome text at the top left of the home page.

4 Click this option to disable the events section next to the welcome text (☐ changes to ☑). This theme offers a number of possible home page sections which are not visible on this screenshot.

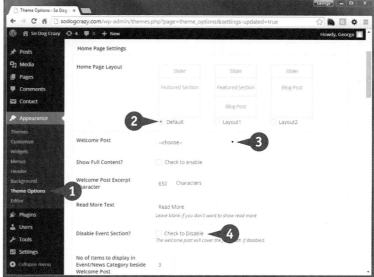

TIPS

I do not see a Theme Options setting or any Home Widgets. Does that mean my theme uses only the Front Page Displays function?
It might use a different name under Appearance. You can also click **Customize** under Appearance and check there, because this is the new way WordPress wants themes to handle options.

My blog is just one category of posts. I do not want all the other categories showing on the Blog page. How do I stop that?
You cannot, without doing some custom coding. However, you do not need anything so elaborate. Just do not assign any Blog page at all, and instead, put the Blog category on the menu.

Use a Page Builder Plugin

Although WordPress themes have continually added more and better choices for site design, the layout and design of post and page content has remained limited. With the introduction of shortcode and page builder plugins, all that has changed. Shortcode plugins make it easy to add elements like columns or tabbed content, whereas page builder plugins add drag-and-drop functionality to the use of shortcodes.

Use a Page Builder Plugin

1 Install and activate Page Builder by WooRockets.com from the Add Plugins screen.

Note: See Chapter 10 for more about plugins.

2 Click **All Pages** under Pages on the left admin menu.

3 Choose a page and click **Edit**.

4 Click the **WR PageBuilder** tab on the content editor.

5 Click **Add Row** to begin adding content.

6 From the list that drops down, choose one column or any of a number of combinations of columns.

Ⓐ If you have more than one row, you rearrange them using the arrow buttons (⌃ and ⌄).

Ⓑ From the menu at the right of each row, you can add columns (▥), edit the row (✎), or delete it (🗑).

7 Click **Add Element** to add content.

The Select Element window opens.

8 From the dropdown at the top left, select which elements or WordPress widgets you want to choose from.

9 Click the item you want.

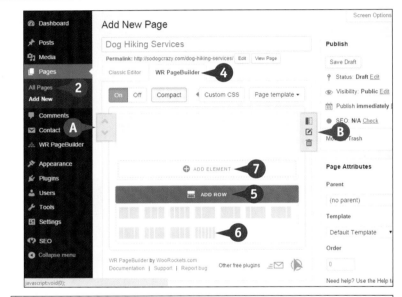

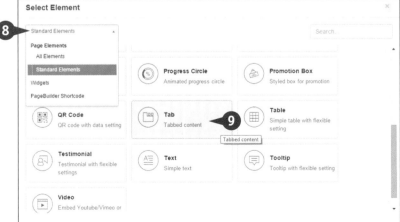

The settings for the element you chose appear.

10 Type your content in the left panel. How it is entered and what options you have depend on the type of element.

C A preview of how your content will appear on the live site is shown on the right.

D The tabs at the top switch you between Content, Styling, and Shortcode, which is the actual coding of the element.

E If there are similar elements, a dropdown allows you to convert your content to one of those other elements.

11 When you are finished, click **Save**.

The window closes and you return to the post or pages you are editing.

12 Click **Publish** or **Update**.

13 View your content on the live site. In this example, tabs are added to the page.

F You can use the regular content editor by clicking the **Classic Editor** tab.

G You can still use the Page Elements in the regular content editor, but they will appear as shortcodes within the text.

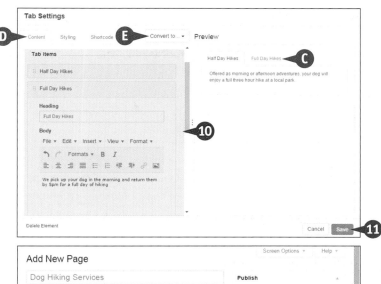

TIPS

What happens to my content if I get rid of a plugin for laying out content?
It depends on the plugin. Many leave their shortcodes in place along with any other coding they create. Others offer the option to strip their coding.

My theme has its own shortcodes for laying out content. Why should I use a plugin?
Because you want the content layout to remain in place even if you switch themes.

Edit Content for Search Engines

Although not specific to WordPress, making your content search-engine friendly is important. The best rule of thumb is to write for visitors and edit for search engines. A large part of that editing involves making sure you are using a keyword or phrase that searchers tend to use.

Focus Every Piece of Content

Keeping web pages narrowly focused is important for visitors, and that makes it important for search engines. If visitors need their kitchen faucet fixed, they do not want to be reading through your air conditioning services to get to their topic. And search engines get blamed if kitchen faucet searchers do not get to the kitchen faucet page right away. The narrower your page topic, the better, and the keyword will describe the topic.

Focus Keyword:	dog sitting
	dog sitting
	dog sitting jobs
	dog sitting on cat
	dog sitting rates
	dog sitting services
	dog sitting prices
	dog sitting tips
	dog sitting business

Write Enough Content

In most cases, if a web page is going to have some value to visitors, it has to have at least a reasonable amount of content. No one knows exactly what search engines consider reasonable, but a common number you will hear is 300 words. Not all pages need this; it does not take a lot to tell visitors how to contact you, for example. But for pages where keywords are important, you need to have a minimum amount of content.

A Tale of Tails

MARCH 19, 2015   GEORGE   0 COMMENTS   EDIT

Tin-pot dictators have their food-testers; we dog ov
to take on that role this past Christmas, when the in
we live with the consequences.

Put Effort into Your Titles

Titles are the gateway to web pages, and in turn to your entire site. If searchers arrive to find a title that seems unrelated to what they are searching for, they hit the Back button and try the next result. The more you can word your titles in a way that directly addresses the kind of search visitors might make for that topic, the more likely they will stop to read more. The keyword for the page should be in the title, near the beginning if possible.

Add New Post

Enter title here

Make Great Openings

Just as the title of a web page is the immediate first impression, so too must the first paragraph confirm that visitors are going to get what they are after. So make sure the keyword is in the first sentence and that the paragraph gives a summary of what visitors will get from the page.

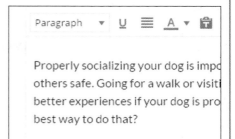

Put Useful Alt Tags on Images

Visitors love images, and to help search engines know an image is relevant to the topic of the page, use the `alt` attribute (**A**) of an image to accurately describe what it shows. Do not simply say "a car," but say what make or model, what color, where it is located, and so on. If you can include the keyword while sounding natural, great.

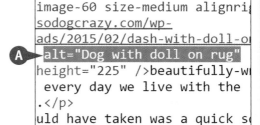

Create Quality Links Inside and Out

HTML stands for *HyperText Markup Language*, and the hypertext stands for text that takes you somewhere else. Linking is how search engines find their way around. So link to relevant, quality external sites and relevant material on your own site. Search engines love both.

Insert/edit link

Enter the destination URL

URL   http://petmd.com

Title

☐   Open link in a new window

Break Up Longer Content with Headings

And longer content means anything more than two or three paragraphs. Headings help to break up the page for visitors so they can jump to specific content or quickly map what is on a page. Search engines do the same. Remember that H1 is the most important heading — the page title — and as the number goes up, the importance goes down: H2 would be a sub-heading, H3 would be a sub-sub-heading, and so on.

cute, but as we heard those sounds moving throughout the hous
triggered by the mouth of a triumphant terrier, **the true nature**
problem became apparent.

The Penny Drops

For Dash, the squeaks and chirps were a reward: bite the doll an
sound. And of course the more often you bite, the greater the re
Looking back, the in-laws foretold as much when they dropped
present:

Use an SEO Plugin

Having focused content that visitors want is the important first step in search engine optimization, but there are also key elements for SEO that need to be in place behind the scenes. For WordPress.org sites, plugins are available that can help with that. This example uses the WordPress SEO by Yoast plugin.

Use an SEO Plugin

1 Install and activate WordPress SEO by Yoast from the Add Plugins screen.

Note: See Chapter 10 for more about plugins.

2 From the Page or Post links on the left admin menu, open a page or post and look for the plugin's meta box just below the content editor.

Ⓐ Snippet Preview shows what the post or page's listing would look like in search results.

Ⓑ The SEO Title field allows you to override the default HTML title tag.

3 Type a meta description. The ideal number of characters and how many you have are both shown.

4 Type a keyword; a series of suggestions appears from actual search terms.

Ⓒ The plugin reports on how the keyword is used on the post or page.

The report tells you where and the total number of times the keyword is found in crucial places: Article Heading, Page Title, Page URL, Content, and Meta Description.

⑤ As you correct missing keywords, the report reflects the changes. For example, as you add the keyword to the meta description field, this report updates the meta description total.

⑥ Click the **Page Analysis** tab to view a report card on the SEO qualities of the post or page.

⑦ Check the colored dots to see where your content could use improvements.

Note: These ratings are combined into a single rating which is shown in the Publish meta box and on page and post listings.

Ⓓ You need to save or update for the report card to reflect any changes you make.

⑧ Click the **Advanced** tab.

Do not touch any of the Advanced tab settings unless you know what you are doing. Setting them improperly can block search engines.

Note: By default, the plugin disables this tab for anyone except Administrators.

⑨ Click links under the SEO section of the left admin menu to control site-wide optimization settings.

Ⓔ Some settings can be used to control all instances of posts, pages, or other WordPress elements.

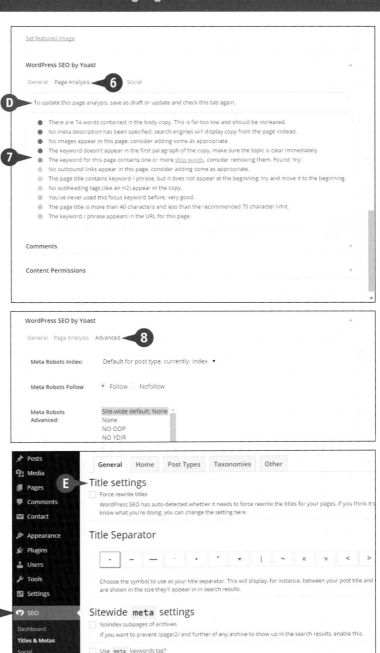

269

Track Site Statistics

Whether you want help to make more money or simply want to know who is visiting, website statistics are crucial. WordPress.com has a built-in visitor tracking system, whereas for WordPress.org sites, you can easily add Google Analytics using a plugin.

Track Site Statistics

Use Google Analytics on WordPress.org Sites

1 Install and activate the plugin Google Analytics by Yoast from the Add Plugins screen.

Note: See Chapter 10 for more about plugins.

2 Click **Settings** under Analytics on the left admin menu.

3 Click to set up the Google Analytics code by authenticating through your Google Account. Log in to Google and accept the terms. You are given a code to paste into the plugin.

4 Click this option to manually enter the UA code you are given when you set up Analytics yourself (☐ changes to ☑).

Note: Manually entering the UA code means statistics from Google cannot display on the plugin's dashboard.

5 Click **Save Changes**.

In a few hours or less you see statistics from Google Analytics.

Ⓐ The left panel displays a list of available reports, of which there are dozens, all of them customizable.

Ⓑ On the right is where report details appear, as well as dashboards. You can create multiple dashboards, pulling in elements of any report.

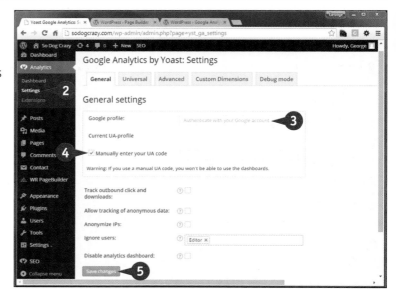

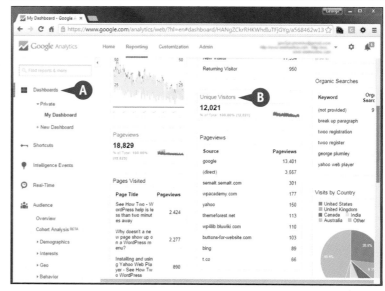

Use WordPress.com and Jetpack Stats

Note: These statistics are also available on WordPress.org sites using the Jetpack plugin.

1 Click **Dashboard** on the left admin menu of your WordPress.com site to see some key statistics in the Stats meta box.

C From any admin screen, the toolbar has a small graph showing visits from the last 48 hours with a link to the statistics screen.

2 From any admin screen, click **Site Stats** under Dashboard on the left admin menu.

D The graph displays statistics according to a chosen time range.

E You can choose which statistics to display on the graph: Views, Visitors, Likes, and Comments.

F A wide range of statistics can be displayed by toggling the individual boxes.

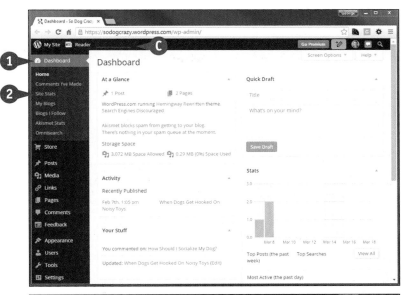

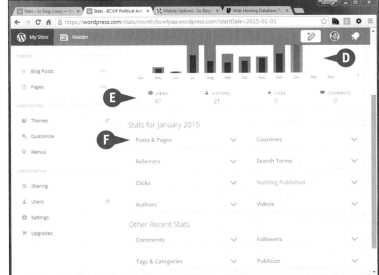

TIPS

My theme has a field where I can enter the code for Google Analytics. Is it better to use that rather than a plugin?

If you switch themes, the new one may not have a Google Analytics field. By using a plugin, you never have to be concerned about that issue.

I can export statistics from Google Analytics, but what about from WordPress.com?

There is no user interface for exporting WordPress.com stats as of this writing, but there is an API you could use to write a script to export to a CSV file: http://phoxis.org/2011/04/24/wordpress-com-stats-api. If you are using Jetpack on a WordPress.org site, the process would be the same.

Understand Site Statistics

The amount of information gathered by statistics services such as Google Analytics or WordPress.com is staggering. Sorting through it becomes the real issue, so here are a few tips. As you will see, the value of statistics is to raise questions and prompt experiments or changes.

How Many Unique and Repeat Visitors?

Unique visitors filters out those who come back to your site more than once in a day, so you have a sense of how many individuals actually visited. A *repeat* visitor is someone who has been to your site on other days. Having a good percentage of repeat visitors is important because it shows your site is holding their interest.

Visits

User Type	Sessions
New Visitor	10,376
Returning Visitor	1,637

What Is the Bounce Rate?

A *bounce* is when someone visits a page for a few seconds and does not go anywhere else on your site. On the face of it, that is not a good thing, but context is important. On a contact page, a high bounce rate may be due to many people simply wanting your phone number or address. Is the bounce rate fairly consistent across all pages? That could mean visitors do not find your site useful, or it could mean visitors are getting to the wrong site.

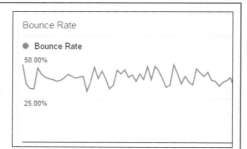

Bounce Rate

● Bounce Rate

50.00%

25.00%

Where Are Visitors Coming From?

There are a number of ways this question applies: What percentage of people arrive from search engines and how many from links on other sites? What sorts of sites are they coming from? What countries or regions are they coming from? Knowing where they are coming from can tell you if current marketing strategies, such as advertising or link building, are working. Not knowing why people are arriving from a certain place is an opportunity to focus more marketing there.

bing	1,088
urbanspoon.com	737
m.yelp.com	348
yelp.ca	182

What Search Terms Are Visitors Using to Find Your Site?

This can tell you if your current keyword strategies are working or if new ones would make sense. Unfortunately, in 2011 Google began hiding the search terms of those who are logged in to their Google accounts. However, if you connect Google Analytics to Google Webmaster Tools, then looking at Acquisition > Search Engine Optimization > Queries can tell you at least something more about search terms.

toastmasters nanaimo	121	(5.49%)
nanaimo toastmasters	43	(1.95%)
toast masters nanaimo	13	(0.59%)
nanaimo toast masters	11	(0.50%)
toastmaster nanaimo	9	(0.41%)
toastmasters	9	(0.41%)

What Are the Most Popular Pages?

Knowing what people like on your site tells you what related material is worth creating. And what they do not visit tells you which content may need more promotion; or if they visit, but only for a few seconds, that suggests you might need to make the content more useful, more focused, and so on.

/member-pages/	471	(2.72%)
/my-books/	298	(1.72%)
/registration/	281	(1.62%)
/about/	228	(1.32%)
/signup-thanks/	218	(1.26%)

How Do Visitors Move through Your Site?

You may have a picture of how visitors use your site, but the truth may be far different. Having a flow chart of the order in which people clicked from page to page is invaluable for considering new ways to promote the pages you want them to click through to, or for placing information at a certain point within a common flow.

Starting pages
11.9K sessions, 10.7K drop-offs

/2011/09/wh...ress-menu/
1.94K

/
1.76K

Are Visitors Fulfilling Your Goals?

All the other statistics aside, the question remains: Are visitors taking the actions you want them to take? Buying products, watching videos, signing up for mailing lists, taking quizzes; these are just a few of the possible goals you would want to track. But if people take these actions, would you know about it from the results? However, the more interesting questions are ones such as: How many people did not try to take the action, or how many did but stopped partway through?

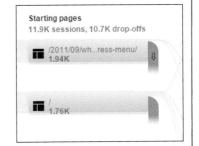

✓ **Goal description**   Edit

Name: *Watched Welcome Video*
Goal type: *Event*

2 **Goal details**

Event conditions
Set one or more conditions. A conversion will be counted if all of the con
You must have at least one Event set up to create this type of Goal. Lea

| Category | Equals to ▾ | Category |
| Action | Equals to ▾ | Action |

Understand User Roles and Capabilities

When you create a WordPress site, you are the Administrator, which means you can do what you want. But there are other types of roles in WordPress, with varying capabilities, and these can be handy when you need others working on your site.

Capabilities

As the name implies, a *capability* is something you are able to do using WordPress, such as write a post or add items to a menu. But being able to write a post is a separate capability from being able to publish a post or to edit other users' posts. By narrowly defining capabilities, it becomes possible to assign very specific tasks to different users.

- delete_published_pages
- delete_published_posts
- edit_dashboard
- edit_others_pages
- edit_others_posts
- edit_pages

Roles

The way that capabilities are assigned to users is through *roles*. WordPress has five different roles by default, each with its own set of capabilities: Administrator, Editor, Author, Contributor, and Subscriber (or Follower for WordPress.com sites). Every user must be assigned one role. You can change a user's role, but there can be only one at a time.

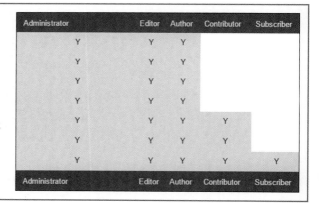

Administrator		Editor	Author	Contributor	Subscriber
Y		Y	Y		
Y		Y	Y		
Y		Y	Y		
Y		Y	Y		
Y		Y	Y	Y	
Y		Y	Y	Y	
Y		Y	Y	Y	Y
Administrator		Editor	Author	Contributor	Subscriber

Use Roles

The point of assigning roles is to limit the actions users can take. For example, you may want a staff person to publish news items to the website, but not be able to edit material he or she has not written, let alone change themes. So you would assign the role of Author. Roles can be used for other purposes, such as to hide content. For example, Subscribers could be shown content that the public cannot access.

Content Permissions

Limit access to this post's content to users of

- ☐ Administrator
- ☐ Editor
- ☐ Contributor
- ☐ Subscriber

*If no roles are selected, everyone can view the cor
users who can edit this post, and users with the*

Add New Users

Y ou can manually add or, in the case of WordPress.com, invite new users to work on your site in various roles.

Add New Users

Add a User to a WordPress.org Site

1 Click **Add New** under Users on the left admin menu.

2 Type a username.

3 Type an email address.

4 Type a strong password.

5 Click ▼ and choose the user role.

A You can send the password to the user by email if you click this option (☐ changes to ☑).

6 Click **Add New User**.

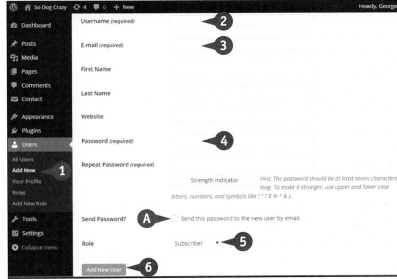

Invite People to be Users on a WordPress.com Site

1 Click **Invite New** under Users on the left admin menu.

2 Type one or more WordPress.com usernames or email addresses.

Note: If the person you are inviting does not have a WordPress.com account, he or she is given instructions on how to register.

3 Click ▼ and choose the role to be assigned to the people you are inviting.

4 You can customize the message sent to each invitee.

5 Click **Send Invitation**.

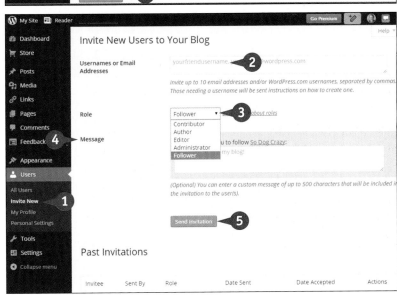

CHAPTER 13

Maintaining Your WordPress Site

Once your WordPress.org site is up and running, there are not a lot of tasks required to keep it safe and running efficiently, but they are important. WordPress.com users have even less to deal with.

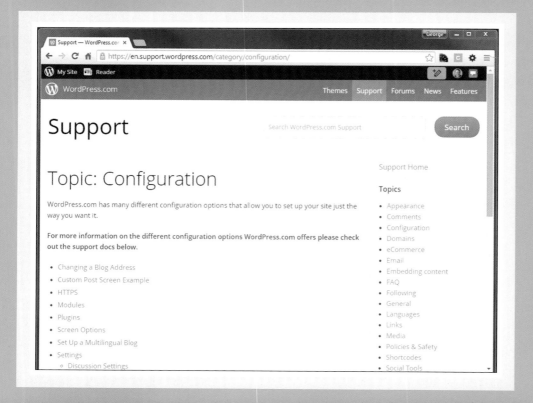

Understand WordPress Backups

The need for backups is not unique to WordPress sites. Backups are the insurance policy every website owner should have, and far too many do not. However, there are some unique aspects to backing up WordPress.

Database and Files

These are the two elements that every WordPress.org backup routine needs to take into account. The database is where your text and settings are stored, whereas the files consist of WordPress, plugins, themes, and your media files. If you do not have both backed up, you will not have a website should some disaster befall.

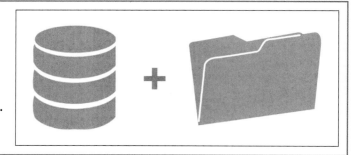

Automatic or Manual Backups?

For the vast majority of site owners, there is no debate on this. You need an automatic backup in place for the simple reason that it will not get done otherwise. Still, manual backups are necessary before doing updates, and for WordPress.com users who want to do a supplementary backup, the only option is a manual one.

Backup Frequency

The short answer is: as often as your site requires. Everyone produces new content at different rates and backups should match that rate. As a rule of thumb, though, a backup once a week would keep current with content as well as any updates to WordPress and its themes and plugins.

Storage Options Online

Storing backups online is an excellent idea, but not on your hosting account. If your server crashes, you are left without any backup at precisely the moment you need one. This does not mean you cannot use a backup service from your hosting company, simply that the backups need to be stored elsewhere. Cloud storage, of course, is the ideal given its redundancies and ease of access.

Storage Options Offline

All backups should be stored in two different locations, ideally one online and one off. The simplest offline backup is a portable hard drive. You do not want the backup on your computer just in case your machine goes down. A portable drive is inexpensive and flexible, and it is easy to store or to take with you on the road.

Toshiba Canvio 500 GB USB 3.0 Basics
Portable Hard Drive - HDTB205XK3AA
(Black)
$47.42 $79.00 *Prime*
★★★★☆ · 3,781

Standard Server Backups

Many people rely on the general backups that all hosting companies make, but this is misguided. Those backups are meant for restoring entire servers, and to restore a single site requires time and money. Also those backups tend to be less frequent than is ideal. Some hosting companies provide daily backups of individual sites, either as a part of their package or as an add-on service, but this needs to be clearly stated in writing. Do not assume it is being provided.

 HostGator backups are provided as a courtesy and are not guaranteed. Customers are responsible for their own backups and web content and should make their own backups for extra protection. For additional information, please refer to our **Terms of Service**.

Backups and Updates

Even if you have a regular, automated backup of your WordPress site, it is still important to do a backup immediately before doing any updating, either of WordPress itself or of even a single plugin. You want a snapshot of your site immediately before the backup so that if you should need to do a restore, you do not have to spend time and money second-guessing what happened between now and the last scheduled backup.

An updated version of WordPress is available.

You can update to WordPress 4.1.1 automatically or download

[Update Now] Download 4.1.1

While your site is being updated, it will be in maintenance mod normal.

Plugins

The following plugins have new versions available. Check the d

Back Up at WordPress.com

Although WordPress.com continually backs up all sites, you may want to keep your own copy of the content. You cannot do a database backup, but WordPress provides an Export function which produces a file that you could use to import your site into a self-hosted WordPress installation.

Back Up at WordPress.com

Back Up at WordPress.com

1 Click **Export** under Tools on the left admin menu.

2 Click **All content** under the Choose What to Export section (○ changes to ⊙).

Ⓐ If you want to back up only certain kinds of content, you can choose from Posts, Pages, or Feedback (○ changes to ⊙).

3 Click **Download Export File** and save it.

Download Media Files

Note: Export does not include media files. Because you uploaded them to WordPress, they should be on your hard drive; but if needed, you can download the originals from WordPress.com.

1 Click **Library** under the Media section of the left admin menu.

2 Switch to Grid view.

3 Click the file you want. The Attachment Details window opens.

4 Highlight the URL for the image and copy it.

5 Paste the URL into a new browser tab.

6 Right-click the image and save it to your hard drive.

7 To download more media files, scroll through them using the navigation arrows.

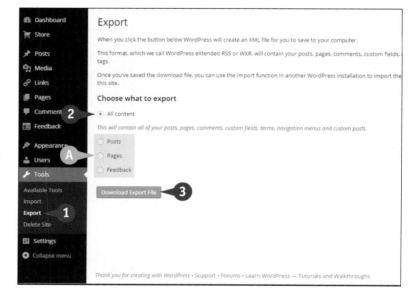

Use Server Backup Tools

ven if you should not store backups on your server, you can still use its tools to do a manual backup on WordPress.org sites. This example uses the cPanel hosting control panel. Your host's version of this or another control panel may have an option to schedule backups. Contact your host if you cannot locate a backup tool.

Use Server Backup Tools

1 From the home page of cPanel, click **Backup Wizard**.

Ⓐ The first step is to choose between backing up or restoring a backup.

2 Click **Backup**.

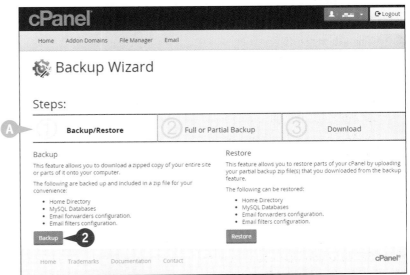

Ⓑ Do *not* click Full Backup. This is used only for moving the entire hosting account to a new host or new server. You would not be able to access it anyway.

3 Click **MySQL Databases** and download the file to the portable hard drive where you keep backups.

Ⓒ Alternatively, you can click **Home Directory** to back up all your WordPress files. Download the file to your portable hard drive.

Note: You are backing up entire sections of your hosting account, including non-WordPress items. If you need to restore, everything is restored, not just WordPress.

Use a Backup Plugin

Numerous backup plugins are available for WordPress.org sites, both free and paid, and they all work in roughly the same way, allowing both automated and manual backups. In this example, you walk through the use of UpdraftPlus.

Use a Backup Plugin

Set Backup Parameters

1 Install and activate UpdraftPlus from the Add Plugins screen.

Note: See Chapter 10 for more about plugins.

2 Click **UpdraftPlus Backups** under Settings on the left admin menu.

3 Click the **Settings** tab.

4 Set the parameters for file backups.

5 Set the parameters for database backups.

A By default, neither type of backup is scheduled. Possible intervals range from 4 hours to Monthly.

B The default backups to be stored is 2.

C All files are included by default in the files backup, but you can change that by clicking an option (☑ changes to ☐).

6 Scroll down to the Copying Your Backup to Remote Storage section.

7 Click ▼ and choose your location for storing files remotely. The free version allows only one choice.

D Depending on the remote storage service you choose, you are asked for its particular credentials.

8 Scroll down and click **Save Changes**.

Do a Manual Backup

1 Click the **Current Status** tab.

E The next scheduled backup is listed.

F The last backup is listed.

2 Click **Backup Now** to do a manual backup, such as before you do any updates.

A window appears. By default, a manual backup includes the database, all files, and sends to any remote storage you have set. But you can override any of these options.

3 Click **Backup Now**.

A progress bar appears, followed by a success message.

4 Click the **Existing Backups** tab to see what backups have been done.

G For each backup, you see the date, available data and its location, and Restore, Delete, or View Log buttons.

Note: If you saved to your server, UpdraftPlus displays buttons for downloading each part of the backup.

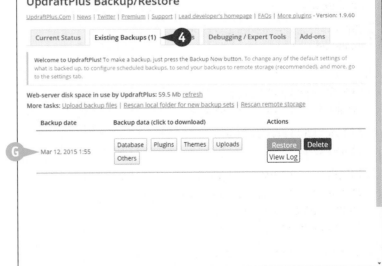

TIPS

If I set up a subdirectory like backups.mydomain.com, could I store backups there?
It is still part of your server space. If your server goes down, you would not be able to access your backup.

Can I be notified every time a scheduled backup runs?
Yes. Many backup plugins have an option to send an email confirming the backup.

Understand Updates

To keep your WordPress.org site safe and able to use new features, updating is crucial. And not only WordPress itself, but plugins and themes need updating too. If you have a WordPress.com site, all updates are handled for you.

Why Are Updates Needed?

Software of any kind requires updating for three reasons: hardened security, fixes, and new features. And although we sometimes bemoan the constant updating of our software, there are good reasons for the changes. Hackers are always coming up with new attacks and the marketplace is always demanding new features or changes. Another way to think of it is this: If your software has no updates, then no one is supporting it, and that is a bad thing.

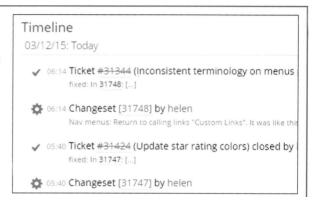

Major versus Minor WordPress Updates

WordPress updates fall into two groups: twice yearly major updates and maintenance release updates as needed. A major update would be from 4.1 to 4.2, whereas 4.2.1 would be a minor update of 4.2. All updates have security and other fixes, but new features tend to be reserved for major updates.

Automatic versus Manual WordPress Updates

An automatic update happens without any action on your part, and administrators are simply notified that the update has occurred. All minor WordPress updates are handled automatically because these maintenance releases typically do not require changes to plugins or themes. Major updates, on the other hand, can involve changes that may affect current site setups, which is why they are left to site owners to do manually. Some server configurations prevent automatic updates, in which case owners simply need to do a manual update.

Plugin Updates

Plugins are each updated according to their own schedules. Some you may never need to update, whereas others seem to have a new version out every month. A major update of WordPress does not necessarily mean a plugin needs to be updated. It all depends on whether some change in WordPress affects the plugin. Plugin authors are given plenty of notice about changes to WordPress so they can do their own updating in a timely manner.

Manual Plugin Updates

While the vast majority of plugins update as easily as they are installed — with a click of a button — sometimes you will need to follow instructions for a manual install. Cases like this typically happen with paid plugins, but the vendor should give you clear details and notification.

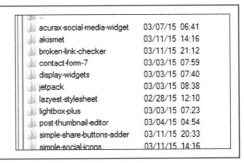

Theme Updates

Updates to themes are much less frequent and tend to be tied either to developments in HTML or CSS, or to major changes in WordPress. Although you may not think of security as an issue for themes, it can be. That is why updating themes is just as important as updating WordPress or plugins. They all interact with one another, so you do not want any weak links in the chain.

What If I Do Not Update?

Failing to do an update does not mean your WordPress site will stop working. It means that you are vulnerable to whatever security issues were fixed, and of course that you do not have any new functionality. The longer you skip updates, the more vulnerabilities. The only time you might not do an update is while you wait for a fix to a plugin that is not working with the latest version of WordPress.

Update WordPress Manually

For major updates or when automated maintenance release updates do not work on your server, you need to manually update WordPress. Luckily, it is as easy as pressing a button. The only work involved is making a backup just before doing the update.

Update WordPress Manually

Ⓐ A notice appears at the top of all admin screens when a WordPress update needs to be done manually. Clicking the **Please update now** link takes you to the Updates screen.

Ⓑ On the Dashboard, a button appears when a manual update is required. Clicking it also leads to the Updates screen.

❶ You can also access the Updates screen by clicking the **Updates** link under Dashboard on the left admin menu.

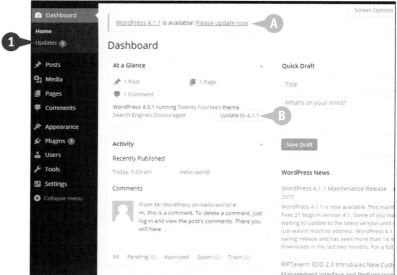

Ⓒ A warning message reminds you to back up your database and files before doing the update.

❷ After you have done the backup, click **Update Now**.

WordPress displays the progress of the update and when it is completed successfully, a welcome screen appears.

The welcome screen lists the highlights of changes in the new version of WordPress.

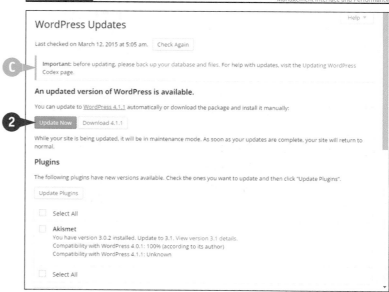

Update Themes

Like with WordPress, updating a theme is easy as pressing a button after making sure you have a current backup of your site. The toughest part is paying attention to the update notices and acting on them.

Update Themes

Update a Single Theme

Ⓐ There is no indication in the sidebar that themes need updating.

① Click the **Update Available** bar on a theme.

A window opens with the theme's details.

An Update Available box appears in the details window.

② Click the **update now** link.

A screen displays the progress of the update.

Update Multiple Themes

① Click **Updates** under Dashboard on the left admin menu.

Note: The numbered circle beside Updates indicates the total updates, whether plugins, themes, or both.

Ⓑ A list appears showing all the themes that have available updates. A thumbnail, current version, and update version are displayed.

② Click **Select All** to select every theme (☐ changes to ☑).

③ Click **Update Themes**.

The progress of each update appears.

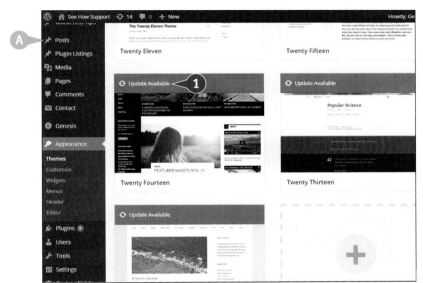

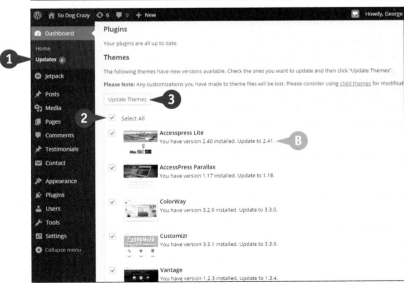

Update Plugins

Backing up your site and pressing a button is all that is involved in updating one or several plugins. However, some paid plugins require manual updating after downloading the new version from the vendor's site.

Update Plugins

Update a Plugin from the Plugins Screen

1 Click **Installed Plugins** under Plugins on the left admin menu.

2 Click the **Update Available** link.

A Active plugins have a colored background, plus an update icon and info bar at the bottom. Inactive plugins just have the update icon and info bar.

3 To update a plugin, click its **update now** link.

Update Multiple Plugins

4 Click the box next to each plugin to update, or click the box in the header to select all (☐ changes to ☑).

5 Click ▼ and select **Update**.

6 Click **Apply**.

A screen listing all the plugins and their update progress appears.

Update a Plugin from the Updates Screen

1 Click **Updates** under Dashboard on the left admin menu.

B A list of all plugins waiting for updates appears.

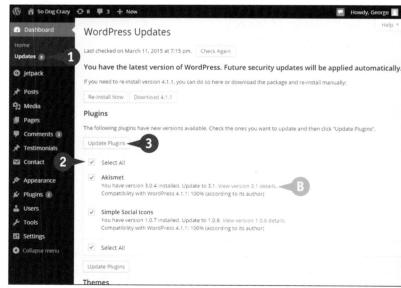

2 Click the box next to one or more plugins you want to update. Click **Select All** to check them all (☐ changes to ☑).

3 Click **Update Plugins**.

The Update Plugins screen opens.

C WordPress displays a success message as each plugin updates.

D When all the plugins have been updated, you see two links: one to the Plugins screen and one to the Updates screen.

Update a Plugin Manually

Some paid plugins may require you to download an update from their site and manually install it.

Usually a manual install requires you to deactivate and delete the old version, and install and activate the new.

The delete and install processes can be handled via FTP.

1 On your hard drive, you need to unzip or unarchive the Zip file you downloaded from the vendor.

2 Delete the folder of the old version that you deactivated.

3 Drag the folder — not the Zip file — to the server side of the screen.

4 Activate the plugin from the Plugins screen.

Note: See Chapter 10 for more about plugins.

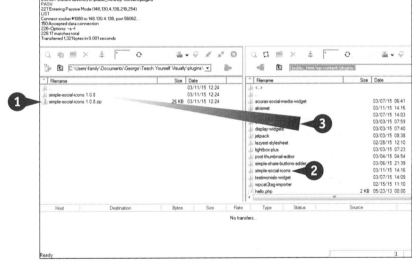

TIPS

Is there a way to automate plugin updates?

There are plugins which will turn on a function in WordPress to auto-update plugins. However, because updating plugins is one of the most common causes of problems in WordPress, you should look for plugins that allow you to exclude individual plugins from updating automatically, or hire someone to write a plugin for you.

I am nervous about updating an important plugin.

You could check the support forum for that plugin to see if anyone else is reporting issues with the update. If it is a paid plugin, contact the vendor and ask.

Check for Broken Links

Broken links are a nuisance for visitors and are frowned on by search engines. But with a growing website, it becomes increasingly difficult to keep track of all your links, let alone test if they are still working. That is why broken link checkers are so valuable. Here is an example of an online checker and a plugin for WordPress.org sites.

Check for Broken Links

Check for Broken Links Using an Online Checker

1 In your browser address bar, navigate to www.drlinkcheck.com.

2 Type the URL of your site.

3 Click **Start**.

The program follows the links on your site and tests to see if they are working.

Note: Online checkers typically have a maximum number of links they crawl — in this case 1,000 — so if you have a very large site, you may need to use a program or the plugin described later in this section.

A Links are listed showing which pages contain the link.

B Problem links are indicated by ✕.

C If the link is external or outbound, an External label appears.

D When you mouse over a Broken label, you see the reason — in this case, "the host name could not be resolved."

Note: Search for "broken link checker" to find an online checker or software to run on your device. Google Webmaster Tools does link checking, if you use it.

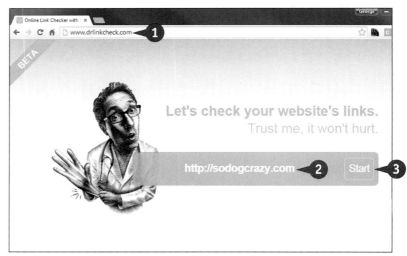

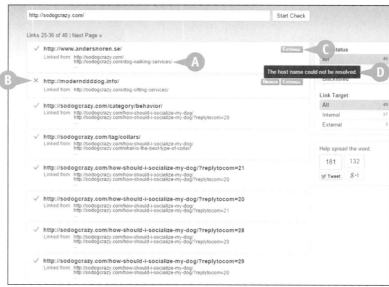

Use a Plugin for WordPress.org Sites

1 Install and activate Broken Link Checker from the Plugin Directory.

Note: See Chapter 10 for more about plugins.

2 Click **Broken Links** under Tools in the left admin menu.

3 Filter problem links.

E Status shows the reason for the problem.

F Link Text displays the anchor text of the link.

G Source shows the page where the link was found. Mouse over to Edit, Trash, or View it.

H Mouse over the link to view a menu.

I Bulk Actions also includes: Fix Redirects and Move Sources to Trash.

Use Broken Link Checker Options

1 Click **Link Checker** under Settings on the left admin menu.

J Current status.

K How often to check existing links. New links are checked when written.

L Whether to send an email when new broken links are found. You can notify authors of their links.

M Where to look for broken links.

N Advanced options to control resource usage.

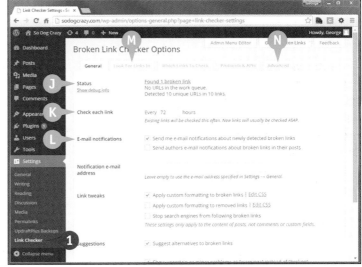

TIPS

Should I use Broken Link Checker? Some servers have banned it.
The plugin contains numerous default settings to minimize the load on the server. If you are concerned about the resources being used, you can deactivate the plugin and reactivate it every so often to do a check.

I have a lot of links on my site. Can I control what the plugin checks?
You can choose whether to check certain areas of the site, such as Posts or Comments, plus you can exclude certain types of links. There is also an exclusion list based on the URL of the link.

Keep WordPress Secure

As the world's most popular content management system, WordPress is also a popular target for hackers. All the more reason for securing your site in several ways. Some of these steps require plugins, whereas others are a matter of getting into good habits.

Stay Updated

Keeping WordPress, plugins, and themes updated is the number one way to protect your site. Unfixed security issues is one of the main ways hackers break into WordPress installations.

Use Strong Passwords

Weak passwords is another common way that hackers gain entry to WordPress sites. This is particularly a problem on WordPress.org sites, because if they can gain administrative access to your site, hackers have access to files where they can plant malware. When you are installing WordPress or adding new users, a strong-password indicator appears. Follow it.

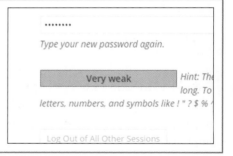

Two-Factor Authentication

A recent option for going beyond strong passwords is two-factor authentication. Your bank card and pin number is a classic example of two-factor authentication — a person needs both to access your account. This is now available on WordPress.com, using Google Authenticator, which sends a one-time unique code to your mobile phone when you log in. Plugins that use various services, including Google Authenticator, are available for WordPress.org sites.

Use Plugins and Themes from Reputable Sources

For WordPress.org sites, a danger exists that themes or plugins have malware embedded in them. That is why it is crucial get them from reputable sources. For example, never download free items except from the WordPress.org directories. One exception would be commercial sites offering free examples. Even in the case of paid plugins and themes, it makes sense to buy from names you have heard of.

Block Repeated Login Attempts

Whether hackers are trying to get into your site or they just want to overload your server, repeated failed login attempts is a sign of trouble. Plugins are available which block someone who tries more than a certain number of times to get in. In fact, more and more servers are taking it upon themselves to do this as a way of preventing server overload. But do not rely on that — set up your own blocking system.

Use SSL for Your Entire Site

Even if you have no e-commerce on your site, getting an SSL certificate and using HTTPS for all your pages, in particular your administrative pages, is a good idea. In fact, Google has been advocating secure sites for some time and many believe Google gives a bit of ranking credit to sites that use HTTPS.

Be Vigilant

One sign that you have been hacked is the appearance of an administrative user you have never seen before. Keeping any eye open for that, or for files you have never seen before while FTP'ing into your site, are just a couple of examples of being vigilant. Not logging into WordPress on public networks or at the very least remembering to log out is another example.

Force Strong Passwords

Although WordPress provides a handy strength indicator when creating passwords, too few people actually follow it. And if you have other administrators and editors on the system, will they follow it? For WordPress.org sites, the solution is to use a plugin that does not allow weak passwords. Most security plugins have this feature, but in this case, the example is for a plugin which does nothing else, called Force Strong Passwords.

Force Strong Passwords

1 Install and activate Force Strong Passwords from the Plugins Directory.

Note: See Chapter 10 for more about plugins.

There are no settings for this plugin — it simply enforces WordPress's password strength rules.

Ⓐ Users are notified that their attempt to reset their password does not meet the strength criteria.

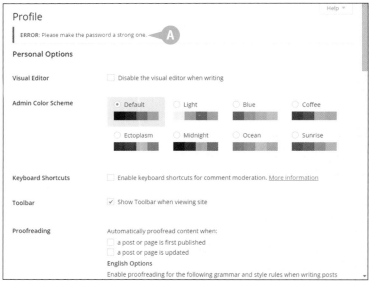

Other plugins, such as Login Security Solution, offer options regarding passwords.

Ⓑ How long must passwords be.

Ⓒ Length a password must be to gain exemption from complexity rules. Default is 20 characters.

Ⓓ It is possible, though not recommended, to set the number of days until a password expires.

Ⓔ If passwords expire, how many minutes a user has to change it.

Ⓕ You can have the plugin remember passwords to prevent people from reusing old ones.

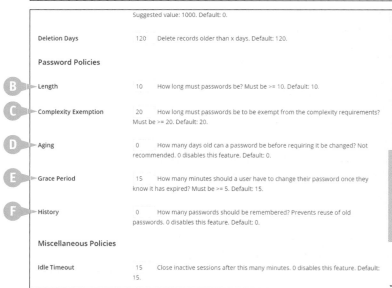

Limit Login Attempts

One of the ways hackers break into WordPress sites is to repeatedly try different passwords. If they do this hundreds or thousands of times in a short period, it can tax the resources of the server and potentially get you shut down. By limiting the number of failed attempts, you can prevent this problem. Most security plugins have this feature, but this example is for a dedicated plugin called Limit Login Attempts.

Limit Login Attempts

1 Install and activate Limit Login Attempts from the Plugins Directory.

Note: See Chapter 10 for more about plugins.

2 Click **Limit Login Attempts** under Settings on the left admin menu.

A Total lockouts appear here. The list of lockouts with the username that attempted to login appears at the bottom of the page.

B You can change the default lockout settings, such as how many retries are allowed, how long the lockout lasts, and more.

3 Click the email option if you want to be notified when someone has been locked out more than the given number of times (□ changes to ☑).

4 Click **Change Options**.

This composite screenshot shows two states of failed logins.

C You are notified how many more login attempts you have before being locked out.

D Once you have reached the login limit, you are told how much time you have before you can try logging in again.

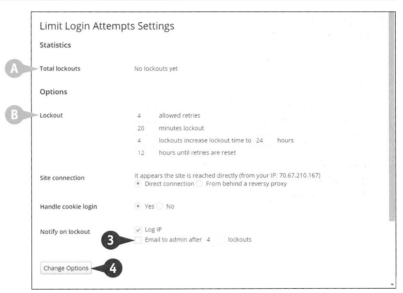

Troubleshoot WordPress

Although it does not happen often, things can go wrong and sites can even crash. On WordPress.org sites, this can be caused by adding a new plugin or from updating WordPress, themes, or existing plugins. Other times problems can be caused by your host's software or issues with other sites on your server. Because you cannot get into the code at WordPress.com, the host must resolve crashes there, but see the table for some issues common to both WordPress versions.

Remain Calm and Take Notes

Take a deep breath and write down exactly what happened. Note any error message you saw or see, and when possible take screenshots. Try to recall what you did just before everything went wrong.

Turn Off Named Culprits

If an error message indicates a particular plugin or theme, try deactivating it and see if your site starts working properly. In the case of themes, you deactivate your current one by activating one of the default WordPress themes — do not use any other themes. If your site starts working, then you know where to start researching solutions.

Turn Off All Plugins

If there is no clear error or no error messages appear at all, try deactivating all plugins. If your site is working, you have a plugin conflict of some sort. Turn on one plugin and check your site. Repeat with the next plugin and so on until the crash recurs. Then, deactivate that last plugin and look into solutions for it.

Activate a Default Theme

If turning off all plugins did not resolve the issue, make sure your current theme is up to date. If updating does not resolve the problem, then activate one of the default WordPress themes. Do not worry, all the settings for your current theme are kept. If the problem goes away, then you need to research solutions for fixing your theme.

Reinstall the Plugin or Theme

Sometimes the code for the problem plugin or theme becomes corrupted. Using your FTP program — because you cannot access your admin screens — delete the plugin folder from the Plugins directory on your server, or the theme folder from the Themes directory. Then, upload the folder for the plugin or theme, not the Zip file.

Support Forums

If your problem is a plugin or theme from the WordPress directories, check the forums for possible solutions. For paid plugins or themes, you need to check your vendor forums or submit a trouble ticket. In all cases it is important to include as much information as possible, in particular the version numbers for everything, including what PHP version your server is running.

If All Else Fails

You may need to restore your site from a backup. Hopefully you chose a backup plugin which includes a restore function; you can also find instructions at http://codex.wordpress.org/Restoring_Your_Database_From_Backup. You may need to restore all the files or only the database, depending on the situation or the plugin.

Troubleshoot Common WordPress Problems

These are some common issues you may encounter and some actions you can take.

Problem	Possible Explanation	What to Do
Incorrect username or password	Brain freeze	Use the lost password function on the WordPress login page. You still need to know the email address from your profile. A password will be emailed to you.
Domain parked screen	Expired domain name	Log in to your domain registrar and re-register.
Browser message says "Page not found"	Server down or interrupted web connection	If you cannot see other sites, call your Internet provider. If you can see other websites, go to www.downforeveryoneorjustme.com and type your site's URL. If it says others can see your site, then your Internet provider is not connecting to your server, so contact your ISP. If it says others also cannot see your site, then the server is down. Wait 15 minutes and try again. If still nothing, contact your web host.
Browser says "Error connecting to database"	Server or WordPress site database issues	If you can get to your login page, but not the front of your site, then it is a problem with your database. If you cannot access either the front or back end, contact your web host to alert it to the problem. If it is not having general database issues, ask your host to check that your particular database is working. If it is, check that your `wp-config.php` file has the right database credentials, and if so, ask the server people to check file ownership issues.
Site displays poorly on mobile devices	Unresponsive theme or a default mobile theme	Switch to a responsive theme. If you want to keep your current theme: on WordPress.com sites, click **Mobile** under Appearance and enable the default mobile theme; on WordPress.org sites, you need a plugin, such as WPtouch, to display a special theme to mobile users.
Theme does not display saved changes	Site *cached* in browser (meaning a previous version is showing up)	You need to refresh your browser. How you do this varies by browser and operating system, but as a general rule, try holding down Shift while clicking the Refresh icon of your browser. For browser specifics, go to http://wiki.scratch.mit.edu/wiki/Hard_Refresh.
Scheduled posts do not appear	Failure to click **Schedule**	After you save a draft to be published at a future date, you not only need to save the draft and okay the time for publication, but you also need to click **Schedule** to make it happen. When you do, the Status will read *Scheduled*.

Find Support at WordPress.org

One of the benefits of a large WordPress community is having a lot of people asking and answering questions. The forums at WordPress.org have been around for many years and contain a wealth of information. And the documentation, called The Codex, has grown substantially in the last few years.

Find Support at WordPress.org

Use the Support Forums

1 Navigate to https://wordpress.org.

2 Mouse over Support and click **Forums**.

3 Log in.

Note: You can browse without registering, but you cannot post. A Register button appears next to the Log In button.

4 Navigate to the forum section you want or use the search function on the opening page.

A Highlighted threads at the top of sections contain important and up-to-date notices.

5 Click **Add New** to start a new discussion.

Note: Be as detailed as possible, and include the version numbers of WordPress and plugins, along with your server's version of PHP.

Use the Codex

1 Mouse over Support on the WordPress.org menu and click **Documentation**.

Scroll through the main index page to find what you need. The Codex is a mix of tutorials and technical explanations of WordPress functions.

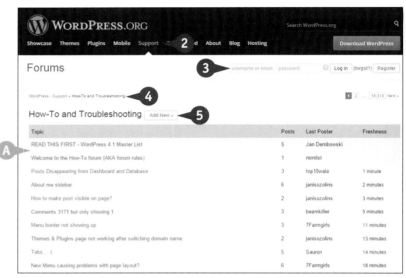

Find Support at WordPress.com

The huge community of millions of WordPress.com users means not only that the staff has an incentive to document the functions well, but that there are a lot of people willing to help in the forums.

Find Support at WordPress.com

Use the Support Knowledgebase

1 You can get to the knowledgebase by clicking the Help button (🔍) at the top right of any WordPress.com admin screen.

A Use the search function to search all the support area, not just the knowledgebase.

B The main topic sections appear on the right.

C On a Topic page, you see a list of individual articles on that topic.

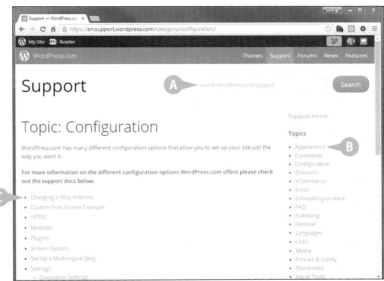

Use the Support Forums

1 Make sure you are logged into WordPress.com so you can post.

D Search the forums.

E A list of the main forum sections appears on the left.

F Important notices appear at the top of forum sections with a distinct background.

G You can click **Add new topic** to begin a new discussion.

Note: If you figure out the answer to your own question, be sure to post it and do not just say "I have solved it" and close the thread.

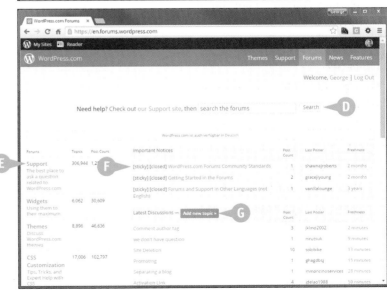

Discover More Support Options

If you still do not find answers at the support forums for WordPress.org or WordPress.com, it is time to look further afield. If you just want to learn more about using WordPress, there are literally tens of thousands of ways to do so.

Search the Web

Searching the web for a specific issue will turn up possible answers in other forums, on individual websites, or in the contents of documents or books, so that is your best starting point. But make sure you use detailed keywords or quotes around key phrases or error messages so that you get results specific to your issue.

Search Sites about WordPress

You could also do a search for WordPress help sites, and on those sites do a search for your issue, just in case the sites did not turn up in your initial search. You can end up finding your answer by browsing these sites. These sites also offer tips for using WordPress, so they can be a great place to learn more.

Online Tutorials

Online tutorials — video or text — have become a popular way to learn WordPress, and there are many free ones available. For a monthly fee or a single course fee, there are also plenty of paid tutorials online. Just on YouTube alone you will find plenty of help. For WordPress.com go to https://learn.wordpress.com.

WordPress.tv

This is an excellent collection of videos on all levels of WordPress issues. Although a lot of the videos focus on WordPress.com, the information quite often applies to WordPress.org sites as well.

Read Books

Just like the one you are reading now, you can learn how to use WordPress or improve your skills by reading print and e-books. A lot of WordPress books are out there now and the quality varies widely. Pay close attention to reviews, but only ones which provide useful information instead of simply saying "It is great."

Premium Support at WordPress.com

When you upgrade your WordPress.com account, you can get different levels of personal support. The Premium plan offers support by email, whereas the Business level has chat.

Premium Support for WordPress.org Sites

When you buy a theme or a plugin, the vendor should provide some level of support. This is usually for one year, after which you would need to pay for continued support. There is no paid support from WordPress.org, but there are many commercial services available offering WordPress support by email, chat, or phone, typically for a monthly fee.

Index

Index